SELF-ESTEEM

by
Matthew McKay, Ph.D.
and
Patrick Fanning

Edited by Kirk Johnson

Cover and illustrations
by Shelby Putnam-Tupper

Publisher's Note

This publication is designed to provide accurate and authoritative information in regard to the subject matter covered. It is sold with the understanding that the publisher is not engaged in rendering psychological, financial, legal, or other professional services. If expert assistance or counseling is needed, the services of a competent professional should be sought.

ISBN 0-934986-41-X (paperback)
ISBN 0-934986-42-8 (hardcover)

First Printing November 1987, 7,000 copies
Second Printing April 1987, 10,000 copies
Third Printing April 1988, 7,500 copies
Fourth Printing July 1989, 7,500 copies
Fifth Printing March, 1990 5,000 copies
Sixth Printing October, 1990 5,000 copies

To my loving parents, Bert and Grace Fanning
—P. F.

In memory of my father, George Edward McKay
—M. M.

Grateful acknowledgement is made to Eugene B. Sagan, Ph.D., who introduced me to the Pathological Critic and some of the important techniques used in this book.
—M. M.

Table of Contents

1

The Nature of Self-Esteem

Self-esteem is essential for psychological survival. It is an emotional *sine qua non*—without some measure of self-worth, life can be enormously painful, with many basic needs going unmet.

One of the main factors differentiating humans from other animals is the awareness of self: the ability to form an identity and then attach a value to it. In other words, you have the capacity to define who you are and then decide if you like that identity or not. The problem of self-esteem is this human capacity for judgment. It's one thing to dislike certain colors, noises, shapes, or sensations. But when you reject parts of yourself, you greatly damage the psychological structures that literally keep you alive.

Judging and rejecting yourself causes enormous pain. And in the same way that you would favor and protect a physical wound, you find yourself avoiding anything that might aggravate the pain of self-rejection in any way. You take fewer social, academic, or career risks. You make it more difficult for yourself to meet people, interview for a job, or push hard for something where you might not succeed. You limit your ability to open yourself with others, express your sexuality, be the center of attention, hear criticism, ask for help, or solve problems.

To avoid more judgments and self-rejection, you erect barriers of defense. Perhaps you blame and get angry, or bury yourself in perfectionistic work. Or you brag. Or you make excuses. Sometimes you turn to alcohol or drugs.

This book is about stopping the judgments. It's about healing the old wounds of hurt and self-rejection. How you perceive and feel about yourself can change. And when those perceptions and feelings change, the ripple effect will touch every part of your life with a gradually expanding sense of freedom.

Causes and Effects

Hundreds of researchers have quizzed thousands of people of various ages and situations, trying to see what causes self-esteem, who has the most of it, how important it is, how it can be increased, and so on.

Studies of young children show clearly that parents' style of child-rearing during the first three or four years determines the amount of self-esteem that a child starts with. After that, most studies of older children, adolescents, and adults share a common confusion: what is cause and what is effect?

Does academic success foster self-esteem, or does self-esteem foster academic success? Does high social status cause high self-esteem, or does high self-esteem help you gain high social status? Do alcoholics drink because they hate themselves, or do they hate themselves because they drink? Do people like themselves because they do well in job interviews, or do they do better in interviews because they like themselves?

These are classic chicken-and-egg questions. Just as eggs come from chickens and chickens come from eggs, it seems that self-esteem grows out of your circumstances in life, and your circumstances in life are influenced strongly by your self-esteem. Which came first? The question has serious implications for your success at raising your self-esteem.

If external circumstances determine self-esteem, then all you have to do to improve your self-esteem is to improve your circumstances. Let's say you have low self-esteem because you never graduated from high school, you're short, your Mom hated herself, you live in the slums, and you're 100 pounds overweight. All you have to do is go to night school and get your degree, grow about six inches, have been raised by a different mother, move to Beverly Hills, and lose 100 pounds. It's a cinch, right?

But you know you'll never make it. There's nothing you can do about your parents or your height. Your only hope is that things are the other way around: that self-esteem determines circumstances. This means that if you improve your self-esteem, your circumstances will improve. So just stop hating yourself, and you'll get taller, your mom will become somebody different, and those 100 pounds will evaporate like the morning dew.

If you feel that this second scenario is also a little unlikely, you can be congratulated on a keen appreciation of the real world.

The fact is that self-esteem and your circumstances are only indirectly related. There is another intervening factor that determines self-esteem 100 percent of the time: your thoughts.

For example, you look in the mirror and think, "Boy, am I fat. What a slob." This thought clobbers your self-esteem. If you looked in the mirror and thought, "Well, all right, it looks good to wear my hair like this," the effect on your self-esteem would be the opposite. The image in the mirror remains the same. Only the thoughts change.

Or let's say that you're discussing the news, and when you make a remark about the right-wing rebels your nitpicking friend corrects you: "No, you mean the *left*-wing rebels." If you tell yourself, "I really sound stupid," your self-esteem will take a nose dive. If you say to yourself, "Oh yeah, I've got to keep that straight next time," your self-esteem will not suffer so much. In either case, you don't change the circumstances, only how you interpret them.

Does this mean that circumstances have *nothing* to do with self-esteem? No. Obviously, in the area of social status, bank vice-presidents have more opportunity to feel better about their careers than cab drivers have. This is why a study of 100 vice-presidents and 100 cab drivers will "prove" that the higher status job leads to higher self-esteem. What is overlooked among the statistics is that there are some vice-presidents who slaughter their self-esteem by telling themselves, "I should have been president of my own bank by now. I'm a failure," just as there are some cab drivers who feel good about themselves because they think, "So I'm just a cab driver—I'm putting bread on the table, the kids are doing good in school, things are going just fine."

This book uses proven methods of cognitive behavioral therapy to raise your self-esteem by changing the way you interpret your life. It will show you how to uncover and analyze the negative self-statements you habitually make. You will learn how to create new, objective, positive self-statements that will foster your self-esteem instead of undermining it.

How To Use This Book

This book is organized logically, with the most important and universally applicable material at the beginning.

Chapter two introduces the pathological critic, the voice inside you that criticizes and keeps your self-esteem low. The next chapter deals with disarming the critic so that you can be free to begin raising your self-esteem without interference.

Chapter four shows you how to make an accurate self-assessment of your strengths and weaknesses, an important first step in changing your self-esteem.

Chapter five explains cognitive distortions, irrational ways of thinking that contribute to low self-esteem.

Chapter six introduces the concept of compassion. Self-esteem is closely tied to compassion for others and compassion for yourself.

Chapter seven is about your shoulds, all the rules you have made for yourself about how you should act, feel, and be. Revising your shoulds is one of the most powerful ways to undo old negative programming.

Chapter eight shows how to handle mistakes by changing how you relate to error and by letting go of mistakes in the past.

Chapter nine teaches you how to react to criticism without losing your self-esteem or having to attack others.

Chapter ten covers asking for what you want, one of the most difficult tasks for people with low self-esteem.

Chapter eleven teaches powerful techniques of visualization, a way of setting and achieving self-esteem goals.

Chapter twelve guides you in learning a simple self-hypnosis technique to reinforce affirmations you have created in earlier chapters.

Chapter thirteen is called "I'm Still Not OK" and is designed to help you stop running away from pain while you develop an attitude of nonjudgment.

Chapter fourteen is for you if you have children. It explains what you can do to give your kids the priceless legacy of high self-esteem.

Using this book is simple. Keep reading until you reach the end of chapter three, "Disarming the Critic." At that point, there is a chart for you to consult. It will direct you to the appropriate chapter to deal with specific problems you may have. If you want to learn about and improve your self-esteem in general, just read the book in sequence from start to finish.

Benefiting from this book is not as simple as just reading it. You have to do some work. Many chapters have exercises to do and skills to learn. When the text tells you to "close your eyes and imagine a scene from your past," you should actually close your eyes and do it. When the book says, "On a separate piece of paper, list three situations in which you have felt inadequate," you really need to go find some paper and a pen that writes and sit down and list your three situations.

There is no substitute for doing the exercises. Imagining yourself doing the exercises is not enough. Skimming through the exercises with the vague intention of coming back to them sometime and trying them is not enough. Doing only the exercises that seem easy or interesting is not enough. If there was a way to improve your self-esteem that was easier than doing exercises, it would be in this book. The exercises that are in this book are here because they are the best, easiest, and only way the authors know to raise self-esteem.

You should take your time reading this book. It is densely packed with ideas and things to do. Read it at a pace that will let you absorb the contents fully. Self-esteem takes a long time to develop in the first place. You've spent your whole life developing the level of self-esteem you have now. It takes time to tear self-esteem down, and it takes time to build it up. Make a commitment right now to take the time you need.

For the Therapist

In his book, *The Shrinking of America*, Bernie Zilbergeld concludes that psychotherapy has only limited effectiveness for many of the problems that it purports to help. But a review of outcome studies led him to find that psychotherapy *does* positively affect self-esteem and that improved self-esteem "may be counseling's most important outcome." (p. 147)

Clients come to therapy wanting help with anxiety, depression, eating disorders, sexual problems, relationship difficulties, and a host of other symptoms. Sometimes the symptoms improve; sometimes they persist despite years of intensive work. But most clients do get a sense of greater personal worth from therapy. While specific symptoms may or may not change, clients at least begin to see themselves as more OK, more deserving, more capable.

The problem with therapy is time. Over the course of months, and often years, a client's self-perception changes in response to consistent positive regard from the therapist. The sense of approval from an authority figure, particularly one who substitutes for the critical parent, has a potential to be enormously healing. Yet this vital process of raising self-esteem, one that can change many aspects of a client's experience, is inefficiently and haphazardly implemented. Often the process takes far longer than it should. Often it is done without a plan and without the specific interventions that could hasten its success.

This book is about hastening the process. You can increase a client's self-esteem more rapidly and more effectively using the cognitive restructuring techniques presented here. Through an exploration of chronic negative self-talk, a systematic confrontation of cognitive distortions, and the development of a more accurate and compassionate self-evaluation, you can intervene directly to raise a client's sense of worth.

An Issue of Diagnosis

There are basically two kinds of self-esteem problems: situational and characterological. Low self-esteem that is situational tends to show up only in specific areas. For example, a person might have confidence in himself as a parent, a conversationalist, and a sexual partner, but expect to fail in work situations. Someone else might feel socially inept, but see herself as a strong and capable professional. Low self-esteem that is characterological usually had roots in early experiences of abuse or abandonment. The sense of "wrongness" in this case is more global and tends to affect many areas of life.

Situational low self-esteem is a problem ideally suited for cognitive restructuring techniques. The focus is on confronting cognitive distortions, emphasizing strengths over weaknesses, and developing specific skills for handling mistakes and criticism. Since the client is not rejecting himself or herself globally, you will find that changing maladaptive thinking patterns will significantly increase a sense of confidence and worth.

Since characterological low self-esteem derives from a basic identity statement, a *feeling* of being bad, changing a client's thoughts is not enough. Identifying and beginning to control the internal critical voice will help, but will not entirely undo the feeling of wrongness. Your main therapeutic emphasis must therefore be on the negative identity that gives rise to negative thoughts. The focus should be on developing self-compassion and a commitment to nonjudgment (see chapter thirteen). These positions can be reinforced through visualization and hypnotic techniques.

Cognitive Restructuring for Self-Esteem

The best place to begin is with the client's thoughts. Ask what he or she was thinking during a recent episode of self-reproach. Get as much detail as you can about the critical self-talk and then introduce the concept of the pathological critic (see chapters two and three, "The Pathological Critic" and "Disarming the Critic"). Encourage the client to develop his or her unique name for the critic as a way to begin to take ownership of the concept. Typical names are "the bully," "the shark," "my kicker," "Mr. Perfect," "Marsha (the client's mother)," and so on.

Personifying the critic helps the client begin to externalize the self-accusing voice. You want him or her to experience the voice as something coming from outside, rather than as a part of the normal flow of thought. It's easier to fight something that is perceived as external. It's also easier to make the critical voice ego dystonic, something the client eventually rejects as "not me."

At the same time that you are identifying and naming the patho-logical critic, you can also introduce the client to his or her "healthy voice." The healthy voice is the client's ability to think realistically. By emphasizing and strengthening this ability you are positioning the client to begin talking back to the critic. Names that are typically used for the healthy voice include "my rational part," "my accepting part," "my compassionate part," "my healthy coach," and so on. Choose a name that fits the client's self-concept (i.e., rational, compassionate, caring, objective, and so on).

By creating this dichotomy between the critical voice and the healthy voice, you can encourage the client to confront his or her critic. The following dialogues exemplify this process.

> *Therapist:* So what did the critic say when you waited and didn't hear from your new friend?
>
> *Client:* That I'm not interesting, that I bored him and he was tired of me.
>
> *Therapist:* What does the healthy coach say back to that?
>
> *Client:* That our conversation *was* lively and fun. That there was nice energy between us. I could feel it.
>
> *Therapist:* What else? Does the coach think you should stew about it, or is there some action you can take?
>
> *Client:* I could call him and try to get a sense of how he feels.

Here's another example:

> *Client:* I didn't get an assignment at work in on time.
>
> *Therapist:* What did the bully say about that?
>
> *Client:* That I'm lazy. Over and over: "You're lazy, you screw up, you'll never get anywhere."
>
> *Therapist:* Can you mobilize the healthy voice to say anything back?
>
> *Client:* All I hear is the bully.
>
> *Therapist:* Right now see if you can find your healthy voice so you can talk back to the bully. Are you really lazy and a screw-up?
>
> *Client:* Well, my healthy voice says, "You did drag your feet, but still you finished it, you turned it in. No one really cared that it was late but you."
>
> *Therapist:* So the bully exaggerated about screwing up?·
>
> *Client:* Yes. He *always* exaggerates.

The next step in cognitive restructuring is to identify the main function of a client's critic (see "How the Critic Gets Reinforced" in chapter two). In every case the critical voice is being reinforced because it serves some positive function—to promote desired behavior, para-doxically to protect self-worth, or to control painful feelings.

A client must understand the reason why he uses the critical voice and how it helps to protect him. Here's an example of how this issue can be discussed.

> *Therapist:* When you were feeling nervous during dinner, what was the critic saying?
> *Client:* She won't like you. You don't know anything and haven't much money. And you're not very funny.
> *Therapist:* Remember we said that the critic always tries to meet some need. What was he trying to protect you from this time?
> *Client:* From the kiss-off.
> *Therapist:* He was trying to protect you from the fear of rejection?
> *Client:* Right.
> *Therapist:* How?
> *Client:* By expecting it and then not getting so hurt.
> *Therapist:* So the critic was sort of desensitizing you, preparing you. You wouldn't feel quite so bad if she didn't like you because you expect her not to. That's something we've seen a lot before. It's one of the main functions of your critic—protecting you from the fear of rejection.

Learning the critic's function sometimes requires an exhaustive inquiry. You have to explain that every thought, no matter how painful, exists because it is rewarded in some way. Critical self-attacks must therefore serve an important function. Ask the client: "What would you be forced to feel or be aware of if the critic weren't attacking you in this situation? How does the critic help you in this situation? What are you afraid you might do or fail to do *without* the critic in this situation?" Some of the main functions of the critic are listed in chapter three, "Disarming the Critic." Using that chapter as a resource, you may want to suggest the major functions you see the critic serving for your client.

Once the function of the critical voice has been unmasked, this information can be used again and again during confrontations. "Once again you are using the critic to push you toward impossible levels of achievement." "Again you deal with the fear of failure by letting the critic tell you that you can't do it so why try." "You are letting the critic punish you again so you won't have to feel so much guilt."

Identifying what reinforces the critic is half the battle. In addition, the client must learn that the important needs his critic helps him meet can be satisfied in healthier ways (see "Making your Critic Useless" in chapter three). The critic is not the only way to deal with the fear of failure, fear of rejection, guilt, and so on. New, nontoxic strategies must be devised.

> *Therapist:* Is there another way of lowering your anxiety about rejection? A way that doesn't use the critic?

Client: I guess so. I could remind myself that we're both probably nervous. And that we're just there to have a pleasant evening and it doesn't have to be anything beyond that.

Therapist: In other words, tell yourself that it's just a date, and you don't necessarily expect her to like you so much that she'll spend the rest of her life with you.

Client: Right.

Therapist: Does reframing it like that lower your anxiety?

Client: I think so.

Identifying distortions. The chapter on cognitive distortions introduces nine specific categories of distorted thinking that contribute to lower self-esteem. Identifying and confronting these distortions can become a major component of your treatment program.

While you may invent your own terms, it's important to define the particular distortion as clearly and with as many examples as possible.

Therapist: I'm saying that words like stupid, fraud, and idiot are toxic labels because they're total indictments of you as a person. They're global put-downs. You're not saying that you're ignorant about taxes, you're saying, "I'm a stupid person." You're not saying that you feel insecure about certain tasks at work, you're saying, "I'm a fraud." These terms are a total dismissal of all your strengths and assets. They're pejorative and brutal because they generalize the negative and forget the positive. They are plain wrong, inaccurate. Part of our work is to find ways to get away from these labels and become more accurate.

The therapist has defined the distortion and is also defining the task. Now she starts teaching the client about how to substitute accurate language for the toxic labels.

Therapist: OK, you're calling yourself a fraud. This is pejorative, a generality. What's the accurate statement?

Client: That I try to look more confident than I am.

Therapist: Continuously, or just in certain things?

Client: Well, mostly in terms of the gas chromatograph. I look like I know more than I really do.

Therapist: So is the accurate statement that you know less than people expect about the gas chromatograph?

Client: Yes.

Therapist: That's very different from being a fraud.

Client: That's true. Fraud is a big exaggeration.

During your first few sessions, ask many specific questions about the content of any self-critical thoughts. "What did the critic say to you when you visited home? When you finished the term paper? When your son got angry? At the end of our last hour?'' The more you learn about the content of the critical voice, the better prepared you will be to confront specific distortions.

When introducing the concept of cognitive distortions, focus only on the most significant ones. Don't overload the client. Most people can't remember to fight more than one or two negative thought patterns at any given time.

When you are first looking at distortions, it's helpful to review three or four self-critical cognitions and show what they all have in in common.

> *Therapist:* Last week you talked about being late and called your-self a *screw-up.* Then you were struggling with your tax forms and said that you were stupid. Today you described yourself as a *fraud* and an *idiot* at work. Screw-up, stupid, fraud, idiot. These are toxic labels that really undermine your self-esteem. They are part of the problem we are working on. Every time you use one of these labels you wound yourself a little bit more, you cut a little deeper into yourself. Have you noticed how much your critic uses toxic labels to put you down?

The therapist in this example has done her homework. She can point to specific examples of toxic labeling so that the confrontation has more impact. She has chosen the term toxic labeling (officially known as global labeling) because her client is an organic chemist and the word toxic has more meaning for him.

Your best technique for helping the client arrive at a more accurate statement is Socratic questioning. This is a method that Socrates used to expose logical inconsistencies in the arguments of his students. There are three main lines of questioning that you can use.

1. Questions that expose overgeneralization. ''Is it true that you *always* screw up? Every single task? You do nothing right, ever?''
2. Questions that expose faulty labeling. ''Is it true that getting a B means you're screwing up?''
3. Questions that expose the lack of evidence. ''What evidence do you have that people think you're screwing up?''

Here's how it might work during a session.

> *Therapist:* So lately the kicker's been telling you that you're ugly.
> *Client:* He's been on me with that a lot.
> *Therapist:* Is every part of your face and body ugly, or just some parts? (*Exposing overgeneralization*)
> *Client:* Mostly my nose, and I think my chin is weak. And my stomach is spongy and out of shape after the baby.

Therapist: Are there any parts of your body that you like?

Client: My legs, I guess. My hair and my eyes.

Therapist: So you're generalizing three features among many and labeling yourself completely ugly.

Client: Yeah, it's kind of crazy.

Therapist: Is it true that your chin and nose are totally ugly and repulsive? (*Exposing faulty labeling*)

Client: Well, they're not real attractive.

Therapist: But are they really *ugly*?

Client: No. Not really.

Therapist: So what's the accurate statement, what would the healthy voice say?

Client: That my legs, hair, and eyes are nice, and I don't like my nose, chin, or stomach.

Refuting the critic. Your objective is to develop specific rebuttals that the client can write down and use for each critical attack. The rebuttals are created through dialogues between the critic and healthy voice, through your Socratic questioning, and through the *three-column technique* (see the "Three-Column Technique" in chapter five). Over time, you can evaluate and modify the rebuttals until they are believable and effective. They are a resource you will use throughout the course of therapy. You should identify and confront distortions every time you hear them. That's because you are modeling in the session what you want the client to begin doing on his or her own. When you consistently confront the client's internal critic, when you let no distortion slip by, you are encouraging the client to fight consistently at home.

Therapist: All right, the critic's telling you that you're ruining your relationship with your son. That's the self-blame again. What can the healthy voice say back to that?

Thought stopping. The internal critic is often so insistent and so caustic that there is literally no room for the healthy voice. To make room for healthy rejoinders, certain thought-stopping procedures may prove useful. Chapter three describes "Howitzer Mantras," a simple technique for thought interruption. Another approach called "Asking the Price" requires the client to refocus on the cost of *listening* to the critic, rather than to the critical message itself. Once the critic has been silenced for a few moments, the client can then use appropriate refutations from the list that the two of you have been creating.

Identifying strengths. Concurrent with your work to defeat the critic must be a program to bolster the client's awareness of genuine strengths and assets. Chapter four, "Accurate Self-Assessment," has a rather detailed methodology for this. The bare minimum you should do includes the following.

1. Work with the client to create a list of genuine strengths and assets. If he or she has difficulty identifying strengths, ask the client to view him or herself as friends and loved ones see him or her.
2. Have the client identify his or her most troubling weaknesses.
3. Point out how the weaknesses are often couched in pejorative language. Revise these using accurate, nonjudging descriptions. Request that the client use only the accurate description when talking to you.
4. Encourage the client to use affirmations taken from the strengths list. These can be reinforced through the use of signs (affirmations displayed on the shaving mirror, the closet door, in the wallet, and so on).

From the strengths list, you should select two to four qualities that you genuinely appreciate in the client. At least one of these should be worked into every session. This means finding a creative way to bring up a particular strength so that it fits into the context of the hour.

- "I'm aware of how much tenacity it has taken to deal with your daughter's drug problem. That's a quality I've seen in you again and again."
- "I'm reminded again of your capacity for genuine caring and support. You gave a great deal to your brother."
- "Again I see this ability to problem-solve and cope in the face of crisis. Remember the last time you did that was . . . "

The repetition of the strengths is a must. Remember that your client's self-esteem was damaged originally when an authority figure (parent) repeatedly attacked his or her worth. It takes a great deal of positive repetition by another authority figure (therapist) to begin to undo this early programming. Saying it once, saying it five times, will probably have no effect. You'll have to remind a client ten, fifteen, twenty times before your praise has much impact. That's why you should only choose two to four positive qualities to focus on. Attempting to praise too many of the client's strengths dilutes the attention given to any one of them.

Self-acceptance. Self-esteem is more than merely recognizing one's positive qualities. It is an *attitude* of acceptance and nonjudgment toward self and others. Chapters three, six, and thirteen contain specific exercises to develop a forgiving, noncritical inner voice. In the end, the only way to really beat the critic is to push the client away from judgment altogether, to create mantras of acceptance that you repeat over and over until a new attitude begins to sink in. The watchword here is consistency. You will need to remind the client, again and again, of the self-accepting mantras you have developed together.

Introducing this issue, then dropping it for the next six sessions, and then mentioning it again will probably have very minimal impact. The concept and language of self-acceptance must be woven all through the fabric of your therapeutic work.

Special focus problems. There are four special problems that impact negatively on self-esteem: (1) inflexible rules and shoulds, (2) perfectionism, (3) extreme vulnerability to criticism, and (4) nonassertiveness. When any of these are present to a significant extent, they should be treated very specifically. Strategies for dealing with these problems are detailed in the following chapters:

1. For shoulds, see chapter seven.
2. For perfectionism, see chapter eight.
3. For vulnerability to criticism, see chapter nine.
4. For nonassertiveness, see chapter ten.

Reinforcing the healthy voice. People with a strong critic will always have contact with their negative inner voice to some extent. The job of the therapist is to diminish the intensity of self-attacks while nourishing more healthy self-talk. In other words, you may never entirely get rid of the inner voice that says, "You made a mistake, you're stupid," but you can reinforce the growth of a parallel and even stronger voice that says, "I'm fine, I'm doing the best I can." As the healthy voice gains strength, it responds more quickly, more forcefully, and more believably to the attacks of the critic.

There are several specific interventions you can use to reinforce the healthy voice.

1. *Teach coping statements.* These can be in the form of affirmations or specific rebuttals to attacks that the critic typically makes.
2. *Hypnosis.* Use or modify the induction in chapter twelve. Hypnosis is effective because it functions as a memory aid for coping statements that you want clients to learn by heart. In addition, because hypnosis is a state of hypersuggestibility, your interventions will penetrate through to a deeper level of acceptance.
3. *Visualization.* Techniques described in chapter eleven will allow the client to begin seeing him or herself as confident, socially comfortable, and competent. Visualization facilitates a more rapid shift in self-concept because the client literally sees his or her body and behavior differently.
4. *Anchoring.* Described in chapter thirteen, anchoring is a technique for retrieving feelings of confidence and self-liking from times in the past and bringing them into the present. An ability to access positive feelings at will has a significant strengthening effect on the healthy voice.

2

The Pathological Critic

The pathological critic is a term coined by psychologist Eugene Sagan to describe the negative inner voice that attacks and judges you. Everyone has a critical inner voice. But people with low self-esteem tend to have a more vicious and vocal pathological critic.

The critic blames you for things that go wrong. The critic compares you to others—to their achievements and abilities—and finds you wanting. The critic sets impossible standards of perfection and then beats you up for the smallest mistake. The critic keeps an album of your failures, but never once reminds you of your strengths or accomplishments. The critic has a script describing how you ought to live and screams that you are wrong and bad if your needs drive you to violate his rules. The critic tells you to be the best—and if you're not the best, you're nothing. He calls you names—stupid, incompetent, ugly, selfish, weak—and makes you believe that all of them are true. The critic reads your friends' minds and convinces you that they are bored, turned off, disappointed, or disgusted by you. The critic exaggerates your weaknesses by insisting that you "*always* say stupid things," or "*always* screw up a relationship," or "*never* finish anything on time."

The pathological critic is busy undermining your self-worth every day of your life. Yet his voice is so insidious, so woven into the fabric of your thought that you never notice its devastating effect. The self-attacks always seem reasonable and justified. The carping, judging inner voice seems natural, a familiar part of you. In truth, the critic is a kind of psychological jackal who, with every attack, weakens and breaks down any good feelings you have about yourself.

Although we refer to the critic as "he" for convenience, your critic's voice may sound female. Your critic's voice may sound like your mother, your father, or your own speaking voice.

The first and most important thing you need to know about your critic is that no matter how distorted and false his attacks may be, he is almost always believed. When your critic says, "God, I'm dumb," this judgment seems just as true to you as the awareness that you're tired this morning, or that you have brown eyes, or that you don't understand word processors. It feels normal to judge yourself because you are so intimately aware of what you feel and do. But the attacks of the critic aren't part of the normal process of noticing what you feel and do. For example, when you examine how you felt on a first date, the critic drowns out any normal, reasonable reflections by shouting through a bull horn that you were a callow bore, a fumbler, a nervous phony, and that your date won't ever want to see you again. The critic takes your self-esteem and puts it through a Cuisinart.

A loud, voluble critic is enormously toxic. He is more poisonous to your psychological health than almost any trauma or loss. That's because grief and pain wash away with time. But the critic is *always* with you—judging, blaming, finding fault. You have no defense against him. "There you go again," he says, "being an idiot." And you automatically feel wrong and bad, like a child who's been slapped for saying something naughty.

Consider the case of a 29-year-old entomologist, recently graduated with a Ph.D., who was applying for a faculty position. During interviews he would observe the dress and manner of the interview committee and make guesses about the sort of people they were and how they were responding to him. He would handle questions by weighing the best possible answer, given what the committee seemed to expect. And while he was doing all that, he was also listening to a continuous monologue in which his critic said, "You're a fraud, you don't know anything. You won't fool these people. Wait till they read that mediocre piece of hogwash you call your dissertation . . . That was a stupid answer. Can't you crack a joke? Do something! They'll see how boring you are. Even if you get the job, you'll only lose it when your incompetence starts to show. You're not fooling anybody."

The entomologist believed every word. It all seemed to make sense. Because he'd heard it for years, the steady stream of poison felt normal, reasonable, and true. During the interview he became more and more stiff, his answers more vague. His voice slipped into a monotone while he perspired and developed a little stammer. He was listening to the critic, and the critic was turning him into the very thing he feared.

Another important thing you need to know about the critic is that he speaks in a kind of shorthand. He might only scream the word "lazy." But those two syllables contain the memory of the hundreds of times your father complained about laziness, attacked your laziness, said how he hated laziness. It's all there, and you feel the entire weight of his disgust as the critic says the word.

Sometimes the critic uses images or pictures from the past to undermine your sense of worth. He shows a rerun of some awkward moment on a date; he pulls out snapshots of a dressing-down you got from your boss, images of a failed relationship, and scenes of the times you blew up at your kids.

A legal secretary found that her critic often used the word "screw-up." When she thought about it, she realized that "screw-up" stood for a list of negative qualities. It meant someone who was incompetent, unliked, a taker of foolish risks, a person (like her father) who would run away from problems. When the critic said "screw-up," she firmly believed that she was all of these things.

One of the strange things about the critic is that he often seems to have more control of your mind than you do. He will suddenly start to sound off, launching one attack after another or dragging you over and over through a painful scene. Through a process called *chaining,* he may show you a past failure, which reminds you of another and another in a long string of painful associations. And though you try to turn him off, you keep being reminded of yet another mistake, another rejection, another embarrassment.

Although the critic seems to have a will of his own, his independence is really an illusion. The truth is that you are so used to listening to him, so used to believing him, that you have not yet learned how to turn him off. With practice, however, you can learn to analyze and refute what the critic says. You can tune him out *before* he has a chance to poison your feelings of self-worth.

An Arsenal of Shoulds

The critic has many weapons. Among the most effective are the values and rules of living you grew up with. The critic has a way of turning your "shoulds" against you. He compares the way you are with the way you ought to be and judges you inadequate or wrong. He calls you stupid if the A you should have had slips to a B. He says, "A marriage should last forever," and calls you a failure after your divorce. He says, "A real man supports his family," and calls you a loser when you're laid off from work. He says, "The kids come first," and calls you selfish when you crave some nights off.

A 35-year-old bartender described how his critic used old "shoulds" he'd learned as a child. "My father was a lawyer, so the critic says that I should be a professional and that anything else is a waste. I feel like I should have forced myself to go to school. I feel like I should read real books instead of the sports page. I feel like I should be *doing* something in the world instead of mixing drinks and heading over to my girlfriend's house." This man's self-esteem was severely damaged by a critic who insisted that he be something other than himself. The fact was that he liked the comradery of the bar and wasn't the least bit intellectual. But he continually rejected himself for not living up to his family's expectations.

The Origin of the Critic

The critic is born during your earliest experience of socialization by your parents. All through childhood, your parents are teaching you which behaviors are acceptable, which are dangerous, which are morally wrong, which are lovable, and which are annoying. They do this by hugging and praising you for appropriate behavior and punishing you for dangerous, wrong, or annoying behavior. It's impossible to grow up without having experienced a great number of punishing events. Personality theorist Harry Stack Sullivan called these punishing events *forbidding gestures.*

By design, forbidding gestures are frightening and rejecting. A child who is spanked or scolded feels the withdrawal of parental approval very acutely. He or she is, for a while, a bad person. Either consciously or unconsciously, a child knows that his or her parents are the source of all physical and emotional nourishment. If he or she were to be rejected, cast out by the family, he or she would die. So parental approval is a matter of life or death to a child. The experience of being bad can be very deeply felt, because being bad carries with it the terrible risk of losing all support.

All children grow up with emotional residues from the forbidding gestures. They retain conscious and unconscious memories of all those times when they felt wrong or bad. These are the unavoidable scars that growing up inflicts on your self-esteem. This experience is also where the critic gets his start, feeding on these early "not-OK" feelings. There is still a part of you willing to believe you're bad just as soon as someone gets angry at you, or you make a mistake, or you fall short of a goal. That early feeling of being not-OK is why the critic's attacks seem to fit in so well with what you already believe about yourself. His voice is the voice of a disapproving parent, the punishing, forbidding voice that shaped your behavior as a child.

The volume and viciousness of a critic's attacks are directly related to the strength of your not-OK feelings. If the early forbidding gestures were relatively mild, the adult critic may only rarely attack. But if you were given very strong messages about your wrongness or badness as a child, then the adult critic will come gunning for you every chance he gets.

There are five main factors that determine the strength of your early not-OK feelings:

1. *The degree to which issues of taste, personal needs, safety, or good judgment were mislabeled as moral imperatives.* In some families, when dad wants things quiet, a child is made to feel morally wrong if he or she is noisy. Other families make a low grade into a sin. Some children are made to feel wrong for needing time with friends or for having sexual feelings. Some children are *bad* if they forget their chores, *bad* if they prefer a certain haircut, or *bad* if they ride their skateboard in the street. When the issue is really a matter of taste, failure to perform tasks, or poor judgment, but parents make a child feel morally wrong, they are laying the foundation for low self-esteem. It's important to recognize that certain words and phrases carry heavy moral messages. If a child hears that he or she is lazy, or selfish, or looks like a bum, or acts like a screwball, the specific situations are very soon forgotten. But he or she is left with an enduring sense of wrongness.

2. *The degree to which parents failed to differentiate between behavior and identity.* A child who hears a stern warning about the dangers of running in the street will have better self-esteem than a child who only hears that he's a "bad boy" when he runs into the street. The child who's a "bad boy" is getting the message that he and his behavior are not OK. He doesn't learn the difference between what he does and what he is. As an adult, his critic will attack both his behavior and his worth. Parents who carefully distinguish between *inappropriate behavior* and the basic *goodness of the child* raise children who feel better about themselves and have a far gentler inner critic.

3. *The frequency of the forbidding gestures.* The frequency of negative messages from parents has an impact on early feelings of worth. Hitler's minister of propaganda once observed that the secret to having any lie believed was merely to repeat it often enough. The lie that you are not OK wasn't learned with your parents' first rebuke. It was learned through repeated criticism. You have to hear "What's the matter with you?" and "Stop screwing around" a good many times before the message sinks in. But after a while you get the point—you're not OK.

4. *The consistency of the forbidding gestures.* Suppose your parents didn't like you to use the word "shit." You may have thought that prohibition rather stuffy, but if they were consistent, you managed to get along without that admittedly versatile word. Suppose, however, that they let you say "shit" sometimes and blew up when you said it at other times. And suppose they were equally inconsistent about other rules. At first you would be confused, but the randomness of the attacks would eventually lead you to a very painful conclusion. It wasn't what you *did*—sometimes that was OK, sometimes it wasn't— it was *you.* There was something wrong with you. Children who have experienced inconsistent parenting often feel an ineffable feeling of guilt. They feel as if they've done something wrong, but because they can never get the rules straight, they have no idea what.

5. *The frequency with which forbidding gestures were tied to parental anger or withdrawal.* Children can tolerate a fair amount of criticism without experiencing much damage to their sense of worth. But if the criticism is accompanied by parental anger or withdrawal (threatened or actual), it has enormous potency. Anger and withdrawal give an unmistakable message: "You're bad, and I'm rejecting you." Since this is the most terrifying thing that a child can hear, he or she is very certain to remember it. Long after the incident has blown over, the child retains the strong impression of his or her wrongness. And the critic will use that sense of wrongness to psychologically beat and kick you as an adult.

Why You Listen to the Critic

You listen to the critic because it is very rewarding to do so. Incredible as it seems, the critic helps you to meet certain basic needs, and listening to his vicious attacks can be reinforcing. But how can so much pain be reinforcing? How can attacking yourself be the least bit pleasurable or help to satisfy your needs?

The first step to understanding the function of your critic is to recognize that *everyone* has certain basic needs. Everyone needs to feel:

1. Secure and unafraid
2. Effective and competent in the world
3. Accepted by parents and significant others
4. A sense of worth and OKness in most situations

People with adequate self-esteem tend to have very different strategies for meeting these needs than people with low self-esteem. If you have adequate self-esteem, you also have a degree of confidence in yourself. You keep yourself secure by confronting or eliminating things that frighten you. You solve problems instead of worrying about them, and you find ways to make people respond positively to you. You cope directly with interpersonal conflicts rather than wait for them to pass. Conversely, low self-esteem robs you of confidence. You don't feel as able to cope with anxiety, interpersonal problems, or challenging risks. Life is more painful because you don't feel as effective, and it's hard to face the anxiety involved in making things change.

This is where the critic comes in. People with low self-esteem often rely on the critic to help them cope with feelings of anxiety, helplessness, rejection, and inadequacy. Paradoxically, while the critic is beating you up, he is also making you feel better. This is why it's so hard to get rid of the critic. He can play a crucial role in making you more safe and comfortable in the world. Unfortunately, the price you pay for the critic's support is very high and further undermines your sense of worth. But you are reinforced to keep listening because every time the critic pipes up you feel a little less anxious, less incompetent, less powerless, or less vulnerable to others.

The Role of Reinforcement

To understand how the critic's painful attacks can be reinforcing, it's necessary first to examine how reinforcement shapes your behavior and your thinking.

Positive reinforcement occurs when a rewarding event follows a particular behavior and results in an increase in the future likelihood of that behavior. If your wife gives you a warm hug and a thank you after you've cut the lawn, she is positively reinforcing your gardening activities. If the boss praises the clean, spare writing style in your last report, she is positively reinforcing the writing behavior she prefers. Because affection and praise are such powerful rewards, you are likely to repeat your gardening and writing behaviors in the future.

Just as with physical behavior, the frequency of cognitive behavior (thoughts) can also be increased through positive reinforcement. If you feel aroused following a particular sexual fantasy, you are quite likely to conjure up that fantasy again. Thinking critically of others can be reinforced by increased feelings of worth. Daydreams of an upcoming vacation, if they are followed by a sense of excitement and anticipation, will be repeated. The increased feeling of worth that follows your memories of success and achievement makes you more likely to return to them. Obsessing about the misfortunes of someone you dislike can be reinforced by feelings of pleasure or vindication.

Negative reinforcement can only occur when you are in physical or psychological pain. Any behavior that succeeds in stopping the pain is reinforced, and is therefore more likely to occur when you feel similar pain in the future. For example, when students are preparing for final exams, they often find that the most boring, mundane activities have become irresistibly interesting. Activities like doodling or scoring baskets in the trash can are being reinforced because they provide relief from high-stress studying. As a general rule, anything that relieves stress and anxiety will be reinforced. Anger is often reinforced by the immediate drop in tension following a blowup. TV watching, eating, hot baths, withdrawal, complaining, hobbies, and sports activities may all at times be reinforced by tension or anxiety reduction. Blaming others relieves anxiety over your mistakes and can be reinforced until it becomes very high-frequency behavior. Macho behavior has the effect of relieving social anxiety for some men, and the decrease in anxiety is so rewarding that the macho style becomes a heavy armor in which they become trapped.

As with positive reinforcement, negative reinforcement shapes how you think. Any thought that relieves feelings of anxiety, guilt, hopelessness, or inadequacy will be reinforced. Suppose, for example, that you feel anxious every time you visit your crusty, judgmental father-in-law. Driving over to his house one day, you begin thinking about what a narrow bigot he really is, how few of his opinions are supported by anything resembling a fact, how tyrannical he is when crossed. Suddenly you feel more angry than anxious, and you experience a strange sense of relief. Since your critical thoughts are reinforced by reduced anxiety, you notice on subsequent visits an increasingly judgmental attitude toward the old man.

A person who feels anxious about mistakes at work may find that devaluing the job ("it's idiot's work") and the boss ("a nitpicking, anal type") reduced anxiety. It's likely that the devaluing thoughts will be entertained again if anxiety should once more increase. Feelings of hopelessness can sometimes be relieved by romantic fantasies, grandiose success fantasies, rescue or escape dreams, or simple problem-solving thoughts. In every case, the particular cognition that succeeds in reducing the sense of hopelessness will be remembered. When the same feelings recur, the same recognition has a high probability of being used again.

The mourning process is a classic example of the power of negative reinforcement. What makes people keep dredging up painful memories of the lost person or object? Why keep thinking and thinking about those sweet days that can never come again? Paradoxically, these obsessive ruminations about the loss have the power of relieving pain. The awareness of a loss creates high levels of physical and emotional tension. The frustration and helplessness build until they must be discharged. Calling up specific images and memories of the lost person or object helps discharge that tension in the form of tears and then a brief sort of numbness. The stage in mourning of obsessive remembering is therefore reinforced by tension reduction and a few moments of relative peace.

In summary, negative reinforcement is basically a problem-solving process. You're in pain. You want to feel better. You keep searching for some action or thought that is analgesic. When you find a thought or behavior that works to decrease your pain, you file it away as a successful solution to a particular problem. When the problem recurs, you will return again and again to your proven coping strategy.

The variable ratio reinforcement schedule. So far, only continuous reinforcement schedules have been discussed. Continuous reinforcement means that a particular thought or behavior is *always* reinforced. Every time you engage in the behavior, you are rewarded by pleasure or relief. An important aspect of continuous reinforcement schedules is that they lead very quickly to *extinction* if the thought or behavior stops being reinforced. Shortly after you cease getting rewarded for a previously reinforced thought or behavior, you simply stop doing it.

The situation is very different with a variable ratio reinforcement schedule. Here reinforcement is not continuous. You may be rewarded after emitting the behavior 5 times, then after 20 times, then after 43 times, then 12 times, and so on. The schedule isn't predictable. Sometimes you might have to engage in the behavior hundreds or even thousands of times before being reinforced. The result of the unpredictability is that you will keep doing a previously reinforced behavior for a long time *without* reinforcement before extinction. It takes a long time to give up.

Slot machines operate on the variable ratio reinforcement schedule, which is why people become addicted and play them to the point of exhaustion. Sometimes it takes only one quarter for a jackpot, sometimes hundreds. People tend to play a long time before giving up because reinforcement *could* occur on any given quarter.

Here are two examples of how the variable ratio reinforcement schedule can have a powerful influence on your thoughts.

1. Obsessive worries are occasionally reinforced when the worry leads to a workable solution that reduces anxiety. This might happen once or twice a year, or even a few times in a lifetime. But the worrier keeps at it, moving from worry to worry, like the gambler who plays quarter after quarter, hoping this one or the next one will finally pay off.

2. The obsessive reliving of an awkward social exchange is sometimes reinforced by those wonderful moments when you suddenly see it differently and don't feel so rejected or incompetent after all. You remember something you did or said that seems, in memory, to save the situation. Your shame melts away, and you feel accepting of yourself again. The sad fact is that your obsessive reliving is hardly ever rewarded by such a reprieve. Usually you suffer, hour after hour, the mental videotapes of an embarrassing exchange, waiting to put in the quarter that makes you feel adequate once more.

How the Critic Gets Reinforced

Your self-critical statements can be both positively and negatively reinforced. Ironically, while the critic is tearing you down, he is also helping you solve problems and meet, in limited ways, certain basic needs. The following are specific examples of how the critic helps meet some of your needs.

Positive Reinforcement for the Critic

The need to do right. Everyone has a rather large inner list of rules and values that regulate behavior. These rules are often useful because they control dangerous impulses and provide a sense of structure and order in your life. The rules create an ethical framework by defining what is moral and immoral. They prescribe how to act with authority figures and friends, how to be sexual, how to handle money, and so on. When you violate these inner rules, life becomes chaotic and you lose your sense of worth. So the critic helps you follow the rules. He tells you how wrong and bad you are whenever you break a rule or feel tempted to break one. He harangues you so much that you try to "do right." As one man put it, "My critic gives me the backbone not to go around lying, cheating, and being lazy. I need that."

The need to feel right. Even while he's telling you that you're no good, the critic can paradoxically help you feel a greater sense of worth and acceptance. The catch is that it's only temporary.

1. *Self-worth.* There are two ways the critic helps you temporarily to feel more worth: by comparing you to others and by setting high, perfectionistic standards.

Here's how comparing works: The critic continually evaluates how you stack up in terms of intelligence, achievements, earning capacity, sexual attractiveness, likability, social competence, openness—virtually any trait or quality you value. Many times you find yourself less adequate than the other person in one or more dimensions, and your self-esteem takes a blow. But once in a while you decide that you are more attractive, smarter, or warmer, and you feel a moment's satisfaction at being higher on the totem pole. Though it comes only occasionally, that moment's satisfaction is reinforcing. The comparing your critic does is being reinforced on a variable ratio schedule. Most efforts to compare yourself to others leave you feeling less adequate, but those times when it pays off—when you look good by comparison—keep you caught in the comparing habit.

The second way the critic boosts your worth is by setting incredibly high standards for how you must perform at work, as a lover, as a parent, as a conversationalist, as a housekeeper, or as a first baseman on the softball team. Most of the time you will fail to live up to the critic's demands, and you'll feel inadequate. But once in a great while, everything comes together in a miraculous perfection. You achieve a milestone at work, you have a deep and lovely conversation with your son, you hit two home runs for your team, and tell six entertaining stories at the pizza parlor afterwards. And that's how you reinforce the critic—with a variable ratio schedule. Every so often you do live up to his lofty standards and, for a brief time, feel at peace with yourself. So the critic keeps insisting on perfection, because it feels so good when you are, for that little while, perfect.

2. *Feeling accepted by critical parents.* To meet this need, your own critic joins your parents in attacking you. If your parents disparaged you for selfishness, your critic will do likewise. If your parents rejected your sexual behavior, the inner critic will also call you immoral. If your parents labeled you stupid or fat or a failure, then your critic will join them by calling you the same names. Every time you use a critical self-statement that agrees with your parents' negative judgments, you are reinforced by feeling close to them. By identifying with their point of view, you may paradoxically feel safer, more accepted, more loved. You are seeing things their way, and in joining them you experience a sense of belonging and emotional security that strongly reinforces your own critical voice.

The need to achieve. The critic helps you achieve goals by whipping you like an old dray horse. He drives you with vicious attacks on your worth. If you don't make three sales this week, you're lazy, you're incompetent, you're a lousy breadwinner. If you don't get a 3.5 average, you're stupid and talentless and will prove to everyone you aren't graduate school material. What reinforces the critic is that you *do* achieve things when driven. You do make sales, you do hit the books. And every time the critic drives you to complete a task, his caustic battering is reinforced.

Negative Reinforcement for the Critic

The need to control painful feelings. When the critic helps you to diminish or entirely stop painful feelings, his voice is highly reinforced. Even though the long-term effect is to destroy your self-esteem, the short-term effect of critical self-talk may be a reduction in painful affect. Here are some examples of how the critic can help you feel less guilty, afraid, depressed, and angry.

1. *Feeling not OK or bad or valueless.* On a very deep level, everyone has doubts about his or her worth. But if you have low self-esteem, those doubts can be magnified so that a good part of your inner life is dominated by feelings of inadequacy and hopelessness. That sense of inadequacy is so incredibly painful that you'll do almost anything to escape it. Enter the critic. The critic helps you cope by creating

impossible standards of perfection. You have to get promoted every six months, cook gourmet meals, spend three hours a night helping your kid with his homework, be a total turn-on to your mate, and make nonstop, spicy conversation straight from the pages of *The New York Times Book Review*. The standard is impossible, but while the critic is driving you to be perfect, you no longer feel so inadequate, so hopeless. You feel instead a kind of omnipotence—if you just worked hard enough, kicked yourself hard enough, fought hard enough to transform yourself, all things would be possible.

2. *Fear of failure.* A woman who was contemplating a job search for a more creative kind of work began feeling very nervous at the thought of leaving the safety of her old job. Her critic came to the rescue. The critic said, "You can't do it. You'll be fired. You haven't got enough artistic talent. They'll see right through you." Under this barrage of self-rejecting statements, she decided to wait for a year before doing anything. Immediately her anxiety level decreased. And the critic was reinforced because his attack led directly to a reduction in her level of distress. The critic is very useful in protecting you against the anxiety inherent in change and risk taking. As soon as he undermines your confidence to the point where you abandon your plan for change, he's reinforced by your feeling of relief.

3. *Fear of rejection.* One way to control the fear of rejection is to constantly predict it so that you're never caught by surprise. The critic does a lot of mind reading: "She won't like you. He's bored to tears. They don't really want you on the committee. He doesn't like your work. Your lover's frown says he is losing interest." The mind reading helps to protect you against being caught by surprise. If you anticipate rejection, failure, or defeat, it won't hurt quite so badly when it comes. The critic's mind reading is reinforced on a variable ratio schedule. Once in a while, the critic does accurately predict some hurt or rejection. And since the anticipation helps desensitize you to the worst of the pain, the critic is reinforced to keep on mind reading.

Another way to cope with the fear of rejection is to reject yourself first. When the critic attacks you for all your flaws and shortcomings, no one else can say anything you haven't already heard. A 38-year-old loan officer described it this way: "After my divorce, I kept calling myself a loser. I think that saying that protected me. It felt like if I kept saying it, nobody else would. They wouldn't have to call me a loser because I was doing it already." A well-known poet described the same feeling: "I always had a sense that if I kept putting my work down it would magically keep other people from doing it." Attacking yourself is very reinforcing if it helps relieve your anxiety about being attacked by others.

4. *Anger.* Feelings of anger toward people you love can be very frightening. As the anger begins to enter awareness, you may feel a huge surge of anxiety. One way of coping is to turn the anger around

and attack yourself. You're the one who's failed, who hasn't understood, whose mistakes caused the problem in the first place. As the critic goes on the attack, your anxiety decreases. Now you won't have to risk hurting someone. Or worse, getting them so angry that they hurt you.

5. *Guilt.* The critic obligingly helps you deal with guilt by providing punishment. You have sinned, and the critic will make you pay. As the critic attacks you over and over for your selfishness, your greed, or your insensitivity, you gradually feel a sense of atonement, sometimes even a sense of undoing, as if the sin never happened. While you sit in the critic's screening room reviewing again and again videos of your transgressions, the feeling of guilt dissipates. The critic is reinforced once more because the violence he does to your sense of worth helps you to conquer for a while that awful feeling of wrongness.

6. *Frustration.* "I've nursed seven sick people all day, I've shopped, I've cooked, I've listened to some blaring lead guitar riffs from my son's room, I've got the bills spread out on the kitchen table. Those are the times I get down on myself. I think of all the stupid decisions I've made, and I get really angry. Like I'm the one who made this life, I lost the marriage, I'm the one who's so afraid I can't change anything. After a while I feel a little calmer and just go to bed." (36-year-old Intensive Care Unit nurse) Notice how the critic's attacks are reinforced by a drop in arousal levels. The self-directed anger has the effect of discharging tension from a tiring day, a noisy house, and anxiety over bills. When you use the critic to get angry at yourself, your covert goal may actually be an attempt to blow off high levels of frustration and negative arousal. The extent to which this strategy works and your tension is reduced is the extent to which the critic is reinforced for beating you up.

These examples of how the critic helps you meet basic needs are not exhaustive. They are designed to get you thinking about your critic and how his attacks get reinforced. It's extremely important that you learn to identify the function of your self-attacks, how they help as well as hurt you. Right now, go back over the list of positive and negative reinforcements for the critic. Put an asterisk by each one that applies to you. When you have determined which needs your critic is helping you to meet, and some of the ways his attacks get reinforced, you can go on to the next step: catching your critic.

Catching Your Critic

To gain control of the critic, you have to first be able to hear him. Every conscious moment of your life, you are engaging in an inner monologue. You are interpreting experience, problem solving, speculating about the future, reviewing past events. Most of this continuous self-talk is helpful, or at worst innocuous. But somewhere hidden in the monologue are your critic's indictments. Catching the critic in the act of putting you down requires a special vigilance. You have to keep listening in on the intercom of your inner monologue. You have to notice the critic when he says, "Stupid . . . another dumb mistake . . . you're weak . . . you'll never get a job because something's wrong with you . . . you're bad at conversation . . . you're turning her off."

Sometimes the critic hits you with images of past mistakes or failures. Sometimes he doesn't use words or images. The thought arrives as an awareness, a knowledge, an impression. The criticism is so lightning quick that it seems beyond the scope of language. A salesman put it this way: "There are times I just *know* I'm wasting my life. I can feel this sense of emptiness. It's like a heavy feeling in my stomach."

Catching the critic will take a real commitment. You'll need to be especially aware of your inner monologue in problematic situations:

- Meeting strangers
- Contact with people you find sexually attractive
- Situations in which you have made a mistake
- Situations in which you feel criticized and defensive
- Interactions with authority figures
- Situations in which you feel hurt or someone has been angry at you
- Situations in which you risk rejection or failure
- Conversations with parents or anyone who might be disapproving

Exercise

Monitor your critic. For one day, stay as vigilant as possible for self-attacks. Count the number of critical statements you make to yourself. You may be surprised at how frequently your internal monologue turns to negative self-appraisal. On days two and three, take a further step. Instead of just counting the critic's attacks, keep a notebook handy and write them down. Here's a sample taken from the notebook of a 24-year-old first grade teacher:

Thought Number	Time	Critical Statement
1	8:15	The principal must be sick of my getting here late.
2	8:40	Skimpy lesson plan. God I'm lazy.

3	9:30	These kids are slow and I'm not helping them much.
4	9:45	Stupid to send Sheila with the lunch list, she'll fool around in the halls.
5	10:00	What kind of teacher are you? These kids are moving ahead *so slow.*
6	12:15	Stupid remark in the lunchroom.
7	12:20	Why am I so inane?
8	2:20	It was a madhouse today. When will I learn to control the class?
9	2:35	Why don't I get some of the kids' drawings on the wall boards? I'm so disorganized.
10	3:10	Parked like an idiot—look at the angle of the car.
11	3:40	Look at the mess. Nice housekeeping.

The more of these self-attacks you write down the better. Congratulate yourself if you catch at least ten of the critic's barbs each day.

At night you will have one more task. On a piece of typing or binder paper, draw a line down the middle. On one side put the heading, *Helps Me Avoid Feeling.* On the other put the heading, *Helps Me Feel or Do.* Now for each critical thought in your notebook, write down the function of that thought—how it is reinforced either positively or negatively, how it either allows you to feel or do something good or avoid feeling something unpleasant. Here's what the school teacher wrote:

Thought Number	Helps Me Feel or Do	Helps Me Avoid Feeling
1		Surprised and hurt if she calls me on my tardiness.
2	Motivated to be more careful with my work.	
3	Motivated to develop a more creative lesson plan, maybe get some consultation.	

4	Motivated to pay more attention to whom I send.	
5	Motivated to work harder at my lesson plan.	
6		Social anxiety. I already know I'm stupid so they can't hurt me.
7		Social anxiety.
8	Motivated to consult with other teachers on discipline techniques.	Surprised and hurt if the principal criticizes me.
9		Surprised and hurt if the principal criticizes me. Guilt at breaking my commitment to being more organized.
10	Motivated to pay more attention to how I park.	Guilt at parking unsafely.
11	Motivated to be more neat.	

As she went over her work, she realized, as you will when you do this exercise, that there were certain basic themes. Many of the critic's attacks were reinforced because the attacks drove her to higher levels of achievement and self-improvement. When she thought about it, she realized that the critic was setting very high standards of performance for her. On the few occasions when she actually met those standards, she had a wonderful feeling of self-acceptance. This feeling was intoxicating, and she knew it reinforced her perfectionism. She also noticed themes of avoiding social anxiety and fear of being surprised by a rejection. Armed with this new knowledge, the teacher was ready for the most important step: disarming the critic.

3

Disarming the Critic

By now you should be getting better acquainted with your critic. Hopefully you've improved at separating the critic's voice from the continuous stream of self-talk that goes on throughout the day. This task is a little bit like tapping the family phone of a suspected Mafioso. You have to sift through a lot of innocuous conversation in order to hear him betray himself. You can't stop listening, because at any moment he could say something incriminating.

Before you can disarm the critic, you have to know him. Secrecy is his greatest strength. So if you can get really good at hearing and identifying his voice, you will have won a major victory. Remember that every time the critic attacks he is doing you real psychological harm. He is further wounding your sense of worth and making it harder to feel competent and happy in the world. You can't afford what he is doing to you. It's costing you too much.

Since it's not really possible to stay on total alert every moment of your waking life, you need to know when you should be especially vigilant. In the last chapter, you were given a list of problematic situations—times when you have made a mistake, been criticized, or dealt with people who might be disapproving. But there's another time when you need to watch for the critic. That's when you are feeling depressed or down on yourself. These emotions are usually triggered by the critic, and their presence indicates that he is at work. In order to catch the critic in the act of making you depressed, you need to do four things:

1. Close your eyes and take some deep breaths. Draw the air deep into your abdomen so that your diaphragm can stretch and relax.
2. Relax your body. Notice and eliminate any tension in your legs and arms, your face, jaw, neck, and shoulders.
3. Notice where you feel depression in your body. Focus on that place and really get to know the feeling there.
4. Listen to the thoughts that go with the feeling in that part of your body. Notice everything that you're saying to yourself. Now try to remember how the feeling began and what the critic was saying then.

If you follow these four steps each time you feel depressed or down on yourself, you'll become much clearer about the specific content of the critic's attacks.

If you did the exercises in the last chapter, you are now more aware of the basic themes of your critical voice. As you analyze your critical thoughts, determining what they help you feel or help you avoid feeling, you'll begin to see a pattern to the attacks. One person may find that his critic's primary function is to help him atone for guilt. Someone else may experience a critic whose main effort is to provide achievement motivation. Another person's critic may help desensitize her to the fear of rejection. Or a critic may harangue you to stay on the straight and narrow path. When you become aware of the theme or themes your critic uses, you are ready to fight back.

Disarming the critic involves three steps: (1) unmasking his purpose, (2) talking back, and (3) making him useless.

Unmasking His Purpose

There are few things more effective for winning arguments than to suddenly unmask your opponent's ulterior motives. A classic example is tobacco company "research" that finds no link between cigarette smoking and heart disease. Since the ulterior motives of the tobacco industry are clear, few people take their arguments seriously.

When you unmask the critic, you expose his true purpose and functions. Here are some examples of ways you might unmask your critic:

- You're kicking me right now to force me to live by the rules I grew up with.
- You're comparing me to everyone so that once in a while I'll find someone lower on the totem pole than me.

- You're slapping me around like my parents used to do, and I believe you because I believed them.
- You're beating me so that I'll achieve more and more and maybe feel better about myself.
- You're insisting that I be perfect because if I did everything exactly right, I might finally feel OK about myself.
- You're saying I can't do it so that I won't bother trying and won't have to worry about screwing up.
- You're telling me they won't like me so that I won't be so hurt if I'm rejected.
- You're saying she's disgusted by me so that no matter what the truth is, I'll be prepared for the worst.
- You're telling me to be perfect so that I'll stupidly think that maybe I could be perfect and for a few minutes feel better about myself.
- You're kicking me around so that I can atone for divorcing Jill.

Getting clear about the critic's function makes everything he says less believable. You know his ulterior motive. No matter how he rants and raves, you've exposed his secret agenda and therefore feel less vulnerable to him. Remember that the critic attacks you because his voice is in some way being reinforced. When you are able to identify the role your critic plays in your psychological life, when you are able to call his game, you are beginning to seriously undermine the credibility of his message.

Talking Back

The idea of talking back to your own critical voice may seem strange to you. But in truth much of this book is about talking back: learning to refute and reject the old negative programming you received as a child. While growing up, Wanda received literally thousands of devaluing messages—first from her father, and then from her own critical voice. Whenever her father was angry, he would call her stupid. In particular, he ridiculed her for doing things "the hard way" and for getting only C's in high school. All of her life, Wanda has believed her father's judgment. These days, her critic constantly berates her for doing things "the stupid way." Wanda's self-esteem can't improve until she stops these messages by learning to talk back to the critic. She needs a psychological cannon to blow the critic away so that he finally shuts up.

What follows are three methods for talking back. Properly delivered, they will render the critic speechless for a few minutes. Experiment with each of them; try them singly and in combination. Find out which ones work best for you.

The Howitzer Mantras. These are selected words and phrases that are designed to hit the critic like a cannon blast. Here are some examples:

This is poison. Stop it!
These are lies.
These are lies my father told me.
Stop this shit!
No more put-downs.
Shut up!
Screw you, asshole.
To hell with these put-downs!
Get off my back!
Stop this garbage!

Choose a mantra that helps you feel angry. It's good to get mad. Profanity is a prefectly healthy response to the critic. When using the Howitzer Mantras, shout them inside. Mentally scream at the critic so that you can drown him out with your anger and indignation.

If the critic continues his assault despite your telling him to "shut up" or "stop this nonsense," it's time for stronger measures. Put a rubber band around your wrist and snap it while subvocalizing your mantra. Let's say, for example, that the critic is kicking you about some aspect of your appearance. One of your mantras is "Stop this shit!" You scream it internally and simultaneously snap the rubber band. By snapping the rubber band, you are emphasizing your "stop" commands and making successful thought-interruption more likely. The sharp stinging sensation breaks the chain of negative cognitions and acts as a punisher so that the critic is less likely to attack in the near future. The important thing is to catch the critic just as he starts, before he is allowed to do much damage. If you snap the rubber band and internally scream your mantra whenever you hear the critic's voice, the frequency of his attacks will greatly diminish.

Asking the price. One of the best ways to disarm the critic is to think about the price you pay for his attacks. What does listening to the critic cost you? A 32-year-old sales representative for a printing firm made the following list as he evaluated the toll the critic took on his work, relationships, and level of well-being.

- Defensive with my wife around any criticism.
- Blow up at my daughter when she doesn't mind.
- Lost friendship with Al because I got hostile.
- Dump on my mother when I detect the slightest criticism.
- Afraid to be assertive with potential clients because they might reject me. (This probably costs me ten thousand a year in commissions.)

- Tend to be cold and distant with bosses and authorities because I am afraid of them.
- Feel anxious and on guard with people.
- Constantly thinking that people don't like me.
- Afraid to try new things for fear that I'll screw them up.

Poor self-esteem was costing the sales representative a great deal in every area of his life. When the critic attacked, he could now talk back by saying, "You make me defensive and afraid of people, you cut my income, you lose me friends, you make me harsh with my little girl."

It's time for you to evaluate the cost of your own critic. Make a list of ways in which your self-esteem has affected you in terms of your relationships, work, and level of well-being. When you've completed the list, combine the most important items into a summary statement that you can use when the critic attacks. Fight back by telling the critic, "I can't afford this, you've cost me . . ."

Affirmation of worth. This method is very hard to practice—especially if you have a deeply held belief that there is something wrong with you, that you are not OK. But you must learn to affirm yourself if you are to fully disarm the critic. The first two methods of talking back are important, but they aren't enough. You can't *permanently* turn off the critic's vitriol by calling him names, telling him to shut up, and insisting that he costs too much. That helps for a while. But you're creating a vacuum by silencing the critic without putting anything in his place. And soon enough his voice will be back, filling that vacuum with more attacks. When the critic has been silenced, you need to replace his voice with a positive awareness of your own worth.

Affirming your worth is no easy task. Right now you believe that your worth depends on your behavior. Metaphorically, you see yourself as an empty vessel that must be filled, drop by drop, with your achievements. You start out essentially worthless, a body that moves and talks. The critic would have you believe that there is no *intrinsic* value in a life, only a *potential* for doing something worthwhile, something important.

The truth is that your value is your consciousness, your ability to perceive and experience. The value of a human life is that it exists. You are a complex miracle of creation. You are a person who is trying to live, and that makes you as worthwhile as every other person who is doing the very same thing. Achievement has nothing to do with it. Whatever you do, whatever you contribute should come not from the need to prove your value, but from the natural flow of your aliveness. What you do should come from the drive to fully live, rather than the fight to justify yourself.

Whether you're a researcher unlocking the cure for cancer or a guy sweeping the street, you have known hope and fear, affection and loss, wanting and disappointment. You have looked out at the world and tried to make sense of it, you have coped with the unique set of problems you were born into, you have endured pain. Over the years you've tried many strategies to help you feel better in the face of pain. Some of your strategies have worked, some haven't. Some have worked short-term, but in the long run brought greater distress. It doesn't matter. You are just trying to live. And in spite of all that is hard in life, you are still trying. This is your worth, you humanness.

The following affirmations are examples of things you might say to yourself to keep the critic at bay.

- I am worthwhile because I breathe and feel and am aware.
- Why do I hurt myself? I am trying to survive, I do the best I can.
- I feel pain, I love, I try to survive. I am a good person.
- My pain, my hope, my struggle to survive links me to every other human being. We are all just trying to live and we are doing the best we can.

One of these may feel right to you. Or none of them. What's important is that you arrive at a statement that you do believe and that you can use to replace your critical voice.

Take time now to write you own affirmation. If you are having difficulty writing an affirmation that's true, chapters four, six, and eight on "Accurate Self-Assessment," "Compassion," and "Handling Mistakes" will help you generate affirmations you can believe.

Remember that you need positive affirmations to fill in for the critic's voice. Try to use an affirmation every time you have successfully shut down an attack from your critic.

Making Your Critic Useless

The best way to disarm your critic is to render him useless. Take away his role and at last he will be silent. Understanding how the critic works isn't enough. You may now be aware that your critic's function is to push you to achieve or protect you from the fear of rejection or atone for your guilt. But knowing that function doesn't change much. Those same needs must be met in new and healthy ways before you will be willing to forgo the services of your critic. This book is about new, constructive ways of taking care of your needs without relying on the critic.

What follows is the list from the previous chapter of needs which the critic may typically help you meet. After each listing is a brief discussion outlining healthy alternative strategies for meeting the need that do not rely on the critic. You will also be directed to chapters in this book that can give specific help.

The need to do right. Your old strategy has been to rely on the critic to coerce you into walking the "straight and narrow." The healthier strategy is to reevaluate your list of shoulds and personal standards to see which ones realistically fit you and your current situation. Chapter seven on "Shoulds" provides a step-by-step method for evaluating the rules you live by. It also describes a healthy system for motivating yourself to live according to your values: basing decisions on a clear understanding of the short- and long-term consequences for each alternative.

The need to feel right. Your old strategy for temporarily feeling more worth has been to compare yourself to others or to set high, perfectionistic standards. The healthier strategy is to learn to see yourself more realistically (chapters four and five on "Accurate Self-Assessment" and "Cognitive Distortions") and with genuine acceptance (chapter six, "Compassion"). Chapters eleven, twelve, and thirteen will reinforce these new ways of viewing and talking to yourself through techniques of hypnosis and visualization and other methods. Much of this book, in fact, is focused on your need to feel right and on helping you develop an accurate and accepting self-evaluation.

The need to achieve. Your old strategy relies on the critic for motivation to achieve more. But you pay by feeling bad and worthless every time you miss a goal, every time you make an error, every time you lose momentum. The greatest problem, though, is that you believe the basic premise of the critic's barrage. You believe the lie that your worth depends on your behavior. The first step, then, toward meeting your need to achieve in healthy ways is to challenge your old belief that what you do is what you're worth (see the "Affirmations of Worth" section in this chapter and chapter six on "Compassion").

The second step involves learning to evaluate your goals to determine if they are appropriate for you. Is it you who wants to own this house, or is it your father or your spouse or some ideal of "the good provider"? Chapter seven, on "Shoulds," will once again provide help in evaluating your goals. You will explore your goals in terms of short- and long-range consequences to determine if they are right for you. An honest exploration will inevitably reveal that some goals simply cost too much.

The last step toward meeting your need to achieve in healthy ways is to find new motivators. Your old motivator was the critic, who attacked if you didn't work hard enough toward your goals. A healthier form of motivation is to visualize the positive consequences of success. When you see yourself reaping the benefits of an achieved goal, when you can imagine each detail of your success, when you can hear the approval of friends and feel the satisfaction, then you have created an extremely powerful motivational force. Chapter eleven, on "Visualization" provides detailed instructions for using imagery to motivate desired behavior.

The need to control negative feelings. In the last chapter you learned how the critic's attack can paradoxically help you control fear, guilt, anger, and other feelings. It's very much like digging your fingernails into your hand to block awareness of some painful injury.

1. *Feeling not OK or bad or valueless.* The critic helps you block this feeling by setting high standards of perfection. The implication is that hard work is all you require to become your ideal self. You can learn to control this feeling without the critic by following the steps outlined in ''The Need To Feel Right'' section above. Again, the strategy involves learning to see yourself accurately and with genuine acceptance.

2. *Fear of failure.* The critic solves your fear of failure by telling you that you "can't do it." As a result, you don't try and your fear recedes. The healthier strategy for controlling the fear of failure is to redefine the meaning of your mistakes. People with low self-esteem consider mistakes to be an indication of a general lack of worth. Each error reaffirms their underlying belief that something is terribly wrong with them. In chapter eight on ''Handling Mistakes'' you will explore one of the fundamental laws of human nature: that *you always choose actions that seem most likely to meet your needs based on current awareness.* You make the best decision you can at any point in time, given what you know and what you want. The secret to coping with any failure is to recognize that each decision you've made was *the very best one available under the circumstances.*

3. *Fear of rejection.* The critic helps you cope with rejection by predicting and thus desensitizing you to hurts. He also helps you cope by making you act in such a way that others are discouraged from any criticism. A healthier strategy for dealing with the fear of rejection is to (1) reframe social errors as the best available decision at the time (chapter eight on ''Handling Mistakes''), (2) develop specific skills for coping with criticism (chapter nine on ''Responding to Criticism''), and (3) learn to check out an assumed rejection rather than mind-read (see the section on mind reading in chapter five). The first step requires that you talk differently to yourself. Social blunders are not an indication of your worth; they are merely decisions that you made that hindsight would lead you to make differently. The second step changes your behavior. You learn how to respond assertively to criticism rather than collapse into an orgy of self-blame. The third step requires a decision not to trust your assumptions about the thoughts and feelings of others. Instead, you develop the skill of checking out; asking specific questions that are designed to clarify suspected negative feelings in others.

4. *Anger.* The critic helps you deal with your fear of anger by deflecting it into an attack on yourself. A healthier strategy for dealing with your anger is to learn to say what you want and negotiate

for change. Anger is so often a byproduct of helplessness because your needs are unexpressed or expressed ineffectually. You have a right to ask for what you want, even though you may not get it. Chapter ten on "Asking for What You Want" will help you to express your needs more effectively. Learning to be assertive will reduce feelings of anger both toward others and yourself.

5. *Guilt.* The critic helps control your guilt by punishing you. A better strategy is to determine if your guilt comes from the violation of a healthy or unhealthy value. Chapter seven on "Shoulds" will give you a framework for exploring your personal value system. You will determine whether the rule you broke and feel guilt over is sufficiently flexible to fit you as a person and apply to your unique situation. You will also find out if the violated rule is realistic, meaning that it is based on the likely consequences and outcomes of your behavior as opposed to absolute dichotomies of right and wrong.

If you find that your rule is an unhealthy one, you can fight your guilt by beginning to question your old value. This is easier said than done, but chapter seven will give you a step-by-step method for coping with unhealthy values. If, after examination, the rule you violated feels healthy and right to you, the only way to stop the critic is to initiate the process of positive atonement,

6. *Frustration.* The critic helps you control frustration by blaming and beating you up until you've discharged enough negative energy to reduce your tension level. The healthier strategy is to relax and calm yourself by using the hypnotic induction in chapter twelve. Some of the key ingredients of the induction are affirmations of your intrinsic worth and a reminder that any mistakes you've made were the best decisions available to you at the time. The main purpose of the induction is to help you toward a sense of personal forgiveness and compassion for your own struggle.

Summary Chart

The following chart is a guide for using the rest of this book. On the left side of the chart are the list of needs that your critic helps you meet. Along the top of the chart are chapter titles that offer specific alternatives for meeting these same needs in healthy ways. The X's indicate which chapters offer help appropriate for a particular need.

NEEDS THE CRITIC HELPS YOU MEET	ALTERNATIVE RESOURCES									
	Accurate Self-Assessment	Cognitive Distortions	Compassion	Shoulds	Handling Mistakes	Responding to Criticism	Asking For What You Want	Visualization	Hypnosis	I'm Still Not OK
The need to do right				X	X					
The need to feel right	X	X	X					X	X	X
The need to achieve			X	X				X		
The need to control negative feelings										
Feeling not OK	X	X	X					X	X	X
Fear of failure					X					
Fear of rejection		X			X	X				
Anger							X			
Guilt				X						
Frustration									X	

4

Accurate Self-Assessment

A singles group had developed the custom of having the women choose the men for their first dance of the evening. The following exchange was overheard when an attractive woman approached a slender, well-groomed man at his table.

> *Woman:* How 'bout a dance?
> *Man:* [*Looking around.*] Me?
> *Woman:* There's nobody else at your table.
> *Man:* I guess so.
> *Woman:* [*Miffed.*] You don't seem too enthusiastic.
> *Man:* I didn't think you'd choose me.
> *Woman:* [*Sitting down.*] Why not, you look nice to me.
> *Man:* Nice? [*Sarcastic.*] This suit is fifteen years old and doesn't fit, I've got Pinochio's nose, I'm losing my hair, and I dance like I'm slipping on gravel.
> *Woman:* [*Silence.*]
> *Man:* You want to dance?
> *Woman:* [*Getting up.*] Let me think about that.

The man in the dialogue was among the most attractive people at the singles group that night. But his self-concept was distorted by an over-emphasis on the negative. He was filtering out all awareness of his positive qualities while focusing exclusively on his perceived flaws.

People with low self-esteem do not see themselves clearly. Like a reflection in a warped funhouse mirror, the image they see magnifies their weaknesses and minimizes their assets. The usual result of seeing such a distorted reflection is a strong feeling of inadequacy, since you seem to compare so poorly with those around you. You see other people far more accurately than you see yourself, because you are aware of their balance of strengths and weaknesses. Compared to all these "normal" people, your distorted funhouse image of yourself seems terribly flawed.

To raise your self-esteem, it is absolutely necessary to throw away the old warped mirrors and learn to accurately perceive your particular balance of strengths and weaknesses. This chapter will help you create a clear and accurate self-description. Instead of filtering out your strengths and magnifying your weaknesses, you can learn to recognize and value the person you really are.

The first step toward accurate self-assessment is to write down in as much detail as possible how you see yourself at the present time. The following *Self-Concept Inventory* will help you organize your self-description.

Self-Concept Inventory

Write down as many words or phrases as you can to describe yourself in the following areas:

1. *Physical appearance.* Include descriptions of your height, weight, facial appearance, quality of skin, hair, style of dress, as well as descriptions of specific body areas such as your neck, chest, waist, and legs.

2. *How you relate to others.* Include descriptions of your strengths and weaknesses in intimate relationships and in relationships to friends, family, and co-workers, as well as how you relate to strangers in social settings.

3. *Personality.* Describe your positive and negative personality traits.

4. *How other people see you.* Describe the strengths and weaknesses that your friends and family see.

5. *Performance at school or on the job.* Include descriptions of the way you handle the major tasks at work or school.

6. *Performance of the daily tasks of life.* Descriptions could be included in such areas as hygiene, health, maintenance of your living environment, food preparation, caring for your children, and any other ways you take care of personal or family needs.

7. *Mental functioning.* Include here an assessment of how well you reason and solve problems, your capacity for learning and creativity, your general fund of knowledge, your areas of special knowledge, wisdom you have acquired, insight, and so on.

8. *Sexuality.* How you see and feel about yourself as a sexual person.

When you are finished with the inventory, go back and put a plus by items that represent strengths or things you like about yourself. Put a minus by items that you consider weaknesses or would like to change about yourself. Don't mark items that are neutral, factual observations about yourself.

Eleanor, a sales representative for a pharmaceutical company, completed her *Self-Concept Inventory* as follows.

1. *Physical appearance*

+ Large brown eyes
+ Dark curly hair
+ Olive complexion
+ Clear, young-looking skin
− Buckteeth
− Fat belly
− Fat thighs
+ Well-shaped hips
  5 feet 5 inches, 130 pounds
− Flat chested
− Ugly nose
+ Look good in 30s style dresses
+ Don't need makeup
  Like jeans and T-shirts, casual dress
  Long neck

2. *How I relate to others*

+ Warm
+ Open
+ Accepting and flexible
− Can't set limits or say no
− Too accepting, then resentful
+ Good communicator
+ Entertaining
− Phony with friends
+ Socially competent
+ Good listener
− Can't ask for what I want
− Uncomfortable with strangers
+ Protective
+ Good at compromising
− Use guilt to get kids to do things
− Sometimes attack and nag at kids

3. *Personality*

+ Responsible
+ Funny
+ Open, outgoing
+ Friendly
− Hate being alone
− Blabbermouth
− Sulky when I don't get my way
− Sometimes irritable
+ Affectionate with family
− Try too hard to please
+ Love to be busy

4. *How others see me*

- – Wishy-washy
- – Overextended
- ≏ Forgetful
- – Lose everything
- + Positive
- + Competent

- + Funny
- + Strong
- + Independent
- + Warm
- – Scattered
- – Irritable
- – Know-nothing

5. *Performance on the job*

- + Prompt
- + Hard-working, motivated
- + Likable
- + Put people at ease
- – Overstressed

- – Lousy on the phone
- – Avoid making sales calls
- + Knowledgeable in field
- + Good at selling
- – Screw up paper work
- – Restless

6. *Performance of daily tasks of life*

- – Forget appointments
- – Put things off
- + Good hygiene
- + Quick, competent cook
- – Lousy housekeeper

- + Conscientious about teeth
- + Conscientious with baby's safety, cleanliness
- – Shop stupidly
- + Don't fret about my appearance

7. *Mental functioning*

- – Lousy at arguing, debating
- – Stupid about current events
- – Mentally lazy
- + Intuitive
- – Illogical

- + Like to learn new things
- + Curious about how things work
- + Quick mind
- – Uncreative

8. *Sexuality*

- + Usually turned on, interested
- + Accepting of partner's sexual turn-ons
- – Inhibited
- – Afraid to initiate

- + Communicate sexual preferences well
- + Can express feelings sexually
- – Can feel very rejected and depressed
- – Passive

It took Eleanor about an hour of concentrated effort to make this list. Right away she learned something very important about herself. She saw that she had almost as many minus as plus items in each category of the inventory. While she was able to recognize her strengths, it was also clear that Eleanor had many negative judgments about who she was in every area of her life.

Not everyone has the same response pattern as Eleanor. You may find that the vast majority of your minus items show up in just one or two areas of the inventory. If that's the case, your self-esteem is generally good but has a few specific weak spots. The more your minus items are spread throughout the inventory, and the larger the proportion of minus to plus items, the more effort it will take to achieve a realistically positive self-concept.

Listing Your Weaknesses

Divide a fresh sheet of paper into two columns. On the left, write down each item that was marked with a minus. Leave three lines between each item so that you'll have sufficient room to rewrite and make changes.

There's nothing wrong with having faults. Everybody has them. There isn't a person on earth who doesn't have a list of ways that he or she would like to be different. The problem is not in having such a list, but the ways in which you use your weaknesses for destructive self-attacks. Saying that you hide your anger with your friends is a reasonable assessment. But to condemn yourself as "phony with friends," as Eleanor did, undermines your self-esteem. Being aware that you have a 32-inch waist and would like to lose 3 inches is a realistic evaluation of something you want to change. But to say that you have a "fat belly" is like sticking pins in your sense of worth.

There are four rules you need to follow when you begin revising the items on your list of weaknesses.

1. *Use nonpejorative language.* The item "buckteeth" should be changed to "prominent front teeth." "Lousy on the phone" should be changed to "I'm uncomfortable when I can't see people to pick up cues; I feel somewhat nervous on the phone." "Shop stupidly" should be rewritten as "too many trips to the grocery store because I buy just what I need for dinner that night." Go through your list and eliminate all words that have negative connotations—*stupid, blabber-mouth, wishy-washy, lousy, fat, ugly,* and so on. These words must be banished from your self-descriptive vocabulary. Like piranhas, these negative labels aren't very dangerous when they occur occasionally in isolation. But in large schools they can literally devour your self-esteem.

2. *Use accurate language.* Don't exaggerate and don't embellish the negative. Revise the items on your weaknesses list so that they are purely descriptive. Confine yourself to the facts. The term "fat thighs" is both pejorative and inaccurate. For Eleanor, the accurate statement was "21-inch thighs." "Screw up paper work" is another inaccurate

statement. Eleanor rewrote it as "*occasionally forget* to fill in items on my order forms." She rewrote "wishy-washy" as "tend to defer to others who have strong opinions." As for being "illogical," she realized that this was her husband's idea and that she didn't really think of herself as "illogical."

3. *Use language that is specific rather than general.* Eliminate words like *everything, always, never, completely,* and so on. Rewrite the list so that your description is limited to the particular situation, setting, or relationship where the trait occurs. General indictments, such as "can't set limits or say no" should be revised to reflect only the specific relationships where the problem occurs. When Eleanor thought about that item, she realized that it was simply untrue as written. She could say no to salespeople, no to her children, no to her mother and no to neighbors who made impossible demands. But she had trouble setting limits with her husband and certain close friends. Eleanor rewrote the item as "difficulty saying no to husband and close friends when they need or ask for help." Eleanor also rewrote the item "use guilt to get kids to do things." She realized there were only two main situations where the problem occurred. "I make the kids feel wrong for hurting each other or not visiting their grandparents." The item "hate being alone" was changed to "nervous and restless being alone in the house after eight or nine o'clock." "Lose everything" got changed to "occasionally lose keys or sweater." Notice how being specific makes a weakness seem less global and wrong. Your problem is no longer all-encompassing. You recognize that it occurs only on *certain* occasions, with *some* people.

4. *Find exceptions or corresponding strengths.* This is an essential step for those items that really make you feel bad about yourself. For example, Eleanor was aware that she had trouble asking for what she wanted. Her pathological critic frequently used this as ammunition for an attack on her self-worth. Eleanor rewrote the item by first noting exceptions: "I'm reasonably assertive with co-workers, with my friends Barbara and Julie, and the kids. But not my husband or other close friends." Another item that made Eleanor feel particularly vulnerable was the label "mentally lazy." She rewrote the item by acknowledging areas of thought where she had no interest and then adding one important exception: "Bored by political and philosophical issues, abstract thought. Do like to think about motivations and drives behind human behavior." Eleanor's item "lousy at arguing, debating" was another area of special sensitivity. The critic used it to kick her for not standing up for herself or defending her position. Eleanor rewrote the item by including a corresponding strength: "Don't have enough facts or a killer instinct. What I like, though, is that I don't have to be right all the time. I don't get miffed when people disagree with me."

Eleanor's Revised Weaknesses List

Original Version	Revised Version

1. *Physical appearance*

Buckteeth	Prominent front teeth
Fat belly	32-inch waist
Fat thighs	21-inch thighs
Flat chested	34B bra
Ugly nose	Proportionately too-large nose

2. *How I relate to others*

Can't set limits or say no	Difficulty saying no to husband or close friends when they need or ask for help.
Too accepting, then resentful	I let my husband do what he needs to do, but if I don't get enough attention I may feel resentful.
Phony with friends	Reluctant to express anger with friends.
Can't ask for what I want	I'm reasonably assertive with co-workers, my friends Barbara and Julie, and the kids; but not with my husband or other close friends.
Uncomfortable with strangers	Uncomfortable with strange men in social settings.
Use guilt to get kids to do things	Make the kids feel wrong for hurting each other or not visiting grandparents.
Sometimes attack and nag the kids	Ninety percent of the time I'm supportive, but several times a week I nag and hassle the kids about homework and kitchen clean-up.

3. *Personality*

Hate being alone	Nervous and restless being alone in the house after eight or nine o'clock.
Blabbermouth	On two occasions in the past year I told something I shouldn't have.

Sulky when I don't get my way	I sulk when my husband works late, otherwise I make a real effort to be cheerful.
Irritable sometimes	Irritable with the kids about homework and chores a couple of times a week.
Try too hard to please	Overextend myself with husband and close friends.

4. *How others see me*

Wishy-washy	Tend to defer to others who have strong opinions.
Overextended	I work, I have three kids, a husband and friends. There's not enough time.
Forgetful	Forget birthdays, doctor appointments on occasion, and certain people's names.
Lose everything	Occasionally lose keys or a sweater.
Know-nothing	Know little about current events or history; don't read the newspaper. Know a lot about psychology, pharmaceuticals, children, modern dance, making a family work.
Scattered	See "Forgetful" and "Lose everything."

5. *Performance on the job*

Overstressed	Usually very tired when I get home, OK on weekends.
Lousy on phone	Uncomfortable when I can't see people to pick up cues, feel somewhat nervous on phone.
Screw up paperwork	Occasionally forget to fill in items on my order forms.
Avoid making sales calls	Aggressive at making sales calls. A few really unpleasant calls I put off for up to a week. Only one doctor have I avoided completely.

Restless	Being restless is not a problem, doesn't bother me.

6. *Performance of daily tasks of life*

Put things off	Put off visiting my mother, cleaning up, and getting the kids to do chores; mostly pretty responsible with family and work obligations.
Shop stupidly	Too many trips to the grocery store because I buy just what I need for dinner that night.
Lousy housekeeper	Dishes sometimes pile up, dining-room table and living room a mess. Do major clean-up once a week.

7. *Mental functioning*

Lousy at arguing, debating	Don't have enough facts and a killer instinct. What I like, though, is that I don't have to be right all the time; I don't get miffed when people disagree with me.
Stupid about current events	See "know-nothing."
Mentally lazy	Bored by political, philosophical issues, abstract thought. Do like to think about motivations and drives behind human behavior.
Illogical	"Illogical" is my husband's idea. I don't really believe it.
Uncreative	Not interested in the arts or in making things. Have done very well at decorating houses, enjoy my modern dance classes.

8. *Sexuality*

Inhibited	Uncomfortable when undressing in front of my husband or having him look at my body too closely. But I enjoy trying new things sexually.

Can feel very rejected and depressed	Feel rejected and depressed if my husband seems cold and cutoff for several days and doesn't seem to want physical contact.
Afraid to initiate	I'm anxious when I initiate, because if he isn't interested I get hurt. But I do initiate at least a quarter of the time.
Passive	I let him set the mood sexually, but that's not really a problem.

Now it's time to revise each weakness on the left side of your list. Do it carefully, taking as much time as necessary. This is an extremely challenging task. You will be taking a major step toward changing the negative self-evaluations that make you feel wrong and not OK.

Remember that each revised item should (1) eliminate all pejorative language, (2) be accurate and purely factual, (3) eliminate general indictments in favor of specific situations where the weakness occurs, and (4) include as many exceptions and corresponding strengths as you can think of.

Listing Your Strengths

The next step in accurate self-assessment is to acknowledge your strengths. But this is no easy task. The American culture has a degree of ambivalence about boasting. Heroes let their actions speak for them. Braggarts are shunned. In addition to these cultural prohibitions, you may have had experiences in your own family that make you reluctant to acknowledge your positive side. Critical parents often punish children for speaking well of themselves. While growing up, some children experience hundreds of interactions like these:

Jimmy: I did good on the spelling test.
Mother: Yes, but you got a D last week and the teacher says you
    aren't doing all your homework.

Susan: I climbed the tree in the backyard, daddy.
Father: Don't do that, it's dangerous.

Mike: I showed my shell collection in school today.
Father: And then did you bring it home or did you lose it?

As a result of cultural and parental conditioning, you may find it anxiety-provoking to give yourself credit for your assets. It feels dangerous, almost as if somebody might hurt you or strike you down for your audacity.

This is the time to be audacious, to toot your own horn, to search for and acknowledge things to appreciate about you. Go back to your *Self-Concept Inventory*. On a fresh sheet of paper, write down all the items marked with a plus. Now look at the items on your revised weaknesses list for which you wrote corresponding strengths. If any of these corresponding strengths are not on your list of assets, add them now.

Read slowly down the items on your list of strengths. Try to think of other special qualities or abilities that you haven't mentioned. Think of compliments you've been given, remember little successes, remember what you've overcome and what you've cared about. Include any prizes, awards, or good marks you've earned. The following exercise may help you to remember some of the things that you value about yourself.

> *Exercise.* For a few moments think about the people you have most loved or admired. What qualities move you to feel affection or admiration? What makes you really like someone? Right now, before reading further, jot down on a piece of paper those qualities that you have most appreciated in these individuals.

At this point your list should be complete. You can now use it as a tool for introspection. Go down the list slowly, item by item, and ask yourself which of these qualities apply to you. Look for examples from your past or present.

You may be surprised to find that a number of the same qualities that inspire you to care for and respect others are descriptive of you as well.

If any of the special qualities that you value in others and recognize in yourself have not been included in your list of strengths, add them now.

Go over your list of strengths one more time. Rewrite them in complete sentences, using synonyms, adjectives, and adverbs to elaborate. Get rid of negatives in favor of positives, and eschew "left-handed compliments." When Eleanor revised her strengths list, she changed "don't need makeup" to "I have excellent natural coloring." She changed "funny" to "I have a quick, perceptive sense of humor that people really appreciate." She elaborated "independent" by writing, "When it really counts, I can depend on myself and not have to ask others for help. I have a strong core of strength and resolve that will see me through."

You've been spending years dwelling on and polishing your list of negative qualities. Now give equal time to your strengths. Dwell on them. Pretend that you are writing a letter of recommendation for someone you really love and really want to succeed. When Eleanor got to items like "like to learn new things" and "curious about how things work," she really went to town. This is an area where you will have to go a little overboard, to counteract your usual tendency to downplay your strengths.

A New Self-Description

It's time now to meld your strengths and weaknesses into a self-description that is accurate, fair, and supportive. It must be a description that
won't run away from the truth. It will acknowledge weaknesses that
you might like to change. But it will also include the personal assets
that are undeniably part of your identity. Your new description should
cover all eight areas of the *Self-Concept Inventory*, including the more
significant strengths and weaknesses (from the revised version only).
The self-description that Eleanor wrote follows.

> I'm five-foot five, 130 pounds, with large brown eyes, a propor-
> tionately too-large nose, full lips, prominent front teeth, dark curly
> hair, and a clear, young-looking complexion. I have excellent
> natural coloring. I have a 32-inch waist, 21-inch thighs, and well-
> shaped hips.
>
> I am a warm, friendly, open person, who communicates well. I
> am reasonably assertive at work and with the kids. I have difficulty
> asking for what I want and setting limits with my husband and
> certain friends. I make friends easily, although I'm reluctant to
> express anger with them. I have a good relationship with my chil-
> dren. At times I nag and hassle the kids about their chores and
> homework. I am a good listener and am intuitive about people,
> especially when I can relate face-to-face.
>
> I'm an extremely responsible person. I have a quick, perceptive
> sense of humor that people really appreciate. I make a real effort
> to be cheerful. I enjoy it when the whole family is home together
> in the evenings, and it's hard on me to be alone after eight or nine
> at night. I really enjoy people, but sometimes I try too hard or
> tell too much when I'm really involved in a conversation.
>
> Others see me as a positive, competent, strong person. But I tend
> to defer to others who have strong opinions. I know little about
> current events and politics, yet I feel knowledgeable about the
> things that really interest me—psychology, children, my job, mod-
> ern dance, and making a family work. When it really counts, I can
> depend upon myself and not have to ask others for help. I have
> a strong core of strength and resolve that will see me through.
>
> On the job I'm hard-working and conscientious and get along well
> with others. I hate the paperwork involved in my job and occa-
> sionally I miss a few of the details. I'm uncomfortable when I'm
> on the phone and tend to delay calls to irritable doctors. I'm a
> great salesperson when I can sit down with people face-to-face.
> I can really sell the products along with myself.

I am fast, casual, and efficient when it comes to cooking, house-work, and grooming. I tend to put off things like visiting my mother and housecleaning. Fortunately I have a high tolerance for the kids' clutter. I do a whirlwind clean-up campaign on Sundays.

I'm fairly intelligent and like to learn new things. My curiosity is insatiable. I like to discover how things work—a new drug we are selling, or the inside of a toaster. This will keep me growing and changing. I avoid political and philosophical arguments and am bored with abstract theory. I love talking about human nature and what makes people tick. I'm not good at arts and crafts, but I en-joy decorating the house.

I feel sexually alive and open to sexual experimentation, although I feel inhibited about undressing or walking around naked—even in front of my husband. I'm intuitive and able to communicate fairly easily about sex.

Indoctrinating yourself. Your new self-description could be worth your weight in platinum. You should read it to yourself out loud, slowly and carefully, twice a day for four weeks. This is the minimum length of time for you to begin changing the ways you spontaneously think about yourself. Just as you learn a song by ''getting the tune in your ear,'' you can learn a more forgiving, more accurate way of think-ing about yourself by reading your new self-description every day.

Celebrate Your Strengths

You've listed the qualities in yourself that you appreciate. But that doesn't mean much unless you can remember them. When the critic is beating on you for being stupid or selfish or frightened of life, you've got to remember your strengths so that you can answer him back. You've got to be able to say, ''Wait a minute, I'm not listening to that. I know I'm creative, I'm generous to my kids, and I tried a new career at forty.''

Remembering your strengths, particularly at the times when you feel most down on yourself, requires you to develop a system of daily reminders. The following three methods will help you stay aware of your positive qualities.

1. *Daily affirmations.* One way to remind yourself of your strengths is to combine several of them into an affirmation. This is merely a one-sentence positive statement that you repeat to yourself at intervals throughout the day. Here are some affirmations that Eleanor developed:

- I am a warm, open, accepting person.
- I'm funny and likable and have good, good friends.

- I'm competent and hard-working and really good at what I do.

Write a new affirmation each morning. Make it something you can believe about yourself, something comforting and supportive. Keep your affirmation in mind throughout the day, as though it were a sort of meditation. Use it when you feel under stress or self-critical. Use it like a touchstone, a reassuring knowledge that you are a good and worthy person.

2. *Reminder signs.* Another method of emphasizing your strengths, and one which can be used together with affirmations, is the reminder sign. Write a brief affirmation in large letters on a piece of typing paper or a six-by-nine file card. Place a sign like this on your mirror. Tape others on the back of your front door, by your nightstand, on your closet or refrigerator door, near a light switch. The idea is to have reminder signs in places where your eye will naturally fall. You can also make smaller signs on three-by-five or business cards. Keep these in your briefcase, under the cellophane on your cigarettes, in your desk drawer at work, in your wallet or money clip. Change or rotate your signs every few days.

While some people will dismiss reminder signs as absurd or silly, many who use them report that they reinforce and strengthen their sense of personal adequacy. The signs are a way of forcing you to notice what qualities in yourself you value.

3. *Active Integration.* A third way to increase awareness of your strengths is to recall specific examples and times when you clearly demonstrated them. Each day, select three strengths from your list. Then look into your past for situations that exemplify those particular qualities. This exercise is called *active integration* because it transforms your list of strengths from a lot of words into specific memories. It helps you to *believe* and remember that these positive qualities really apply to you. You can go through your list, finding examples, as many times as you want. But try to make it through the entire list at least once. In her process of active integration, Eleanor thought of examples like these:

- *Likable.* The time Jeanne said I had a sparkling personality and then Ellen spoke up and said I made it fun in the office.
- *Competent.* I'm third best rep in my area, which is damn good considering I've only been doing this for four years.
- *Independent.* Like when my husband was sent to Saudi Arabia for three months. I took care of the family without him.

A commitment to accuracy. Accurate self-assessment involves two things: (1) acknowledging and remembering your strengths and (2) describing your weaknesses accurately, specifically, and nonpejoratively. This second aspect requires a major commitment on your part. When the critic is kicking you, when he's exaggerating and using those negative generalizations, you've got to stop him. The truth will stop him: accuracy, specificity, nonjudgment. Stay vigilant. Those old, negative ways of talking to yourself are well-entrenched habits. You will need to answer them, over and over again, with the new and accurate language you have learned.

5

Cognitive Distortions

Cognitive distortions are the tools of the pathological critic, the means by which the critic operates, the weapons that the critic brings to bear against your self-esteem. If irrational beliefs can be said to be the pathological critic's *ideology* (a thesis explored in a later chapter), then cognitive distortions can be considered the critic's *methodology*. The critic uses distortions the way a terrorist uses bombs and guns.

Cognitive distortions are actually bad habits—habits of thought that you consistently use to interpret reality in an unreal way. For example, when a colleague declines to be on a committee you are chairing, you can take his refusal as the simple decision it is. Or you can employ your habit of thinking about any type of rejection as a personal insult, and thus take another swipe at your beleaguered self-esteem.

Distortions are a matter of style. They may be based on deeply held unrealistic beliefs, but the distortions are not beliefs themselves— they are habits of thinking that get you into trouble.

Distorted thinking styles are hard to diagnose and treat because they are bound up tightly with your way of perceiving reality. Even the sanest, most rational person on earth operates at some distance from reality. It's unavoidable, given the built-in programming of the human mind and senses.

One way of thinking about this is to say that everyone looks at himself or herself through a telescope. If your telescope is right-way-round and in good repair, you see yourself looming relatively large and important in the universe, clearly focused, and with your various parts in correct proportion. Unfortunately, few people have perfect telescopes. The telescope can be wrong-way-round, so that they see themselves small and diminished. The lenses can be smudged, lopsided, chipped, or out of focus. Obstructions in the tube can block your view of certain aspects of yourself. Some people have kaleidoscopes instead of telescopes. Others can't see at all, because they've pasted pictures of a false self over the lens of their telescope.

Distorted thinking styles cut you off from reality in several ways. Distortions are judgmental; they automatically apply labels to people and events before you get a chance to evaluate them. Distortions also tend to be inaccurate and imprecise. They are invariably general in scope and application, failing to take special circumstances and characteristics into account. They allow you to see only one side of a question, giving an unbalanced view of the world. And finally, distortions are based on emotional rather than rational processes.

This chapter will discuss the nine most common cognitive distortions that affect self-esteem. It will teach you how to recognize them and develop effective rebuttal techniques to pierce through the veil of distortion and deal with reality in a more balanced, accurate, self-compassionate way.

The Distortions

1. *Overgeneralization*

Cognitive distortions change the very nature of the universe you live in. Overgeneralizations create a shrinking universe in which more and more absolute laws make life more and more confining. It is a universe in which the scientific method is turned upside down. Instead of observing all available data, formulating a law that explains all of the data, and then testing the law, you take one fact or event, make a general rule out of it, and never test the rule.

For example, a chief accountant named George asked a bookkeeper in his department to go to dinner with him. She declined, saying she never went out with the boss. George concluded that none of the women in his department would ever want to go out with him. From one rejection he overgeneralized and made it a rule never to ask again.

If you overgeneralize, one faux pas means that you're a social incompetent. One unsuccessful date with an older woman means that all older women will find you shallow and inexperienced. One wobbly table means that you'll never master furniture making. One accidentally deleted file means that you're a computer illiterate. And your habit of overgeneralizing doesn't let you test these rules.

You can tell that you're overgeneralizing when your pathological critic uses these key words: *never, always, all, every, none, no one, nobody, everyone, everybody.* The critic uses absolutes to close the doors of possibility, blocking your access to change and growth: "I *always* screw up." "I *never* get to work on time." "*Nobody* really cares for me." "*Everybody* thinks I'm awkward."

2. *Global Labeling*

Global labeling is the application of stereotyped labels to whole classes of people, things, behaviors, and experiences. People who practice global labeling live in a universe populated by stock characters who act out unrealistic melodrama. Global labelers with low self-esteem often cast themselves in the role of the villain or the simpleton.

This thinking style is closely allied with overgeneralization, but the distortion takes the form of a label instead of a rule. Global labeling is even more deadly in the way it creates stereotypes and cuts you off from the true variety of life. For example, an aspiring writer was working in a warehouse and writing at night. He had a touch of asthma and a slight limp. He had labels for everything: The warehouse owner was a Capitalistic Slime. Editors who rejected his short stories were part of the Literary Establishment. His job was a Treadmill. His writing was Neurotic Scribbling. He himself was a Wheezing Gimp. He thought he suffered from an Inferiority Complex. His favorite words were all pejorative ones. He had a million slogans, and they were all cliches of loss and dissatisfaction. With so many labels pasted on his life, he was too bound into the status quo to change any part of it.

You should suspect yourself of global labeling if the messages from your critic are pejorative cliches about your appearance, performance, intelligence, relationships, and so on. "My love affair is a hopeless tangle." "I'm just a failure." "My house is a pigsty." "My degree is a worthless piece of paper." "I'm neurotic." "I'm stupid." "I'm a spineless jellyfish, a quitter." "All my efforts to improve are futile grasping at straws."

3. *Filtering*

When you filter reality, you see your universe as through a glass darkly. You can see and hear only certain things. Like a voice-activated tape recorder, your attention is awakened only by particular kinds of stimuli: examples of loss, rejection, unfairness, and so on. You selectively abstract certain facts from reality and pay attention to them, ignoring all the rest. You have blind spots that obscure evidence of your own worth. Filtering makes you a particularly bad reporter of your life experience. Your own accounts of your experience are as biased as political journalism in a banana republic. Filtering is as dangerous to your self-esteem as driving a car with all the windows painted black would be to your physical well-being.

An example of filtering is Ray and Kay's intimate dinner at home. Kay praises Ray's choice of wine and the flowers he bought. She compliments him on grilling the steaks to perfection and for picking out the sweetest corn on the cob. Then she suggests that next time he might put a little less salt in the salad dressing. Ray suddenly feels let down and incompetent because Kay doesn't like his salad dressing. He can't console himself by recalling her several compliments because he literally didn't hear them—he was too busy filtering the conversation for its critical content.

You should suspect filtering when your pathological critic returns again and again to certain themes or key words: *loss, gone, hurt, dangerous, unfair, stupid.* Examine your memories of social events or conversations to see whether you remember all of what happened or was said. If out of a three-hour dinner party you can only clearly recall the fifteen minutes when you spilled your wine and felt mortified, then you are probably filtering your experiences for evidence of unworth.

The negative things about yourself that you focus on become the leitmotifs in the symphony of your life. You listen for them so hard that you lose track of the larger, more important melodies and movements. It's like the piccolo player who never heard the cannons in the *1812 Overture*.

4. Polarized Thinking

If you habitually indulge in polarized thinking, you live in a black-and-white universe, with no colors or shades of gray. You divide all your actions and experiences into either/or dichotomies, according to absolute standards. You judge yourself as either a saint or a sinner, a good guy or a bad guy, a success or a failure, a hero or a villain, a noble or a bastard.

For example, Anne was clerk in a fabric store. She sometimes drank a little too much at parties. One Monday she stayed home from work with a hangover. She was severely depressed about this incident for a week because she tended to judge people as either sober citizens or alcoholics. By falling off the wagon once, she became, in her own eyes, a bottomed-out drunk.

The trouble with polarized thinking is that you inevitably end up on the negative side of the equation. No one can be perfect all the time, so at the first mistake, you must conclude that you are all bad. This "one strike and you're out" style of thinking is death to self-esteem.

You can catch yourself doing polarized thinking by listening for "either/or" messages from your pathological critic. "I'm either going to win the scholarship or completely blow my future." "If you can't be funny and 'on' then you're a bore." "If I can't be calm I'm hysterical." Sometimes only one half of the dichotomy is stated, and the other half is implied: "There's only one right way to live (and all the others are wrong)." "This is my big chance for a good relationship (and if I blow it, I'll be alone)."

5. Self-Blame

Self-blame is a distorted thinking style that has you blaming yourself for everything, whether you are actually at fault or not. In the self-blaming cosmos, you are at the center of a universe of bad things, and they're all your fault.

You blame yourself for all your shortcomings, for being coarse, fat, lazy, scatterbrained, incompetent, or whatever. You blame yourself for things that are only marginally under your control, such as your bad health or how others react to you. If self-blame is a firmly ingrained habit, you may even find yourself feeling responsible for things that are obviously out of your control, like the weather, plane schedules, or your spouse's feelings. It's good to take responsibility for your life, but in a case of serious self-blame, you see yourself as pathologically responsible.

The most common, observable symptom of self-blame is incessant apologizing. Your hostess burns the roast, and you apologize. Your spouse doesn't want to see the movie you prefer, so you apologize. The clerk at the post office says you don't have enough postage and you say, "God, I'm so stupid, I'm sorry."

Self-blame blinds you to your good qualities and accomplishments. One man had three sons who grew up to become a dedicated social worker, a talented chemist, and a drug addict. The father poisoned his later years by brooding over the ways he had failed his third son. He discounted any influence he may have had over the lives of his other, more successful sons.

6. Personalization

In a personalized universe, you *are* the universe. Every atom in it is somehow related to you. All events, properly decoded, seem to have something to do with you. Unfortunately, there is very little sense of power or of being in control of events. It feels more like you are under pressure, under siege, or under observation by everyone around you.

Personalization has a narcissistic component. You enter a crowded room and immediately begin comparing yourself to everybody else— who is smarter, better looking, more competent, more popular, and so on. Your roommate complains about how cramped the apartment is, and you immediately assume that she means that you have too much stuff. A friend says that he's bored and you think he means that he's bored with you.

The big drawback to personalization is that it makes you react inappropriately. You might start a fight with your roommate over a nonexistent issue. You may try to be less boring by cracking tasteless jokes, and thus become *really* boring. Inappropriate responses like these can alienate those around you. Their hostility or disapproval, imagined at first, can actually become real, fueling another round of distorted interactions.

It's difficult to catch yourself indulging in personalization. One way is to pay close attention when someone is complaining to you. For example, if someone at work were complaining about people not returning tools and supplies to their proper place, what would your reaction be? Would you automatically assume that the person was complaining about you? Would you automatically assume that the person wanted you to do something about the problem? Then you might be personalizing. You might be automatically relating the complaint to yourself and never have it cross your mind that the person was just blowing off steam and that it had nothing to do with you personally. Another way to catch yourself is trying to notice when you are comparing yourself negatively to others, concluding that you are less smart, attractive, competent, and so on.

7. *Mind Reading*

Mind reading is a distorted thinking style which assumes that everyone in the universe is just like you. This is an easy mistake to make, since it's based on the phenomenon of projection—you assume that others feel the way you do, basing your assumption on a belief in a commonality of human nature and experience that may or may not actually exist.

Mind reading is fatal to self-esteem because you are especially liable to think that everyone agrees with your negative opinions of yourself: "I'm boring her. She can tell I'm really a dull guy trying to fake it." "He's quiet because I was late and he's angry about it." "He is watching my every move for the slightest mistake. He wants to fire me."

Mind reading leads to tragic miscalculations in your relationships. Harry was an electrician who often assumed that his wife, Marie, was angry with him when she bustled about the apartment with a frown on her face. He handled this supposed rejection by becoming very terse and withdrawn. In fact, Marie frowned when she was having menstrual cramps, when she was rushed, and when she felt worried about finances. But Harry's withdrawal made it hard for her to tell Harry why she was frowning. She interpreted his withdrawal as lack of interest, and kept quiet. Harry's initial mind reading destroyed the chance for any real communication.

When you're mind reading, your perception *seems* right, so you proceed as if it *were* right. You don't check out your interpretations with others because there seems to be no doubt. You can tell you're mind reading by listening closely to what you say when pressed, when asked why you made an assumption: "I just had a strong hunch." "I can just tell." "I just know." "It's my intuition." "I'm sensitive to these things." These kinds of statements show that you are leaping to conclusions without any real evidence.

8. *Control Fallacies*

Control fallacies either put you in charge of the whole universe or put everyone *but* you in charge.

The distorted thinking style of overcontrol gives you a false feeling of omnipotence. You struggle to control every aspect of every situation. You hold yourself responsible for the behavior of every guest at your party, for your child's grades in school, for your paperboy's punctuality, for your mother's coping with menopause, and for the outcome of your United Way campaign. When guests put their feet on the furniture, when your child flunks algebra, when the newspaper is late, when your mother calls you up in tears, or when your motion is voted down at the committee meeting, you feel a loss of control. You may experience resentment, anger, and a keen sense of personal failure that erodes your self-esteem.

You should suspect your pathological critic of using the fallacy of overcontrol when you think things like "I've got to make them listen," "She has to say yes," "I'll make sure he arrives on time" in situations where you are not really in control. You should suspect that overcontrol is the problem if you feel a keen sense of personal failure when someone close to you fails.

The distorted thinking style of undercontrol takes control away from you. You put yourself on the fringes of every situation, unable to influence others. You feel that the outcomes of events are out of your hands most of the time. Molly was a receptionist for the phone company who frequently fell into this fallacy. Her habit of thinking that she could do nothing about her life usurped her power and cast her in the role of perennial victim. She was in trouble with her boss for coming in late too often, her bank account was overdrawn, and her boyfriend had stopped calling her. When she thought about her situation, she felt helpless. It seemed that her boss, the bank, and her boyfriend were all ganging up on her. Her pathological critic kept saying things like, "You're weak, you're helpless. There's nothing you can do." She was literally unable to make plans for getting up earlier, refinancing her debts, or calling up and confronting her boyfriend.

Of the two control fallacies, undercontrol is the worst for your self-esteem. Abdication of power has its cost in a feeling of helplessness, a bleak sense of hopelessness, feeble resentment, and numbing depression.

9. *Emotional Reasoning*

An emotional universe is chaotic, governed by changeable feelings instead of rational laws. The distortion in this thinking style is to avoid or discount your thinking all together. You rely instead on emotions to interpret reality and direction action.

Susie was a fashion designer who lived on an emotional roller-coaster. She'd feel happy one day, so she figured her life was going well. The next day she might be sad, and if you asked her, she'd tell you how her life was a tragedy. Next week she'd be a bit nervous and be convinced that her life was dangerous in some way. The actual facts of her existence didn't change much from day to day. Only her emotions changed.

The implication for self-esteem is disastrous: You *feel* useless, so you must *be* useless. You *feel* unworthy, so you must *be* unworthy. You *feel* ugly, so you *are* ugly. You are what you feel.

Here's how the pathological critic uses emotions as weapons: He whispers in your mental ear, "Weak, spineless." This faint thought triggers the emotion of depression. You feel helpless and stuck. Then the critic pipes up again with a devious piece of circular reasoning: "You are what you feel. You feel helpless, so you are helpless." By this time, you've forgotten that the critic started the whole vicious circle. You fall for a circular argument that you would dismiss out of hand if you read it in a book.

The real error in emotional reasoning lies in tuning out those first thoughts introduced by your pathological critic, the thoughts that cause your painful emotions in the first place. The way to correct the error is to tune back into your self-talk and notice how it distorts reality to trigger negative emotions.

Combating Distortions

The most important single skill to master is vigilance. You must constantly listen to what you're telling yourself. You must not give in to depression, but persevere in analyzing the thoughts that arouse your painful emotions.

It helps to remember that low self-esteem involves some short-term gains. When you begin to thwart the pathological critic and refute the distorted thinking styles that are his weapons, you are cutting yourself off from these short-term gains. You're taking a chance. You're betting your current discomfort against future gain. This risk will feel scary at times, boring at others. The process will seem hopeless, or just like too much trouble. You will come up with a series of rationalizations for why it won't work, why it isn't working, and how silly the whole thing is anyway. These are the death struggles of the pathological critic.

Combating distorted thinking involves a commitment. You must commit yourself to being constantly on guard, even when you don't feel like it. This commitment is more important than your commitment to your family, your friends, or your ideals, because it is a commitment to *yourself.*

The Three-Column Technique

This technique for rebutting cognitive distortions is as simple as the commitment to use the technique is difficult. At first, write all your responses down on paper. Later, when this technique becomes a habit, you may be able to do it in your head.

When you're in a situation that makes you feel depressed or discouraged, when your opinion of yourself is low, take time out to get a pencil and a piece of paper. Make three columns like this:

Self-statement   *Distortion*   *Rebuttal*

In the first column, write down what your pathological critic is saying to you about the situation. Even if nothing immediately comes to mind, keep reliving the situation until you get a word or two. Your self-statements may be extremely fast or condensed, so that you will have to slow them down and write them out in full.

Then examine your self-statements for the distortions that murder your self-esteem. Here is a summary of the nine most common distortions for your quick reference:

1. *Overgeneralization.* From one isolated event you make a general, universal rule. If you failed once, you'll always fail.
2. *Global labeling.* You automatically use pejorative labels to describe yourself, rather than accurately describing your qualities.
3. *Filtering.* You selectively pay attention to the negative and disregard the positive.
4. *Polarized thinking.* You lump things into absolute, black-and-white categories, with no middle ground. You have to be perfect or you're worthless.

5. *Self-blame.* You consistently blame yourself for things that may not really be your fault.
6. *Personalization.* You assume that everything has something to do with you, and you negatively compare yourself to everyone else.
7. *Mind reading.* You assume that others don't like you, are angry with you, don't care about you, and so on, without any real evidence that your assumptions are correct.
8. *Control fallacies.* You either feel that you have total responsibility for everybody and everything, or feel that you have no control, that you're a helpless victim.
9. *Emotional reasoning.* You assume that things are the way you feel about them.

In the last column, write rebuttals to your self-statements, specifically attacking each distortion in turn.

Example. Joan had trouble joining in at work. Others would gather in the employee's lounge for coffee and go out to lunch together. Joan stayed at her desk or took walks alone at lunch time. She liked and admired many of her co-workers, but felt awkward about joining them. One day at lunch she stayed at her desk and tried the three-column technique. This is what she wrote:

Self-statements	*Distortions*	*Rebuttal*
They'll reject me. They'll see how nervous and awkward I am. They	Mind reading	I have no way of knowing what they'll think. That's up to them.
already think I'm weird. I'll be tongue-tied, nothing to say. I'm always like that.	Overgeneralization	Not so! Sometimes I'm quite articulate.
I'm such a dud.	Global labeling	No, I'm not a dud. I'm just quiet.
They'll all be looking at me, at my weird clothes that don't fit, my dishrag hair.	Mind reading	They couldn't care how I look. That's all in my head.
It's hopeless. There's nothing I can do about it.	Control fallacy	Nothing is ever totally hopeless. Enough defeatism.

Creating Your Rebuttal Voice

After making a commitment, the next hardest task facing you is to develop effective rebuttals to your self-statements. It will help greatly to imagine a person as your rebuttal voice—someone else who can stand up to your pathological critic when you're down. This person becomes the champion of your cause, your advisor, your teacher or coach. Here are some suggestions.

Healthy Coach. If you are athletically inclined, you might like the idea of a healthy coach. This is the person of experience who is committed to helping you win. He or she gives you pointers and pep talks, sets up a regimen of healthy things to do each day, and keeps you fit and motivated.

Accepting Friend. This is a friend who has known you for years and accepts all your quirks and failings. There's nothing you can't say to this friend and nothing your friend says can hurt you. This friend is totally on your side, ready with understanding, and able to remind you of your good points when you forget them yourself.

Assertive Agent. Picture a Hollywood or Broadway agent who is totally dedicated to you. He or she is out there shouting your praises from dawn to dark. Your agent thinks that you're the greatest, you can do anything, you're going right to the top, you can't fail. Your agent is a shoulder to cry on, a reservoir of confidence.

Rational Teacher. This is the stern but kindly, rational but warm teacher who lives only so that you may learn. He or she points out opportunities to learn and grow. Your teacher's comments are always factual and insightful, enlightening you and showing you how the world works and how you work in it.

Compassionate Mentor. This is an older, wiser person who has chosen to guide you in your development as a whole and healthy human being. This mentor has seen everything, lived through everything, and is an invaluable source of good advice. The chief characteristic of your mentor is a deep and abiding compassion for you and all living things. You are totally safe with your mentor.

You can choose one of these personae for your rebuttal voice or make up a voice based on somebody you know, read about, or saw in a movie. It could be a priest or rabbi, an admired movie actor, or even an alien from another galaxy—whoever you feel safe with, whoever will help. You can even imagine an entourage of these people who go everywhere with you, speaking up to give advice and support as needed.

When you rebut your pathological critic, hear your imaginary support person speaking to you in the second person, addressing you by name: "No, John, you're not weird. You have a vivid imagination and a unique way of looking at things. You have a right to your own point of view and your own feelings." Then paraphrase the statement in your mind, using the first person and changing the words to make them stronger and drive the point home: "That's right, I'm not weird. I have a vivid imagination. I have my own slant on things, and that's a valuable trait. I have a right to be different if I feel like it, and I refuse to call myself names anymore."

Rules for Rebuttal

But what should these rebuttal voices say? How do you refute distortions like mind reading or emotional reasoning that seem so right, so unassailable?

In composing an effective rebuttal to a distorted self-statement, there are four rules to take into consideration.

1. Rebuttals must be strong. Imagine your rebuttals spoken in a loud, forceful voice. If you invent a coach or trainer or mentor to be your rebuttal voice, make that person strong and forceful. Your pathological critic is powerful, with years of experience in delivering devastating messages to you. You need to counter with equal or greater force. Try beginning your rebuttals with a loud mental exclamation that will shock your critic into silence: "NO!" or "SHUT UP!" or "LIAR!" See "The Howitzer Mantras" in chapter three for more suggested retorts of this kind. You might even do something physical to interrupt your negative train of thought—snap your fingers or pinch yourself.

2. Rebuttals must be nonjudgmental. This means that if you have been indulging in global labeling, all those pejorative adjectives and adverbs—"awful, disgusting, horrible"—have got to go. Get rid of notions of right and wrong. Concentrate on what is, not what should be. You are not "stupid," you merely got a C in sociology. You are not "selfish," you just wanted some time for yourself.

Being very exact in your statements, rather than exaggerating or minimizing, will help remove the judgmental quality from your self-statements. You are not fat, you weight 198 pounds. Your blood pressure is not astronomical, it is 180 over 90. You are not a boob at parties, you just don't like to talk to strangers unless they speak first.

3. Rebuttals must be specific. Think in terms of specific behavior or a specific problem. If your self-statement is "Everything I do turns out wrong," make it specific: "Only three out of the eight people I invited came to my party." Instead of saying, "Nobody will ever love me again," say, "At this moment, I am not in a relationship." You are not without friends, you have three people you can call up if you want to. Your date wasn't cold and rejecting, he just said that he was tired and wanted to make it an early night.

Constantly ask yourself, "What are the facts? What would stand up in court? What do I know for sure?" This is the only way to find mind reading and emotional reasoning. If you feel that your boss disapproves of you, examine the facts: all you really know is that he didn't say anything about the memo you sent him and that he blinks a lot when he looks at you. Beyond that, it's all fantasy.

4. Rebuttals must be balanced. Include the positive as well as the negative. "Five people didn't come to my party, but three people did come and had a good time." "I'm not in a relationship right now, but I have been in the past and will be in the future." "I weigh 198 pounds, but I have a kind heart." "I'm not the best-looking guy in my class, but I know I'll achieve something in life."

When you use these rules to compose your own rebuttals, write them out on paper using the three-column technique. You will probably have a long paragraph of analysis, refutations, and positive statements to rebut each negative self-statement. When you are finished, underline or star the parts of your rebuttal that seem the strongest. These stronger statements are the ones you should memorize and use the next time your pathological critic starts attacking you.

Rebuttals

At the beginning, you can use the rebuttals suggested in this section word for word. Later you will find that the rebuttals you compose yourself will be the most effective.

1. Overgeneralization. To fight overgeneralizations, first get rid of absolute terms such as *all, every, none, nobody, everybody, never, always*, and so on. Pay special attention to the rules about being specific and balanced. Finally, avoid statements about the future—you have no way of predicting the future. Here are some examples:

- What evidence have I got for that conclusion?
- Do I really have enough data to make a rule?
- What other conclusion could this evidence support? What else could it mean?
- How can I check this conclusion?
- No absolutes—quantify exactly.
- I can't predict the future.

Here's an example of how a plumber named Harold fought against some powerful negative self-statements. He habitually told himself, via his pathological critic:

- Nobody likes me.
- Nobody ever invites me anywhere.
- Everybody looks down on me.

- I'm just a dumb plumber.
- I haven't got a friend in the whole world.
- I'll never have any friends.

The first thing that Harold noticed after writing down these self-statements was the number of absolutes: "Nobody . . . anywhere . . . everybody . . . whole world . . . never." He asked himself, "What evidence do I have for these absolute conclusions?" He found he could be more accurate and take the sting out of the statements by substituting less general words: "Few people . . . some places . . . some people . . . few friends . . . "

Harold applied the rule about being specific by listing the people he felt looked down on him, and those he wished would include him in social functions. He applied the balance rule by listing people who did like him and spent time with him. He made his rebuttal strong by prefacing it with "Stop it!" shouted loudly in his mind.

Finally, Harold deleted the judgmental label "dumb plumber," balanced it with his good points, and warned himself against predicting the future. Here is Harold's full rebuttal:

- Stop it!*
- What evidence do I have for these absolute conclusions?
- I haven't met everybody in the world.
- I haven't been everywhere in the world.
- *Some* people like Bob seem to dislike me.
- But others like Gordon like me a lot.
- Ralph and Sally didn't invite me to their picnic.
- But my Dad, Molly, and Mr. Henderson often invite me over.
- So I *do* have some friends.*
- I probably will have friends in the future.
- So stop it! Stop predicting loneliness.
- I'm a *good* plumber.*
- Plumbing is a respectable trade.*

The statements marked with an asterisk are the parts of the rebuttal that Harold found most powerful. These are the parts that he memorized and remembered to use whenever his pathological critic started telling him that he was "friendless" and "dumb."

2. Global labeling. When you write your negative self-statements down on paper, look for nouns, adjectives, and verbs that are judgmental global labels. Look for nouns such as *slob, failure, bum, ingrate, coward.* Adjectives can be the worst: *lazy, stupid, ugly, weak, clumsy, hopeless.* Even verbs can function as global lables: *to lose, to err, to fail, to waste, to disgust.*

When fighting global labels, being specific means realizing that your label is referring only to a part of yourself or of an experience. Be specific by replacing the label with an accurate definition of what you don't like. For example, instead of "I'm fat," say, "I'm fifteen-and-a-half pounds over my ideal weight." Instead of saying to yourself, "I acted like a jerk," say, "I stammered when she asked me about my old girlfriend."

Being balanced involves describing some of the many parts of yourself to which your label does *not* apply: I'm fifteen-and-a-half pounds overweight, but I carry it well and look good in my new clothes." "I stammered when she asked me about my old girlfriend, but I told the story about the old doctor well."

Here are some self-statements to get you started in rebutting global labels:

- Stop! That's just a label.
- That's not me, that's just a label.
- Labels exaggerate a tiny part of me.
- No more labels—be specific.
- I refuse to call myself names.
- Exactly what do I mean by _____ ?
- My experience is too limited for global labels ever to be true.
- Labels are mistaken opinions based on limited experience.
- I have far more good points than bad.

Here is an example of a global labeler who broke the habit. Peg was a mother of four whose critic typically assaulted her with a barrage of labels:

- Call yourself a mother? You're the Wicked Witch to your kids.
- You've failed Billy. He's backward.
- You ignore the older kids. They're running wild.

Peg wrote these self-statements down and underlined all the global labels: "Wicked Witch . . . failed . . . backward . . . ignore . . . wild." She began her rebuttal by replacing the labels with the facts: she sometimes raises her voice to her kids, she worries about Billy because at two years old he doesn't talk much. She spends her available time with Billy and Susan, her youngest kids, and thus has little time for her older children.

To balance her shortcomings, Peg included her good points: maintaining consistent rules for her kids, providing them with good clothes and nutritious food, and taking a real interest in their educations. Here is Peg's complete rebuttal:

- Enough already!*
- These are harsh, distorted labels.*

- Sometimes I yell at my kids.
- I do provide my kids with consistent rules and enforce them fairly.*
- I worry about Billy not talking, but that's just his way.
- It's not my fault Billy doesn't talk much.*
- Billy will talk when he's ready.*
- I wish I had more time for Jim and Andrea, but they actually do fine with what time I can give them.
- They will benefit from the freedom.
- I refuse to call myself names anymore.*
- I've always done my best, and will keep trying.*

Peg marked the strongest rebuttals with an asterisk and used them whenever she started criticizing herself for being a poor mother.

3. Filtering. The most important rule for forming rebuttals to filtering is to look for balance. Since you are stuck in a rut from which you can only see negative things, you must make a strong effort to climb out and look around. Look for the opposite of what you filter for. If you tend to focus on loss in your life, make up rebuttals that stress all the good things that have not been lost. If you see rejection all around you, write descriptions of the times when you were accepted and loved. If you obsessively look for instances of failure, make up rebuttals that remind you of your successes.

Here are some general rebuttals to use to fight filtering:

- Wait! Open your eyes! Let's see the whole picture.
- I may have lost things in my life, but there are many treasures I still have and cherish.
- There I go again, looking for rejection.
- This one defeat can serve to remind me of my victories.
- There's more to life than pain (or danger, sadness, etc.)
- I can choose to stop blanking out the good things.

Bill always filtered his reality for signs of rejection. A typical morning would net for him these kinds of negative self-statements:

- The bus driver was irritated because I didn't have correct change.
- Maggie's mad at me for not wanting to buy a new dryer.
- The new accountant won't like my bookkeeping.
- God, Stan is grouchy. Better pussyfoot with him.

Upon analysis, Bill found that there were other aspects to all these relationships that he was only dimly aware of. He replayed conversations and situations in his mind until he could identify the positive elements: although the bus driver may have been rejecting, most drivers were neutral or even friendly if you yourself were pleasant. His wife, Maggie, actually wasn't mad about the dryer, she had a different opinion and appeared willing to discuss it rationally. Furthermore, he and

Maggie had been rather close and playful over the past week. Having not even met the new accountant, Bill was filtering the future, predicting rejection without evidence. Regarding his friend Stan, Bill reminded himself that Stan was frequently grouchy. So what else is new? Here is Bill's full rebuttal as he first wrote it out:

- So what if a bus driver doesn't like me? In half an hour we'll have forgotten each other.
- Maggie and I are feeling close; that's what counts.
- Disagreements don't necessarily imply rejection or anger.
- Don't predict rejection.*
- Others are just as likely to like as to not like me.
- What's important is that I like myself.*
- The only serious rejection is self-rejection.*
- People don't have to like me.*
- Look on the loving side. Look for the smiles.
- Stan and I have been friends for ten years, why should I worry?

The items marked with an asterisk are the ones that Bill found especially telling. He recalled them whenever he felt the familiar feeling of impending rejection, or whenever he felt depressed after a social interaction that seemed to have gone poorly.

4. Polarized thinking. The rule about being specific will guide you in fighting polarized thinking. Instead of describing life to yourself in absolute blacks and whites, describe specific shades of gray. As soon as you find yourself making a snap judgment about yourself, say, "Wait a minute. Let me be more precise."

A helpful technique in writing rebuttals of polarized thinking is to use percentages. The car show wasn't a total disaster, your Packard got eighty out of a hundred points. The meal you cooked wasn't garbage, rather the entree was 50 percent OK, the salad was 80 percent, and the dessert was 40 percent. Your party wasn't a complete bore— 60 percent of your guests had a good time, 30 percent were bored, and the remaining 10 percent never admit to having fun no matter where they are.

These general rebuttals show the tack to take against polarized thinking:

- Wrong!
- Nothing is totally anything.
- Let me be more precise.
- Remember the gray zone.
- No more absolutes.
- What are the percentages?
- There are infinite gradations of good and bad in all I do.

An example of polarized thinking is Arlene. She was a loan officer at a bank, a job that unfortunately reinforced her tendency toward polarized thinking—applicants either qualified for their loan or not, with no middle ground. Arlene's problem was that she applied this same rule to her own performance—she was either perfectly competent at her job, or she was incompetent. Her pathological critic put it like this:

- You've got to get these loan packages together by three o'clock.
- If you don't, you've totally screwed up.
- You're either competent or you're not.
- The packages were late. What a disaster.
- You can't do anything right.
- You're completely disorganized. Just look at this desk.
- If you don't do this job right, you'll end up on welfare.

Arlene countered this polarized thinking by creating a rebuttal voice. She imagined a patient, wise teacher, similar to a favorite professor she once had in college. This teacher was with her all the time at work, like an invisible guardian angel. This is the rebuttal she wrote and imagined spoken in her teacher's voice:

- Slow down, now.*
- Stop thinking in black and white.*
- Sometimes you're perfectly competent.
- Sometimes you're less competent.
- You're never totally incompetent.*
- Not every job is life and death.*
- Not every missed deadline is a disaster.
- You're punctual 90 percent of the time.
- Your job is secure and you do it well.
- Everybody makes mistakes.
- This is not the end of the world.*

At work when she heard her pathological critic start up, Arlene had her teacher rebut with the starred statements.

5. Self-blame. To rebut self-blaming statements, you must rigorously weed out judgmental statements and replace them with balanced ones. State the facts of the situation without judging yourself, and use reinforcing self-statements like the following:

- No more blaming!
- Everyone makes mistakes—it's just human.
- No brooding. The past is over and I can do no more about it.
- I can acknowledge my mistakes and move on.
- I always do my best according to my awareness at the moment.
- Let it go.
- I am not in charge of others.
- I don't have to blame myself for others' behavior.
- I accept the consequences of my actions, but I will not wallow in guilt for past errors.

George was an unemployed waiter who blamed himself for all his own problems and for his girlfriend's problems as well. He blamed himself for losing his job, for failing to find another, for being depressed, for depressing his girlfriend, and for making her over-eat because she was worried about him. Whenever he thought about work or his girlfriend, the simple phrase "It's all my fault" flashed into his mind like a neon sign. A wave of guilt and depression would come over him.

To rebut this recurring thought, George wrote a sort of pep talk that he imagined his old high-school coach might say to him:

- Bullshit!*
- It's *not* all your fault.*
- Stop bad-mouthing yourself.
- You were laid off because business is slow—which isn't your fault.
- It's hard to get restaurant work for the same reason—which also isn't your fault.
- Pity and guilt are just sapping your strength.*
- Polly's a big girl. She's in charge of her own life and feelings.*
- You can't *make* her feel one way or another.
- Accept her support, and stop kicking yourself.

George starred and memorized the statements he needed to hear most often.

6. Personalization. If your pathological critic is constantly comparing you to others, your rebuttal should stress that people are individuals, with unique combinations of strengths and weaknesses. You should concentrate on affirming your own right to be exactly as you are, without apology or judgment.

If your personalization takes the form of assuming that every situation or interaction involves a judgment of you personally, you should compose rebuttals that point out the fact that most of what goes on in the world has nothing to do with you. Encourage yourself to check things out, to assume nothing.

Here are some typical rebuttals effective for countering a pathological critic who is given to personalization:

- Hold it! No comparisons!
- Everybody's different, with different strong and weak points.
- I am just me, without comparisons.
- I can describe myself accurately, without reference to others.
- Assume nothing!
- Check it out.
- Most of the universe has nothing to do with me.
- Don't be so paranoid!
- Everybody else is too concerned with their own act. They're not watching me.

Gracie was a poor tennis player made poorer by personalization. She felt that everyone on adjacent courts was aware of her play. She was constantly comparing herself to the others around her and nearly always deciding that her play was inferior. This is what her pathological critic had to say:

- All eyes are on you.
- Wow, what a serve. Mine isn't half as fast.
- Look how Denny is always in position, while I'm tripping over my own feet.
- My partner's quiet. What did I do?
- Missed! Damn, I look like an amateur.

It got so bad that finally Gracie avoided playing. She had to spend a week thinking about her pathological critic's attacks and getting them down on paper. Then she composed the following rebuttal:

- Stop this!*
- It's just a game, to have fun.*
- Everybody else is concentrating on his game.
- Athletic ability doesn't determine worth.
- Stop comparing.*
- Everybody's game is uneven sometimes.
- Everybody's an individual, with unique strengths and weaknesses.*
- They're not watching me, they're watching the ball.*

Gracie found that she could remember the starred items and use them when she returned to the courts. Her game improved when she stopped comparing and just concentated on hitting the ball. And her self-esteem fared better because she had fun and didn't suffer from so many unfavorable comparisons.

7. Mind reading. If you have the habit of mind reading, you need to make up especially strong rebuttals that will shock you back to reality. The most important rule is the one about being specific and accurate. Concentrating on the known facts is the best way to stop assuming that others are thinking ill of you.

Here are some general rebuttals that are effective against mind reading:

- Stop it! Nonsense.
- I have no way of knowing what they're thinking.
- The only way to know others' opinions is to ask them straight.
- Assume nothing.
- Check it out.
- What else could that mean? Why assume the negative?

- What are the facts? Spell them out.
- "Intuition" is just an excuse for guessing.

Josh was a librarian who dreaded having to work the front desk. He felt that the patrons were irritated at him if he couldn't answer questions, had to charge them fines, or had to make them wait during busy times. Words would pop into his head: "Slow . . . stupid . . . mean . . . arrogant," and so on. He would feel very anxious and flustered. When he examined the words that popped into his head, he found they stemmed from mind reading. He was then able to slow them down and elaborate them. This is the stream of negative self-talk that he wrote out in full:

- She thinks I'm slow.
- She hates me.
- He thinks I'm stupid not to know that author.
- He's being nice, but it's just patronizing. He's really seething inside because I was mean enough to charge the full fine.
- She thinks I'm an arrogant civil servant because I made her wait while those little kids checked out their books. She'd like to report me to the head librarian.

Josh's rebuttal took the form of repeated shouts inside his head, and careful observation of the observable facts. Here is his full written rebuttal:

- Stop it!
- This is just somebody's grandmother trying to get through the line in a hurry.
- I don't know what she thinks, and I don't care.
- Stop it!
- This is just some guy who doesn't know who wrote the book he wants. That's all I know about him.
- Stop it!
- This is just some poor slob who forgot to get his books back on time. He's being nice about paying the fine. Who knows how he really feels?
- Stop it!
- This is just some girl in a pink sweater who had to wait till the kids were through. She doesn't know me from Adam, and I don't know what she's thinking.
- If it's important to know what these people are thinking about me, I could ask them. But it's a waste of time trying to invent their opinions for them.

When he was actually at work, Josh couldn't run such long monologues through his head. When the negative word "Stupid" flashed into his mind, he would just mentally shout back, "Stop it! He's just a guy who needs info . . . that's all."

8. Control fallacies. If your pathological critic uses the fallacy of undercontrol, your rebuttal must emphasize your real and actual control over your life. The most crucial rule is the one about being specific—tell yourself exactly what you can do to regain control of a given situation. Here are some general rebuttals to get you started:

- Wait! I'm doing it again.
- No more victim crap.
- I got myself into this mess and I can get myself out.
- Let's see, what can I do?
- This helpless feeling is just the critic talking.
- I refuse to let my critic take away my power.
- This situation is the result of a long series of actions or inactions on my part. It can be changed by direct action.

Randy was a new father who felt overwhelmed. The new baby had upset his habitual routine, he was short on sleep, and his pathological critic was taking the opportunity to whittle away at his self-esteem. Here is what Randy's critic was saying:

- You're exhausted.
- You're not coping.
- You'll never get organized.
- You're helpless.
- You're just barely treading water.
- There's nothing you can do.
- There's always another chore for you to do.
- It will be like this for at least the next two years.

Randy knew he would need a strong rebuttal to arrest this constant stream of defeatism. Instead of "No!" or some other mental interrupter, he imagined a bomb going off inside his head. When the smoke cleared, he imagined a wise, compassionate mentor who would calmly rebut his pathological critic. His mentor, he realized, looked a lot like the alien Yoda from *Star Wars*. This is what Randy wrote down for his mentor to say:

- (BOOM!)
- Randy, relax and take a deep breath.
- Stop thinking about all the things you feel you have to do.
- Find that calm place inside yourself. Breathe deeply and enjoy a moment of peace.*
- You are in control, not the baby.

- True, you must respond to your child, but you have choices as to how. You will get better and better at this.
- Muster your resources and take charge.*
- Remember your options: setting up alternating shifts with your wife, babysitters, letting the grandparents help, new parents' groups, hiring someone to do house and yard work.
- You can cope.
- You can get enough rest and enjoy your baby.

The fallacy of overcontrol, where you take responsibility for the pain and unhappiness of those around you, is functionally similar to self-blame. Use the suggested rebuttals in the self-blame section to cope with overcontrol.

9. Emotional reasoning. To fight the distortion of emotional reasoning, you need to follow the rules about being nonjudgmental and specific. Create rebuttals that omit emotionally loaded words like *love, hate, disgusting, furious, depressed,* and so on. Constantly encourage yourself to look for the thoughts that underlie and create the painful emotions you feel. Those underlying thoughts are where the pathological critic does his work. Those thoughts are what you need to ultimately refute.

Here are some rebuttals for calming emotional turmoil and countering the underlying distorted thoughts:

- Lies! My emotions are lying to me.
- Distrust all sudden feelings.
- There is nothing automatically true about my feelings.
- Look for the underlying thoughts.
- What am I telling myself that makes me feel so sad, so anxious, so angry?
- Correct the thoughts and the pain will go away.

Marjorie was a baker at a gourmet bakery. The other people in the bakery never knew whether Marjorie would be on cloud nine or down in the dumps. She was ruled by her feelings. She would see a headline about an airplane crash, think about death, feel a wave of sadness, and emotionally reason that her life wasn't worth much, since it could be snuffed out in a moment. Someone would ask her a perfectly innocent question about her muffins in the oven, and she would tell herself that some criticism was implied, feel threatened and anxious, and emotionally conclude that her job was in danger. She would tell herself that her credit cards would never be paid off, feel depressed, and emotionally decide that she was a failure, that she would always be poor and miserable.

Marjorie's problem was exacerbated by the fact that she was not very aware of the chain reaction from experience to thoughts to emotions to emotional reasoning. She just felt lousy and figured she would always feel lousy. When she started writing down her self-talk, she had a hard time getting back to the thoughts. This is all she came up with at first:

- I feel sad, hopeless. Life is so fragile.
- I'm afraid of losing my job. I don't know why, I just feel on edge whenever someone looks over my shoulder.
- I must be a failure. I feel overwhelmed by my debts.

To go further, Marjorie had to literally invent her thoughts. She would make up a thought that sounded like it might account for her feelings. Once she did this, she found that she could say, "Yes, that's it," or "No, it's more like this . . ." Eventually she completed this list:

- I'm going to die.
- It's horrible.
- I can't stand it.
- They'll throw me out on the street with no references.
- I'll starve.
- I'll lose my apartment, my bike, everything.
- I'll be bankrupt and on welfare.
- All my friends will hate me.

These are the catastrophic messages from her pathological critic that triggered Marjorie's depression. She began creating her rebuttal by crossing out the emotionally loaded words: "die, horrible, throw me out, lose, bankrupt, hate."

Then Marjorie made up a strong beginning for her rebuttal to shock her out of her emotional funk. Finally, she created reminders to be specific and a balanced list of her rational resources to counter the critic's catastrophic predictions. Here is her full rebuttal:

- Stop! Just stop this right now, Marjorie!*
- This garbage is 99 percent feelings.*
- There's nothing automatically true about feelings. My feelings change when my thinking changes.*
- How did I get into this? What was I thinking about?*
- That's ridiculous. That's my critic talking.*
- I have more on the ball than I give myself credit for.*
- I'm in good health. I can take care of myself.*
- I'm a good baker. They depend on me around here.
- I'm still young and smart enough to straighten out my finances.

Marjorie used the starred rebuttal points whenever she felt overwhelmed. Depending on the thoughts that started the whole episode, she would improvise the rest of her rebuttal. Sometimes she couldn't pinpoint the thoughts that started her down the familiar path of emotional reasoning. She would then have to get out the pencil and paper again and use the three-column techniques.

Sometimes Marjorie didn't need to know the original negative thoughts. She found that she could say to herself, "These are feelings, not facts. They will pass in a little while. Wait it out." And in a few hours the emotional storm usually began to abate and she felt more confidence in herself again.

6

Compassion

The essence of self-esteem is compassion for yourself. When you have compassion for yourself, you understand and accept yourself. If you make a mistake, you forgive yourself. You have reasonable expectations of yourself. You set attainable goals. You tend to see yourself as basically good.

Your pathological critic cannot stand compassion. To him, compassion is like water to the Wicked Witch of Oz or garlic to a vampire. When your self-talk is compassionate, your pathological critic is gagged. Compassion is one of the most potent weapons you have for keeping your pathological critic at bay.

When you learn to feel compassion for yourself, you begin exposing your sense of worth. You literally uncover the hidden jewel of your own value. Compassionate self-talk can wash away the sediment of hurt and rejection that may have covered your innate self-acceptance for years.

This chapter will define compassion, show how compassion for yourself and compassion for others are related, discuss how to achieve a sense of self-worth, and present exercises designed to increase your compassionate skills.

Compassion Defined

Most people think of compassion as an admirable character trait like honesty, loyalty, or spontaneity. If you have compassion, you show it by being kind, sympathetic, and helpful to others.

This is certainly true. However, as it relates to self-esteem, compassion is much more. First of all, it is not an unchanging character trait. *Compassion is actually a skill*—a skill you can acquire if you lack it or improve if you already have it. Second, compassion is not something you feel only for others. It should also inspire you to be kind, sympathetic, and helpful to yourself.

There are three basic components to the skill of compassion: understanding, accepting, and forgiving.

Understanding

An attempt to understand is the first step toward a compassionate relationship to yourself and others. Understanding something important about yourself or a loved one can totally change your feelings and attitudes. Consider the case of Sean, a brick mason who finally realized why he overate in the evenings. One day he had a particularly hard job. After working until dark, he realized that he still had a full day's work left for the next day, when he was supposed to start yet another job. He drove home with one eye on the temperature gauge because his car had been overheating and he couldn't afford to get it fixed. He felt exhausted, anxious, and defeated. He thought about stopping at the liquor store and getting some nuts, some corn chips, and some dip to snack on before dinner. As he pictured himself ensconced in front of the TV with his snacks piled on the arms of the chair, he began to feel better. But the critic had also started kicking him for his "junk food binges." At this point Sean did something different. He asked himself why the thought of food made him feel better. Then he had an insight: he overate in the evenings to escape his feelings of pressure and inadequacy during the day. While snacking, he felt comforted and safe.

This sudden understanding was Sean's first step toward a more compassionate view of himself. He understood his overeating as a response to unbearable pressures, rather than an expression of gluttony or weakness.

Not all understanding comes so easy. Sometimes it comes as the result of a plodding, sustained effort to figure things out. Your decision to buy and read this book is an example of a conscious, step-by-step approach to understanding.

Understanding the nature of your problems doesn't mean that you have to come up with solutions to them. It merely means that you have figured out how you operate—what you are likely to do in a given situation and why you probably do it. It means you have some sense of how you came to be the person you are.

Understanding others is mostly a matter of listening to them instead of listening to your own self-talk about them. Instead of saying to yourself, "What a blabbermouth! Will she ever shut up?" you listen instead as your mother tells you about her trip to the doctor. You ask her questions about her symptoms and the tests she had to take. You gently probe for the feelings underneath the facts. Gradually you realize that she is not just complaining about the nurse and the receptionist. She is worried about getting older, about death. You are able to empathize and offer some sympathy, instead of your usual impatience. This makes her feel better and you feel better about yourself.

Acceptance

Acceptance is perhaps the most difficult aspect of compassion. Acceptance is an acknowledgement of the facts, with all value judgments suspended. You neither approve or disapprove—you accept. For example, the statement "I accept the fact that I'm out of shape" does not mean "I'm out of shape and that's perfectly OK with me." It means "I'm out of shape and I know it. I may not like it. In fact, sometimes I may feel like a barrel of flab. But right now I'm putting my feelings aside, editing out value judgments, and just facing the bare facts."

Marty is a good example of the power of acceptance. He was an auto body worker who constantly put himself down for being a "short, fat, ugly little man." As part of his struggle to gain self-compassion, he composed a brief description of himself to use every time his pathological critic started whispering "short . . . fat . . . ugly." He would counter by saying, "I'm five-foot-six, and I accept that. I'm 182 pounds, and I accept that. I'm getting bald, and I accept that, too. These are all facts. These facts are to be accepted, not used to beat myself up."

Acceptance of others involves acknowledging the facts about them without your usual judgments. For example, Laurie usually thought of a particular teacher as a "cold fish, totally without feelings. He never gives a word of encouragement or extra time for assignments." However, she made a great effort to accept this man because she had to work with him on an important student-faculty committee. First, Laurie got rid of the derogatory labels in her mind. Then she mentally ran down the facts: "Doctor Sommers is quiet, reserved, and detached. He usually gives help only when formally asked. He takes deadlines very seriously. I may not like his style as a teacher, but I accept him for what he is. I can work with him and still accomplish something." This exercise in understanding helped Laurie get some important joint resolutions passed by her committee. The whole experience boosted her self-esteem as well, because she felt that she had learned the value of being a little more detached and reserved herself.

Forgiveness

Forgiveness flows out of understanding and acceptance. Like those two traits, it doesn't mean approval. It means letting go of the past, reaffirming self-respect in the present, and looking toward a better future. When you forgive yourself for screaming at your child, you don't change wrong to right or forget all about it. Your tantrum was still the wrong thing to have done, and you will remember your mistake so that you can do better in the future. But you do write "case closed" and proceed with today's business without dwelling on the incident and feeling rotten all over again.

Alice was a young woman who had trouble accepting dates. Men would ask her out to dinner or the movies, and she would invent some excuse for why she couldn't go. Then her pathological critic would start up: "Chicken. He's a nice guy. Why can't you take a chance? You've blown it forever with him." Alice would suffer this attack repeatedly for days. When she began fighting back, forgiveness was one of her most powerful weapons. She would say to herself, "OK, I made a mistake. I would have liked to go out with John, but I felt too shy and scared. That's in the past. There's nothing to do about it now. I forgive myself, and I can go on to the next opportunity. I refuse to atone forever for my shyness."

True forgiveness of others means that the accounts are balanced. The person who harmed you no longer owes you anything. He or she is no longer in a one-down position to you regarding what happened. You have given up any idea of retaliation, reparation, restitution, or revenge. You face the future with a clean slate between you.

Charlie was a landscape architect whose relationship with his dad was poisoned by a long-standing disagreement over some money they had earned when they were in the gardening business together. His self-esteem suffered whenever he compared himself to friends who had closer relationships with their fathers. Finally, he realized that the key to raising his own opinion of himself and getting back in touch with his dad was to sincerely forgive him. "I had to stop rehashing all the old arguments," Charlie explained. "They were hanging around both our necks and keeping us apart." When he forgave his dad and put the past behind him, Charlie's self-esteem and his relationship with his father improved.

Toward a Compassionate Mind

Understanding, acceptance, and forgiveness: these are three big words that seem almost platitudinous. No one becomes more understanding or forgiving because he or she reads somewhere that this is a good way to be. Abstract concepts, no matter how laudable, have little effect on behavior.

To develop a compassionate mind, you must make a commitment to a different way of thinking. The old way was to judge and then reject. The new way requires that you suspend judgment for a few moments. When confronted with a situation that you traditionally evaluate in a negative way ("She's stupid . . . I screwed up again . . . He's selfish . . . I'm incompetent . . ."), you can instead use a specific series of thoughts that are the *compassionate response*.

The Compassionate Response

The compassionate response begins with three questions you should always ask yourself to promote an understanding of the problematic behavior.

1. What need was (he, she, I) trying to meet with that behavior?
2. What beliefs or awarenesses influenced the behavior?
3. What pain, hurt, or other feelings influenced the behavior?

Next come three statements to remind yourself that you can accept a person without blame or judgment, no matter how unfortunate his or her choices have been.

4. I wish _____ hadn't happened, but it was merely an attempt to meet (his, her, my) needs.
5. I accept (him, her, myself) without judgment or feeling of wrongness for that attempt.
6. No matter how unfortunate (his, her, my) decision, I accept the person who did it as someone who is, like all of us, trying to survive.

Finally, two statements suggest that the slate can be wiped clean, that it is time to forgive and let go of it.

7. It's over, I can let go of it.
8. Nothing is owed for this mistake.

Try to memorize this sequence. Make a commitment to use it whenever you notice that you are judging yourself or others. Revise it, if you wish, so that the language and suggestions feel right for you. But be sure to maintain the basic thrust of the compassionate response: understanding, acceptance, forgiveness.

The Problem of Worth

Learning compassionate skills helps you to contact your own sense of self-worth. But that sense can be very elusive if you suffer from low self-esteem. At times it seems like you're just not worth anything. It may seem that nobody is worth much.

What makes people worthwhile? Where do you look for evidence of worth? What are the criteria?

Many criteria for human worth have been devised throughout history. The ancient Greeks valued personal virtue in a human and political sense. If you conformed to ideals of harmony and moderation and contributed to society's order, you were considered worthy and might enjoy high self-esteem. Worthy Romans were expected to display patriotism and valor. Early Christians valued love of God and mankind over allegiance to worldly kingdoms. Worthy Buddhists strive to rid themselves of all desire. Worthy Hindus contemplate ways to deepen their reverence for all living beings. Worthy Muslims respect law, tradition, and honor. Liberals value love of man and good works. Conservatives value industry and respect for tradition. The worthy merchants are the rich ones. The worthy artists are the talented ones. The worthy politicians are the powerful ones. The worthy actors are the popular ones. And so on.

In our culture, the most common solution to the problem is to equate worth with work. You are what you do, and other positions and professions are more or less worthy than your own. Doctors are better than psychologists are better than lawyers are better than accountants are better than stockbrokers are better than disk jockeys are better than hardware clerks and so on.

Within a given profession or social level, our culture next awards worth based on accomplishments. Getting a raise, a degree, a promotion, or winning in competition are worth a lot. Acquiring the right house, car, furnishings, boat, or college education for your kids—all these accomplishments are worth a lot too. If you get fired or laid off, lose your home, or in any other way slip down the accomplishment ladder, you are in deep trouble. You lose all your counters and become socially worthless.

Buying into these cultural concepts of worth can be deadly. For example, John was a bank examiner who equated his worth with his accomplishments at work. When he was late in meeting an important deadline, he felt worthless. When he felt worthless, he got depressed. When he got depressed, he worked slower and missed more deadlines. He felt more worthless, got more depressed, worked less diligently, and so on in a deadly downward spiral.

John wasn't worthless. He was crippled by an irrational concept of worth. And because his irrational concept was a very common one in our society, he had no one close to him to point out the dilemma. John's supervisor agreed that he was worthless to the company if he couldn't meet deadlines. His wife and brother agreed that something was wrong with him. Even his therapist tended to agree that poor performance at work was certainly something to get depressed about. In subtle ways, they all reinforced John's belief that he was worthless. He was on a self-propelled merry-go-round of depression, and they weren't helping pull him off. They were helping push.

When you're in this sort of cultural jam, it may help a little to remind yourself that every criterion ever devised for measuring human worth is dependent on its cultural context. The Zen monk of great virtue is worthless in Wall Street. The highly respected stockbroker is worthless in the jungles of Borneo. The most powerful witch doctor is worthless in the halls of the Pentagon. John tried reminding himself of this: "What does it matter if the First Intercity audit is finished this week or next? Are stars going to fall from the sky? Is my total worth as a human being really so dependent on whether two columns of numbers balance? I wouldn't even have this problem on the beach at Pago Pago or in Shakespeare's London."

This self-talk gave John some distance on the situation, but it didn't boost his self-esteem much. The fact was, he had chosen to operate and compete in the arena of bank examination, not beachcombing in Pago Pago or Renaissance playwriting. He was a member of a western, urban culture, and he felt that he had to measure up to the prevailing standards of success, even if those standards were irrational or subjective.

A more fruitful place to turn is to your own experience and observations. The most "obvious" and "reasonable" cultural criteria for worth can often be confounded by observation. For example, if pediatricians are more worthy than the people who wash their windows, then it follows that pediatricians should have a higher sense of self-worth. All the pediatricians should be basking in the warm glow of their high self-esteem, while the window washers should all be diving off their scaffolds in despair. But it just isn't so. Statistics show that your profession is only slightly related to your level of self-esteem or mental health. The observable fact is that there are both pediatricians and window washers who like themselves, and there are similar ratios of pediatricians and window washers who don't like themselves.

John's personal observations bore this out. He knew other people in financial occupations who had good self-esteem, but weren't really any more competent or successful than himself. On the negative side, one of John's classmates in college was a vice president of a major corporation, but John knew him to be haunted by a sense of worthlessness despite his accomplishments.

Obviously, some people have solved this problem of personal worth and some haven't. If you want to enjoy high self-esteem, you too will have to come to terms with the concept of human worth. When you conclude that the solution must lie outside of culturally determined criteria, that leaves four ways you can approach the concept of worth and come out with your self-esteem intact.

Affirming Your Worth

The first way to deal with the problem of worth is to throw it out the window. Accept that human worth is an abstract concept that, upon examination, turns out to have an extremely fragile basis in reality. It's just another global label. All the criteria turn out to be subjective, culturally variable, and damaging to your self-esteem. The idea of identifying a universal standard of worth is a tempting illusion, but you and everybody else are better off without it. True human worth is impossible to determine.

The second way to deal with the problem of worth is to realize that worth exists, but that it is equally distributed and immutable. Everyone at birth has one unit of human worth, absolutely equal to everyone else's unit of worth. No matter what happens in your life, no matter what you do or is done to you, your human worth can't be diminished or increased. Nobody is worth more or less than anybody else.

It's interesting to note that these two options are *functionally* the same. They both free you to live without having to compare yourself to others and make constant value judgments about your relative worth.

Of course, these first two options are *essentially* different. The first is a kind of practical agnosticism: one person may or may not be "worth" more than another, but this judgment is a hopelessly difficult and dangerous one to make, and you refuse to make it. The second option is more in line with traditional western religious teaching, and results in a comforting, nondenominational "feeling" that people are worth something, that they are special, that they are more akin to angels than to animals. For the purpose of fostering self-esteem, you can choose either option and succeed.

The third choice is different from the first two options without negating either of them. In this option you acknowledge your own internal experience of human worth.

Recall a time when you felt good about yourself, when human worth seemed real and you had a good piece of it. Recall the feeling that you were OK, with all your faults and failings, in spite of others' opinions. You may have had only a glimpse of this emotion in your life. You may be, at this moment, totally out of touch with the feeling of personal worth. You may have only a dim, colorless, purely intellectual memory that once-upon-a-time you felt good about yourself.

The point is to admit that your personal worth exists, as evidenced by your own internal experience, however brief and occasional it has been. Your worth is like the sun, always shining, even when you are in the shade and can't feel it. You can't keep it from shining, you can only keep yourself in the shade by letting your pathological critic throw up clouds of confusion or by crawling under the rock of depression.

John, the bank examiner, was able to contact his inner sense of worth by remembering a neighbor he had when he was twelve. She was an old woman named Ackerson who lived next door. She would often look at John's school projects and drawings when his mother and father didn't have time or were not forthcoming with praise. Mrs. Ackerson always had great enthusiasm for his creations, telling him what a clever boy he was and how he would go far. John remembered the pride he felt, and his sense of confidence about the future. Sometimes it was possible for John to reach back to the memory of Mrs. Ackerson and tap into his early feelings of pride and competence.

The fourth way to deal with the problem of worth is to take a good look at yourself through the lens of compassion. Compassion exposes the essence of your humanness.

What do you understand about yourself? First, you live in a world in which you must constantly struggle to meet basic needs—or you will die. You must find food, shelter, emotional support, rest, and recreation. Almost all of your energy goes into these major need areas. You do the best you can, given your resources. But the available strategies you have for meeting your needs are limited by what you know and don't know, your conditioning, your emotional make-up, the degree of support you receive from others, your health, your sensitivity to pain and pleasure, and so on. And all through this struggle to survive you are aware that both your intellectual and physical abilities will inevitably deteriorate—and despite all your efforts you will die.

In the course of your struggle you make many mistakes and are rewarded with pain. Often you feel afraid—both of very real dangers and the vaguer dreads that come from a life without guarantees, where loss and hurt can slap you down at any time. There are so many kinds of pain, and yet you carry on, seeking whatever emotional and physical sustenance is available.

The last point is key: you carry on. In the face of all the pain, past and to come, you continue to struggle. You plan, you cope, you decide. You continue to live and to feel. If you let this awareness soak in, if you let yourself really feel the struggle, you may begin to get a glimmer of your real worth. It is the force, the life energy that keeps you trying. The degree of success is irrelevant. How good you look how psychologically or physically nourished you are is irrelevant. The only thing that counts is the effort. And the source of your worth is the effort.

After understanding comes acceptance. Nothing one does in the quest to survive is bad. Each approach is only more or less effective, painful or not painful. Despite your mistakes, you are doing a good job—because it is the best job you *can* do. Your mistakes and the pain that follows teach you. It is possible to accept everything you do without judgment because every minute of your life you are engaged in the inescapable struggle.

You can forgive and let go of your failures and mistakes because you have already paid for them. It is our condition that we do not always know the best way—and even knowing the way, we may not have the resources to follow it. Your worth, then, is that you were born into this place. And that you continue to live here despite the enormous difficulty of the struggle.

Compassion for Others

To be complete, compassion must be directed toward others as well as toward yourself. At present you may find it easier to understand, accept, and forgive others than to understand, accept, and forgive yourself. Or you may find that it's relatively easy to feel compassion for yourself, but that you're constantly irritated at the failings of others. Either kind of imbalance can lower your self-esteem.

Fortunately, this imbalance is self-correcting. Feeling increased compassion for others will eventually make it easier to feel compassion for yourself. Learning to give yourself a break will lead naturally to a more compassionate view of others. In other words, the Golden Rule operates in both forward and reverse: "Love thy neighbor as thyself" or "Love thyself as thy neighbor."

If loving yourself seems like misplaced affection, then start with increasing your compassion for others. After you have learned to understand, accept, and forgive the foibles of others, your own shortcomings won't seem so enormous.

Empathy

A more convenient term than compassion for others is *empathy.* Empathy is clearly understanding the thoughts and feelings of another person. Empathy involves listening carefully, asking qustions, setting aside your value judgments, and using your imagination to understand another's point of view, opinions, feelings, motivations, and situation. The insight gained by the exercise of empathy leads naturally to the compassionate process of understanding, accepting, and forgiving.

Empathy is *not* feeling the same way somebody else feels. That's sympathy, a related but different activity that is not always possible or appropriate. Empathy is also not acting in a tender, understanding manner. That's support, another activity that's not always possible or appropriate. Empathy is not agreement or approval either. Empathy operates outside of and prior to sympathy, support, agreement, and approval.

True empathy is the ultimate antidote to anger and resentment. Remember, anger is caused by your thoughts, not others' actions.

When you take the time to thoroughly understand another's thoughts and motivations, your mind reading and blaming are short-circuited. You see the logic behind others' actions. You may still not agree with the logic or like the actions, but you understand. You come to see that real evil and meanness are very rare, that the vast majority of people are seeking pleasure or avoiding pain in what seems to them to be the best way at the time. You see how little your own worth or actions enter into the equation. You are free to accept the facts of the matter, forgive the offender, and move on.

June was a social worker who frequently had run-ins with her supervisor. June felt that the clients had to come first and paperwork second, and so she was often late with her weekly and monthly statistics and reports. She felt very critical about her supervisor's insistence that she keep up with the paperwork, feeling that he didn't really care for her clients as much as he cared about looking good on paper.

This state of affairs improved after June had a long conversation with her supervisor at a staff picnic. She consciously made an effort to listen and understand the supervisor's point of view. As they talked, she refrained from making her usual accusatory or sarcastic remarks. Her supervisor gradually unbent, letting some of his commitment and feelings show. He told a story of how he had once lost a lot of grant money and killed a valuable outreach program because he messed up the paperwork. This major failure had taught him that looking good on paper was a necessary precondition for doing good as a social worker. After this conversation, June was much more kindly disposed toward her supervisor. Her exercise in empathy paid off in a better working relationship.

Exercises

This chapter concludes with four exercises. The first two will train you in feeling compassion for others, and the last two combine compassion for others with compassion for yourself. Go with your strength: try the exercise that seems easiest first. Then proceed to the more challenging exercises.

Video Encounter

This is a perfectly safe, nonthreatening way to practice empathy for others. Watch a TV show you hate, one you normally wouldn't be caught dead watching. If you normally watch game shows, pick a serious drama. If you normally watch only news, tune in some cartoons. If you prefer comedies, watch a TV preacher, or a cop show, or a soap opera.

Watch and listen carefully. Every time you feel irritated, disgusted, bored, or embarrassed, set your feelings aside and refocus your attention. Say to yourself, "I notice I'm feeling very irritated by this. That's OK, but it's not what I'm interested in right now. I can set the irritation aside and just observe for a while, without judging."

Suspend your value judgments for a time and imagine why the faithful fans watch this show. What do they get out of it? Do they watch for excitement, enlightenment, diversion, escape, identification with the characters, confirmation of their prejudices? Try to understand the attractive features of this show and what kind of person likes it.

When you arrive at an empathetic understanding, switch to another kind of show and try again. Remember, you don't have to approve of what you see—just see it clearly and understand its attractions.

The goal of this exercise isn't to expand or corrupt your viewing taste. The purpose is to provide a safe, nonthreatening situation in which you can practice setting aside your snap judgments and gain insight into a point of view you would ordinarily dismiss out of hand.

Active Listening

With a friend. Choose a friend who likes to try new things. Explain that you want to improve your listening skills. Ask your friend to tell you a story about something that is important in his or her life: a traumatic experience, an important childhood memory, or a hope for the future.

As your friend talks, your job is to listen carefully and ask questions about any parts that you don't understand. Ask your friend to clarify or expand. Dig beneath the facts by asking for information on thoughts and feelings: "Why was that important to you?" "How did you feel about that?" "What did you learn from that?"

From time to time, paraphrase what your friend has said: "So in other words, you . . . " "Wait, let me see if I understand: you thought that . . . " "What I hear you saying is . . . " Paraphrasing is an important part of listening with empathy because it keeps you on track. It helps you remove your own false interpretations and clarify your friend's precise meaning. Your friend gets the satisfaction of knowing that he or she has really been heard, and a chance to correct any errors you have made. You then incorporate the corrections in revised paraphrases.

With acquaintances. Now you can go on to a more difficult exercise. Choose people that you don't know as well and practice your empathetic skills without their knowledge of what you are doing.

Whatever they are talking to you about, ask for clarification and amplification. Resist your impulse to argue or jump in with an anecdote of your own. Notice when you start judging them in your mind and set the judgments aside. Remember that you don't have to love them, that you are just trying to understand something without your own self-talk getting in the way. Especially watch out for any comparisons with yourself that you find yourself making.

With someone you don't know well, paraphrasing is even more important. It helps you remember an unfamiliar story, assures the speaker of your interest, and helps you separate your own mental processes from what was actually said. As your acquaintance clarifies and corrects, your understanding deepens and the conversation will often shift to a more personal, intimate level. True opinions, feelings, and areas of uncertainty or vulnerability will be gradually uncovered as the speaker learns that you are a careful, interested listener who can be trusted to hear a person out without jumping all over the conversation. Do this exercise often enough, and acquaintances become friends.

With strangers. At a party or other gathering, pick someone you don't know or someone you don't like. Engage that person in conversation and use your listening skills to really try to comprehend what he or she has to say. Follow the instructions given for listening to friends and acquaintances, realizing that it will probably be more difficult to suspend judgment and concentrate on asking for information and paraphrasing.

When you are listening to someone you actually don't like or with whom you have nothing in common, it is important to remind yourself of the basis of compassion: *Everyone is just trying to survive like you are.* Ask yourself the three questions that begin the *compassionate response.* Ask yourself, "What need is this person meeting by saying this? How is it making this person feel more secure, more in control, less anxious, less in pain? What beliefs are influencing him or her?"

Compassion for Things Past

This is an exercise that you can do over and over to develop skills of understanding, acceptance, and forgiveness.

This moment, as you are reading, is the present. Every other event of your life is in the past. Some of these events you label bad and use to reject yourself: not visiting your father more before he died, the demanding way you dealt with your first wife, things you said as you were separating, your eating binge last week, your failed effort to stop smoking, your argument with your son, and so on. But you don't have to go on hurting yourself with the past. These events can be reexperienced by using the compassionate response.

Here's what you do. First, select an event from the past, one that the critic has used to make attacks. Now get into a comfortable position. Close your eyes and take a few deep breaths. Scan your body for tension and stretch or relax any tight areas. At this point, let yourself begin drifting into the past. Go back to that time when your selected event was unfolding. See yourself doing whatever it was you now regret. See how you were dressed, see the room or the environment, see whoever else is present. Hear any conversation that is taking place. Notice any feelings you are having in the past event—either emotional or physical. As best you can, let yourself relive the event. See the action unfolding, hear the words, notice your reactions.

Now, while still holding on to the image of yourself in the middle of the event, ask yourself this question:

What need was I trying to meet?

Think about it. Were you trying to feel more secure, more in control, less anxious, less guilty? Take your time with the answer. Now ask:

What was I thinking at the time?

What were your beliefs about the situation? How were you interpreting things? What did you assume to be true? Don't rush your answer. Now ask:

What kind of pain or feeling was influencing me?

Take your time and think about the emotional context of the event.

When you have some answers to these questions, when you know the needs, thoughts, and feelings that influenced you, it's time to accept and forgive yourself for who you were at that moment in time. Stay focused on the image of yourself in the middle of the event and say this to the person you were:

I wish this hadn't happened, but I was trying to meet my needs.

I accept myself without judgment or any feelings of wrongness for my attempt.

I accept myself at that moment as trying to survive.

Really try to feel each of these statements. Allow them to sink in. Now it is time to let go of the past. Say to yourself:

I owe no debt for this mistake.

It is over, I can forgive myself.

If this exercise works at all for you, use it with as many past events as you can. As you keep using it, the compassionate response will become more automatic. Forgiveness will come easier. And you will feel less caught in the painful regrets of the past.

Compassion Meditation

This exercise has three parts: visualizing and feeling compassion for someone who has hurt you, for someone you have hurt, and for yourself. You can have someone read this to you, or make a tape recording and listen to it. Speak slowly, in a low, distinct, relaxed tone.

For someone who has hurt you. Sit or lie on your back with your hands and arms uncrossed and your legs stretched out side by side. Close your eyes and take several deep breaths. Continue to breathe deeply and slowly as you scan your body for tension. As you notice tight areas, relax your muscles and settle into a heavy, warm, relaxed state. Let your breathing slow even further, and suspend your judgments. Accept whatever images come to you, even if they don't immediately make sense.

Imagine that there is a chair in front of you. Someone is sitting in the chair, someone you know who has hurt you in some way. Imagine that person who has hurt you sitting silently in the chair. Notice all the details: how big or small the person is, the clothes, the colors, the posture. The person who has hurt you is looking calmly, expectantly at you. Say to the person:

> You are a human being like me. You are trying to survive. When you hurt me, you were trying to survive. You do your best, given your limitations and your understanding of the situation at the time. I can understand your motivations, your fears, your hopes. I share them because I am human too. I may not like what you did, but I can understand it.
>
> I accept the fact that you hurt me. I do not like it, but I do not make you bad for doing it. Nothing now can change what happened.
>
> I forgive you. I may not approve or agree, but I can forgive. I can let go of the past and wipe the slate clean. I know better than to expect atonement. I let go of revenge and resentment. Our differences are in the past. I am in control of the present and I can forgive you in the present. I can leave my anger behind.

Continue looking at the person who hurt you. Gradually let the person enter your heart. Open yourself. Let anger and resentment fade out like music being turned down. Open further. If it's difficult to empathize or let go of your anger, don't judge yourself for how difficult it is. Take a moment more if you need to, and go at your own pace. When you are ready, say "I forgive you" one more time. Let the image of the person in the chair fade from sight.

For someone you have hurt. Imagine that the person in the chair is now someone whom you have hurt, someone from whom you want understanding, acceptance, and forgiveness. See all the details of clothing and appearance. Make the vision as real as you can. The person you have hurt is looking at you calmly, expectantly. Say to the person:

I am a human being, worthy but imperfect. I am like you. We are both just trying to survive. When I hurt you, I was just trying to do what seemed best for me at the time. If I had then the awareness I do now, I would have chosen differently. But at the time, I could only do what I did. I understand that I hurt you, and I want you to know that hurting you was not my goal.

Please accept the fact that I hurt you and nothing can change that. I would undo it if I could. You would undo it if you could. But we can't. Nothing now can change the past.

Please forgive me. I don't ask you to approve of what I did, or agree with me, but I do ask you to forgive me. I want to put our differences in the past, wipe the slate clean, and start fresh.

Please open your heart to me. Understand, accept, and forgive.

As you look at the person you hurt, see that person slowly smile. Know that you are understood, you are accepted, you are forgiven. Let the image of the person fade away until the chair is empty.

For yourself. For the final part of this meditation, imagine yourself sitting in the chair. Again, see all the details: see yourself dressed as you are dressed, looking as you look now. Imagine that the image of yourself is saying:

I am a human being. I am worthwhile just because I exist and try to survive. I take care of myself. I take myself seriously. I correctly take myself into consideration first in all matters.

I have legitimate needs and wants. I can choose what I need and want without having to justify it to anybody. I make choices and I take responsibility for them.

I always do my best. Each thought and action is the best I am capable of at the time. Because I'm human, I make mistakes. I accept my mistakes without blame or judgment. When I make a mistake, I learn from it. I am imperfect and I forgive myself for my mistakes.

I know that others are equally worthy, equally imperfect. I have compassion for them because they are engaged in the same struggle for survival that I am.

Imagine the figure of yourself in the chair getting up, coming over to where you are, and sitting or lying down in your body, merging into one whole person.

Relax and rest. You are at peace with yourself, at peace with others.

When you are ready, open your eyes and get up slowly, feeling refreshed and relaxed, with a sense of compassionate acceptance toward yourself and others.

Do this exercise at least five times over the next two weeks.

7

The Shoulds

On a chilly November evening in 1952, a middle-aged black doorman was hailing a taxi for a white family that had just come down the steps from the Sheraton. Before anyone could stop her, their six-year-old child darted into the street. She was chasing her windblown hat directly into the path of an oncoming tour bus. Suddenly, with the reflexes of a much younger man, the doorman launched into the street, tackled the child, and rolled with her to safety.

What's interesting about this event is the very different reactions it elicited. The doorman's wife was furious. She told him he was risking his life on some fool stunt when he had a wife and children who needed him. "It's just wrong, your family's always got to come first." A brother also disapproved, but mostly because the rescued child was white. "If you're going to kill yourself, do it for one of our own." The hotel manager, on the other hand, declared the rescue a "selfless act" and that year provided a rather substantial Christmas bonus. The doorman's pastor heard the story and described it as heroic in his Sunday sermon. "Whoever saves a child," he said, "saves the world. Because who knows which of our children will grow up to be the great healer, the great leader, or the saint?"

The same event triggered these very different reactions because of the unique belief systems through which people filter the world. Reality hardly matters. What really counts are the values and rules of conduct that you use to judge behavior. That's why the same act can be selfish to the wife while selfless to the manager, stupid to the brother while heroic to the pastor.

Looking back, one is afforded the luxury of knowing the consequences of an act. And outcomes are the only sure form of judgment. The pastor was right. Thirty years later that little girl received an award for a major contribution to her medical specialty.

The pathological critic uses your beliefs and values to attack you. The "shoulds" that make up your rules for living form the ideological basis of the critic's effort to destroy your self-esteem. The critic is constantly evaluating what you say, what you do, and even what you feel by comparing you to an ideal of perfection. Since you never live up to the ideal of how you ought to speak, act, or feel, the critic has endless grounds for indicting you as bad or worthless.

Consider the case of the young man who gets three A's and a C+ on his report card. His beliefs about grades and success will entirely determine his reaction. If he uses the criteria of a B average as his standard for reasonable performance, then he'll be delighted to see that he has far exceeded his goal. If he believes that a C is a totally unacceptable grade, a sign of stupidity or laziness, then his critic will have all the punch it needs to make his self-esteem feel like it went fifteen rounds with Muhammad Ali.

How Values Are Formed

Woodrow Wilson brought America into the First World War in order to "make the world safe for democracy." U.S. soldiers took their places in the trenches and foxholes of Europe believing that they were fighting against the forces of tyranny. Thousands died in the Argonne Forest and at St. Mihiel. The belief in nationalism, in the superiority of the American political system, and in such abstract values as duty and honor produced in 1917 a zealousness for the righteous war, a war that would forever end war. On the other side, young men were also dying for deeply held beliefs in German nationalism, in ideals of bravery and duty to the fatherland.

Looking backward seven decades, none of it seems worth fighting for. Why should young Germans die because of the Kaiser's political ambitions? Why should American lives have been lost so that the allies could use the treaty of Versailles to punish and humiliate Germany and in so doing plant the seeds for World War Two? Yet there is nothing new in this. Throughout history men have been dying for their beliefs, and rarely has the cause proved worthy of such sacrifice.

Why are beliefs and values so powerful? What is it about the nature of belief that makes a man willing to surrender comfort, safety, even his life so that he will not be guilty of doing wrong? The answer is that while the content of a belief may be arbitrary and is often erroneous, the motivation for believing springs from the deepest human drives.

Most beliefs are formed in the same way—in response to some basic need. Your first beliefs were generated out of the need to be loved and approved of by your parents. In order to feel safe and cared for, you adopted their beliefs about such things as how to work, how to handle anger, mistakes, and pain, how and when to be sexual, what one can and cannot talk about, what are the proper goals in life, how to act in a marriage, what is owed to parents and other family members, and how self-reliant one should be. Some of the rules and beliefs you acquired from your parents were promoted by value-laden words such as *commitment, honesty, generosity, dignity, intelligence,* or *strength.* Those terms, as well as their negative opposites, were used by your parents as value yardsticks to measure people and behavior. They applied some of them to you. And in your need to please your parents, you may have accepted even such negative labels as *selfish, stupid, weak,* or *lazy.*

A second group of beliefs is generated by the need to feel belonging and approval from peers. To ensure peer acceptance, you learn to live by rules and beliefs governing such areas as how to act with the opposite sex, how to handle aggression, how much to reveal, what you owe your community and the world at large, and what are appropriate sex-role behaviors. The approval of peers often depends on your willingness to accept the group's beliefs.

If your friends oppose American intervention in Latin America, for example, there is a strong pressure to either support that belief or face ostracism.

A number of studies have shown that beliefs change dramatically in response to changes in role or status. For example, pro-union employees who are for workers' rights undergo a change in viewpoint when promoted to managerial positions. Within six months, they have often shifted significantly toward pro-management beliefs and values. Again, the need for belonging and safety literally creates new patterns of belief in order to fit in with the new reference group.

There is a third major force that helps to shape your beliefs. This is the need for emotional and physical well-being. Included here is the need for self-esteem; the need to protect yourself from painful emotions such as hurt or loss; the need for pleasure, excitement, and meaning; and the need to feel physically safe. Consider the example of the aspiring city councilman. He explains to his wife that during the next year of campaigning he will have little time for her and the family. But it's a necessary sacrifice, he argues, because once elected he will do so much for the community. The truth is that the few trivial changes a councilman could make might not be worth giving up a year with his children. But the truth is irrelevant. His belief is forged from a need for meaning, pleasure, and excitement.

Now consider the case of a man recently fired from his job as a bookkeeper. He reports to a friend that he was crazy to ever take a job like that, that it was "boring, soul-destroying, and politically incorrect. I've never met an accountant type," he says, "who wasn't an unmitigated nerd." He vows not to sell out again, and some months later berates his sister for "working in some downtown numbers' factory." These opinions are an obvious rationalization. They are created entirely by the need to maintain self-esteem. This man must either devalue his employers or see himself as a failure.

A woman's lover tells her that he needs three nights a week to be alone or visit friends. She says to herself, "You can't let a man take you for granted," and tells him that maybe they should call off their relationship. Her sudden conviction that she must assert herself is really in response to her need to avoid hurt and loss.

A man is in danger of losing his leg due to complications of diabetes. He concludes that God is punishing him for a long-standing extramarital relationship. He forms the belief that breaking off the affair will save his leg. His need for physical safety and a sense of control is generating what he would call in better times "stupid, magical thinking."

As a last case, consider a woman who believes in full commitment to every task and hates the smallest sign of laziness. She works long hours trying to meet impossible deadlines. But her hard-work rule is really protecting her rather fragile self-esteem. Her need to see herself as competent and to feel safe from criticism is the fuel for her belief.

The Tyranny of the Shoulds

Since most beliefs and rules are formed in response to needs, they have nothing to do with truth or reality. They are generated by parental, cultural, and peer expectations and by your needs to feel loved, to belong, and to feel safe and good about yourself.

While the process that generates shoulds has nothing to do with the literal truth, it depends on the *idea* of truth for its power. In order to feel motivated to act on a should, you have to be convinced of its veracity. Take, for example, the case of Mrs. L. She is an ardent supporter of a Christian group that promotes the idea of chastity before marriage. Mrs. L. has three very strong needs that help to generate her belief about premarital sexuality. The first need is to win the love and acceptance of her mother, who is very uncomfortable with sexuality of any kind. The second need is to protect her children from environments and associations which she considers dangerous. A "strict conscience'' is a good way to keep them safe. A third need is to feel a close identification with her children. She knows that they will seem strange and foreign to her if their sexual behavior differs markedly from her own. These three needs create the belief for Mrs. L. But her conviction that the belief is absolutely right in God's eyes gives it its power. She can insist on her values because they are true, and not only true for her children, but for everyone, everywhere in the world.

This is the tyranny of shoulds: the absolute nature of belief, the unbending sense of right and wrong. If you don't live up to your shoulds, you judge yourself to be a bad and unworthy person. This is why people torture themselves with guilt and self-blame, this is why they are willing to die in wars, this is why they become paralyzed when forced to choose between unbending rules and genuine desire.

Here is a list of some of the most common pathological shoulds:

- I should be the epitome of generosity and unselfishness.
- I should be the perfect lover, friend, parent, teacher, student, spouse, and so on.
- I should be able to endure any hardship with equanimity.
- I should be able to find a quick solution to every problem.
- I should never feel hurt. I should always feel happy and serene.
- I should be completely competent.
- I should know, understand, and foresee everything.
- I should never feel certain emotions such as anger or jealousy.
- I should love my children equally.
- I should never make mistakes.
- My emotions should be constant—once I feel love, I should always feel love.
- I should be totally self-reliant.
- I should never be tired or get sick.
- I should never be afraid.
- I should have achievements that bring me status, wealth, or power.
- I should always be busy; to relax is to waste my time and my life.
- I should put others first: it is better that I feel pain than cause anyone else to feel pain.
- I should be unfailingly kind.
- I should never feel sexually attracted to _____ .
- I should care for everyone who cares for me.
- I should make enough money so my family can afford _____ .
- I should be able to protect my children from all pain.
- I should not take time just for my own pleasure.

Notice which of these shoulds apply to you. In the section on healthy versus unhealthy values, you can explore why these shoulds are unreasonable.

Healthy Versus Unhealthy Values

You can tell whether your beliefs, rules, and shoulds are healthy or unhealthy by applying the following criteria.

Healthy values are flexible. Flexible rules allow for exceptions where circumstances warrant, while unhealthy rules are unbending and universally applied. For example, the rule that you should avoid causing other people pain could be workable if exceptions were made in cases where your own vital needs were at stake. But if the rule is unbending and you are obliged to protect others from pain at any personal cost, then you have an unhealthy value. Unhealthy values are rigid. They often include words like *never, always, all, totally, perfectly*, and so on. You must either follow the rule or feel worthless and bad.

A second way to measure the flexibility of your rules is to look at your failure quotas. Flexible rules include a built-in awareness that a certain percentage of the time you will fail to live up to the ideal standard. Rigid rules have no such quota system. You are crucified if you deviate one millimeter from the straight and narrow. As an example, consider the rule "I should never make mistakes." Striving for excellence is a worthy ambition, but you need a healthy quota for mistakes and failures. Without such a quota your stress level will be high, and your self-esteem will be destroyed by the smallest error.

Healthy values are owned rather than introjected. Owning a belief or should means that you've critically examined this rule for living and it still makes sense to you. This is in contrast to *introjected rules*, where you accept parental values without determining how well they fit your own unique circumstances, personality, and needs. Unquestioning acceptance of parental rules and values is like buying a car without a test drive. You just accept everything the salesman says, and never find out how the car handles, whether the ceiling's too low for your height, if it has enough power, or if the transmission works smoothly. With introjected values you accept your parents' word for things that you should test and evaluate yourself.

Healthy values are realistic. This means that they are based on an assessment of positive versus negative consequences. A realistic value or rule promotes behavior that leads to positive outcomes. It encourages you to do things that result in long-term happiness for the people involved. That's the *purpose* of a value. You follow it because in your experience the value guides you toward a way of living that *feels good*. Unrealistic values and shoulds have nothing to do with outcomes. They are absolute and global. They prescribe behavior because it is "right" and "good," not because it leads to positive consequences. Unrealistic values require you to act "on principle," no matter how much pain the act brings to yourself and others.

Consider the value "marriage should last forever." As a rule governing your behavior, it's unrealistic. That's because it isn't based on outcomes. It doesn't take into account the fact that struggling to maintain your marital commitments may make you and your spouse unhappier than divorcing. The "marriage should last forever" rule is based on the unbending principle that marital commitment is the highest good. Your happiness is irrelevant. Your pain is irrelevant. All that counts is doing the "right" thing.

Now consider the rule "I should be honest with my spouse." This value could be either realistic or unrealistic, depending on how you frame it. The rule might be realistic if you believe that it promotes intimacy, helps to solve problems before they get too large, and encourages you to voice your needs. In other words, you can adhere to the value of marital honesty because you know it usually makes you feel good in the long run. But because your value of honesty is based on outcomes, you might not always choose to be honest. At certain times you might withhold your feelings because the prospect of greater intimacy would be outweighed by negative consequences of hurt or discord. In contrast, your honesty-in-marriage value would be unrealistic if it were based on principle rather than outcomes or consequences. You'd force yourself to adhere to the rule because it was right and dishonesty of any kind was wrong.

In the study of ethics, this approach is called *consequencialism*. What makes consequencialism appealing is that ethical systems based on absolute principles inevitably reach a point where some of the principles contradict each other. This problem can be demonstrated on a very simple level. Consider the conflict a child must face when trying to decide whether the highest good is telling his parents the truth or keeping a confidence with his brother. He will have to break one of his principles by either lying or betraying a sibling. The only realistic way you can escape such an ethical quandry is to evaluate the negative and positive consequences of each choice for all parties concerned.

Healthy values are life-enhancing rather than life-restricting. This means that the rules you live by must take into account your basic needs as a human being. Healthy values give you the flexibility to pursue your emotional, sexual, intellectual, and recreational needs. Your rules for living should not diminish or narrow you. They shouldn't leave you feeling depleted by self-sacrifice. Life-enhancing values encourage you to do what is nourishing and supportive, except in situations where the long-term consequences are painful for yourself or others. As an example, take the rule that "you should always put your children first." This is not a life-enhancing value. There are many times when your needs are in conflict with needs of your children. Staying healthy and balanced requires that you sometimes take care of yourself—even though your children will suffer a minor deprivation. Men who believe that they should never feel afraid are stuck with a life-restricting value. This belief denies the reality that a man can feel fear in many circumstances and has a right to acknowledge and accept that feeling. The same difficulty occurs when you have rules demanding that you be universally bright and cheery. The value isn't life-enhancing, because it denies you the right to feel a full range of emotion—including times when you're sad, frustrated, or angry.

Exercise

In the following exercise, you will read vignettes about real-life situations and the values that people use to guide them. In each case, the protagonist of the story uses a rule which violates one or more of the criteria for healthy values. See if you can spot which criteria is being violated. To refresh your memory, here again are the criteria for healthy versus unhealthy values.

Healthy Values	*Unhealthy Values*
1. Flexible (exceptions and quotas)	Rigid (global, no exceptions or quotas)
2. Owned (examined and tested)	Introjected (unquestioned acceptance)
3. Realistic (based on consequences)	Unrealistic (based on "rightness")
4. Life-enchancing (acknowledge your needs and feelings)	Life-restricting (ignore your needs and feelings)

Situation 1. Ellen is a thirty-year-old craftsperson. She loves working with her hands and specializes in making customized lamp shades. Last year she opened a small shop and is very much enjoying her first experience as an enterpreneur. Ellen's father is a full-time professor. He's always been disappointed that she didn't study harder and express a greater interest in academics. Despite the pleasure that she gets from her craft, Ellen has a nagging sense of failure. She feels that she should be teaching English, like she planned and her father wanted. She feels embarrassed that she isn't "using her brain." She had tried to go back to college three different times, and on each occasion dropped out. She confides to friends that in some ways her life "has been a waste."

What's wrong with Ellen's values? Which of the following apply?

RIGID   INTROJECTED   UNREALISTIC   LIFE-RESTRICTING

Ellen's problem is that she has introjected her father's value system without examining how it fits her unique needs and abilities. For years, Ellen has been tortured by values and rules that she never critically examined. If Ellen had developed her own realistic values, she would have recognized the positive consequences of working at her craft. She has a job that she enjoys and does well, as opposed to struggling with the rigors of an academic career.

Situation 2. Arthur has been an insurance broker for the past eight years. He has been moderately successful but has never made "the big money." Arthur's biggest problem is that he feels like a failure every time he loses an account. While losing accounts is inevitable, and every broker anticipates a certain attrition rate for old accounts, Arthur feels that a good broker must please every one of his clients. When a client cancels, Arthur concludes that he is "screwing up," and hasn't been sufficiently attentive.

What's wrong with Arthur's values? Which of the following apply?

RIGID   INTROJECTED   UNREALISTIC   LIFE-RESTRICTING

Arthur's rules are too rigid. He expects to be perfect, and when he is not 100 percent effective in reenlisting clients, he labels himself a failure. Flexible values allow a quota for being human. You expect to make mistakes, and so you build a realistic failure rate into your expectations. If Arthur's values were flexible, he would find out the renewal percentages for other brokers. Then he could build a quota for lost accounts into his performance standards.

Situation 3. Every year Cynthia spends a week in Ann Arbor visiting her mother. Always she stays in her mother's home, where she feels continually attacked and undermined by criticism. After the first 24 hours of good behavior, the relationship quickly degenerates to the point where Cynthia and her mom are having several blowups a day. If Cynthia doesn't respond, her mother rebukes her for not listening. If she tries to defend herself, her mother simply shifts the ground and discusses another of Cynthia's "failings." This year Cynthia has decided to handle the visit differently. She stays at a motel, even though her mother insists that she stay at home. She spends more time visiting friends and taking breaks from her mom. She also refuses to see her aunt, who often joins forces with her mother for a two-on-one fight. Despite the fact that there are far fewer fights and an unusually sweet goodbye, despite feeling safer and less beat up, Cynthia experiences guilt about her decision. "I hated myself for doing it. I ought to be loving and sort of endure things for mom's sake."

What's wrong with Cynthia's values? Which of the following apply?

RIGID   INTROJECTED   UNREALISTIC   LIFE-RESTRICTING

Cynthia's values are unrealistic. They are based on the principle of doing right, rather than a realistic assessment of consequences. If Cynthia looked at the consequences, she would conclude that she felt safer and happier with her new strategy. She would realize that there was much less conflict and that for once she and her mother felt good about each other when they parted.

Situation 4. Will is an upholsterer by day, a delivery man by night, and a security guard on the weekend. He feels he has to be busy every minute in order to "achieve something in life." Will hates "wasting time" because "I'll keep feeling like I'm nothing till I earn some money and respect." Will is in a relationship that he doesn't like, but has no time to look for anyone new. He lives "on the cheap" in the "Hotel Roach Haven."

What's wrong with Will's values? Which of the following apply?

RIGID   INTROJECTED   UNREALISTIC   LIFE-RESTRICTING

Will's values are life-restricting. They don't take into account his basic needs for recreation, intimacy, or friendship. Will is leaving a lot of himself on the road to die in his headlong race for wealth and status.

Situation 5. At 69, Sonya has a number of friends who've lost their spouses. One recently widowed friend has been phoning constantly and staying on the line for hours. The problem has continued to the point where Sonya's husband has become quite annoyed. Recently, Sonya told her friend that she wanted to cut the telephone contact down to maybe once a week. But she felt terribly wrong and guilty. She has always believed that above all a person must be kind. To salve her conscience, she began phoning her friend nearly every day "just to see how she is."

What's wrong with Sonya's values? Which of the following apply?

RIGID   INTROJECTED   UNREALISTIC   LIFE-RESTRICTING

Sonya's values are too rigid. They don't allow for worthy exceptions. It's clear that Sonya needs to set limits on her needy friend, but the rule of kindness doesn't permit her. She needs to evaluate this situation to see whether the negative consequences make it a special case.

Situation 6. Arlene lives in a very poor school district where children have consistently scored below the national norms for reading and math. She has decided that she wants to send her children to a private school, but she needs her mother's help with the tuition. Arlene is torn by conflicting values. Her number one rule is "get the best for your children," but her number two rule is that "you should be self-reliant." She's determined to have her children get a good education, but she feels like a failure as a parent because she hasn't the financial means to provide it. She also feels guilty that she's "taking advantage" of her mother and "being dependent."

What's wrong with Arlene's values? Which of the following apply?

RIGID   INTROJECTED   UNREALISTIC   LIFE-RESTRICTING

Arlene's values are both rigid and unrealistic. Being independent is a reasonable life rule, but there are times when the consequences warrant making an exception. The outcome of getting a good education for her children by far outweighs the general principle of independence.

Situation 7. Jarrett has been unhappy in his marriage for the past six years. His mother, who made many sacrifices for her family, used to say that it's "better to hurt yourself than hurt the ones you love." Jarrett can't bear the thought of causing his wife pain. He imagines her alone and overwhelmed with grief after the divorce. But at the same time, he finds himself avoiding the family, working late, and being easily annoyed at home. He feels caught. Even though he's attempting to "do the right thing" to protect his wife, he feels that he is failing her with his absence and irritation. Jarrett says, "I'm unhappy, so I keep staying out. But I'm kicking myself the whole time I'm away."

What's wrong with Jarrett's values? Which of the following apply?

RIGID   INTROJECTED   UNREALISTIC   LIFE-RESTRICTING

Jarrett's values are introjected, rather than owned. He has never examined his mother's value of self-sacrifice to see if it applies to his unique situation and needs. If he could look at the value critically, he might see that it does not apply to him, that he is a person who is strongly inclined to run away from emotional pain, and that it is better to end the relationship than continue the pattern of avoidance.

Situation 8. Jim is in a new relationship. Recently his lover told him that she had not been able to reach orgasm during their lovemaking. Jim has a very strong feeling that he should be a perfect sexual partner and should be able to bring his lover to orgasm at all times. Her distressing news has left Jim with a sense of failure and inadequacy. In fact, he feels so uncomfortable that he has experienced a sharp decline in sexual interest. He tells his girlfriend that he needs "space" and suggests that they spend a week apart.

What's wrong with Jim's values? Which of the following apply?

RIGID   INTROJECTED   UNREALISTIC   LIFE-RESTRICTING

Jim's rule about sexual performance is too rigid. There is no quota for anything less than perfection. Jim believes that he should immediately understand and meet every lover's sexual needs. A healthier value would be that he should work toward understanding his partner's unique sexual needs. He should expect this process to take time and not expect to succeed in perfect responsiveness every time.

Situation 9. Julie has recently moved to another city. She is increasingly distressed about her son's problems in his new school. A bully has shoved and hit him in the schoolyard and has sometimes chased him on the walk home. Julie has a deeply held belief that a good parent should be able to protect her children from all pain. She blames herself and feels that she should do something to stop the harassment. She tries complaining to the principal, picking her boy up straight from school, and speaking to the bully's parents. But the problem persists. Julie writes to her brother that she condemns herself when she sees the boy drag in from another hard day.

What's wrong with Julie's values? Which of the following apply?

RIGID   INTROJECTED   UNREALISTIC   LIFE-RESTRICTING

This is another case of a life rule that is too rigid to work. It is simply not possible to protect a child from every unpleasant experience in growing up. The value that one should protect children is a good one, but there are exceptions. There are many hurts that children suffer at the hands of their peers, and it is both inappropriate and impossible for Julie to protect her son from every mean kid.

Situation 10. Jorge owns a small factory that produces Christmas novelties. The business was founded by his father, who was a man of unlimited energy and drive. His father used to work fourteen hours a day and told Jorge that the owner must set the example "by working harder than any one else." Like his father, Jorge puts in twelve to fourteen hour days. At 38, he has an ulcer. His marriage is strained because his wife never sees him. He misses his children and feels a growing sense of emptiness.

What's wrong with Jorge's values? Which of the following apply?

RIGID   INTROJECTED   UNREALISTIC   LIFE-RESTRICTING

Jorge has introjected his father's rules without determining if they fit him. His "work hard" rule is both unrealistic (because the negative outcomes far outweigh the benefits) and life-restricting (because it blocks his need to be with his family). Jorge has symptoms of stress, depression, and marital discord. He's paid too big a price for keeping faith with his father's entrepreneurial ideals.

How Shoulds Affect Your Self-Esteem

The shoulds attack your self-esteem in two ways. First, your shoulds and values may not fit you. For example, the social mores of Cedar Falls, Iowa, may be quite appropriate for that area but serve you poorly if you move to Manhattan. Your father's rule about hard work may have served him well, but now it's killing you with high blood pressure. A rule against expressing anger might have worked in your very gentle family, but the same rule limits your effectiveness as a foreman. The value that you be slender and well-shaped could be very damaging if you have a different body type.

The fact is that many of the shoulds you grew up with simply don't apply to you. They don't fit because you live in a different time and place and have different hopes, hurts, and needs than your parents. The values you've inherited were created by others to fit their needs in their unique circumstances—not yours. When your shoulds don't fit you and begin to conflict with your basic needs, you are then put into an impossible bind. Either you choose deprivation, the giving up of your need, or you choose to break faith with your values. Loss or guilt. If you choose to meet your needs at the expense of strongly held values, you may label yourself as weak, a screw-up, or a failure.

Shoulds often demand behavior that is impossible or unhealthy for a given individual. To illustrate how values can sometimes be impossible ideals, consider the case of Al. He's an ex-airline mechanic who's been drinking heavily for thirty years. He held his last job eight years ago, and lives on Social Security disability in a downtown hotel. He spends his day in one of the plastic chairs in the lobby ruminating about past sins. He hates himself for continuing to drink, for not working, and for not putting his daughter through college. But the truth is that alcohol is the only pleasure he has. Peripheral neuropathy has destroyed his fine motor coordination, and he will never work his trade again. Al's shoulds are demanding the impossible. They provide a daily torture. If Al could create values that fit the person he really is, he might demand of himself what was possible: to visit his daughter when clean and sober; to call her frequently to lend encouragement and support. Those things Al could do, but because his shoulds require him to be something he is not, he is immobilized to the point of giving his daughter nothing.

Rita has a set of shoulds that demand behavior which is essentially unhealthy for her. Rita believes that she should have unlimited energy to work. So in addition to caring for three children, a house, and an ailing father-in-law, she does all the books for her husband's large construction company. She feels exhausted, depressed, and seems to fall further and further behind. "But it's wrong not to help. And I keep asking myself what's the matter with me that I can't push myself and keep up with things. I'm just lazy or tempermental or something. Think of the women toiling in the fields. All over the world women toiling, and I can't even finish his books."

An article that appeared a few years ago in the *National Enquirer* illustrates this unhealthy variety of shoulds. A man had just completed building his own motor home from scratch. It was two stories, about the size of a Trailways bus, and towed a "three-car garage." He had worked between thirty and fifty hours a week on the project for ten years and was enormously proud of building and owning something "that no working man could ever afford." But the cost was enormous.

He'd been disabled by a heart attack, he had strained relations with his wife and family, and he hadn't taken a vacation in ten years. His goal had become a consuming obsession. His rule that "a man should finish what he begins" had cost him far too much in terms of stress, family happiness, and time for the little pleasures.

A second way shoulds attack your self-esteem is by attacking moral concepts of rightness and wrongness to situations, behaviors, and tastes that are essentially nonmoral. This process starts in childhood. Parents tell you that you are good when you follow their rules and bad when you break their rules. You are told that certain actions are right and certain behaviors are wrong. The right-wrong, good-bad dichotomy has been built into your values and system of personal rules by an accident of language. The decision to make your bed or leave it messy as a child is lifted into the moral dimension when your parents label you as bad for your negligence. Family rules that are established to promote safety, convenience, or efficiency often get misrepresented as moral imperatives. For example, it is not morally wrong for a child to get mud on his clothes. It is a matter of inconvenience and extra work for his parents. But a muddy pair of pants can precipitate a moralistic monologue: "What's wrong with you? Look what you've done to your clothes! You don't deserve television tonight for being such a bad boy."

Even worse is the tendency of many parents to confuse matters of taste and preference with moral ideology. Hairstyles, music, and choices in friends and recreational activities are often judged in terms of right and wrong instead of seen as normal intergenerational conflicts in taste.

Many parents label poor judgment as moral error. For example, a child who puts off a school project until the very end and is then forced to stay up late doing a rather slipshod job is guilty of poor judgment or poor impulse control (or both). But a parent who labels this behavior as lazy or stupid or "screwed up" is communicating to the child that he is morally bad. When you catch your nine-year-old smoking in the garage or playing with matches, these are errors in judgment that are dangerous to health and safety. But there is nothing moral about these issues and no badness or wrongness involved.

The more your parents confused matters of taste, preference, judgment, and convience with moral issues, the more likely you are to have fragile self-esteem. Over and over you've gotten the message that your taste or decisions or impulses are bad. The shoulds your parents handed down to you made you the captive of an impossible dilemma: "Follow the rules we've created about how you should look and act or be condemned as worthless and bad."

Discovering Your Shoulds

What follows is an inventory that will help you identify some of your shoulds and personal rules. Each item on the inventory represents a particular area of your life. Ask yourself the following four questions for each of these areas:

1. *Do I have feelings of guilt or self-recrimination in this area—* either past or present?
2. *Do I feel conflict in this area?* For example, do I feel torn between doing something I should do versus something I want to do?
3. *Do I feel a sense of obligation or owing in this area?*
4. *Do I avoid something I feel I ought to do in this area?*

When you recognize the presence of guilt, conflict, obligation, or avoidance in a particular area of your life, it's usually fairly easy to identify the underlying should. For example, for the item "activities in the home" you might recall that you feel rather *guilty* about not helping your wife enough with the dishes and the laundry. You might also notice that you feel *conflict* about child care; part of you believes you should do more child care in the evening, while another part wants to drink a beer and read the paper. The underlying should, you realize, has to do with the belief that you should split the work exactly fifty-fifty. As another example, consider the item "friends." You might notice that you've been feeling a strong *obligation* to visit a recently divorced friend. You know that this feeling comes from a should that requires you to take care of anyone in pain.

Sometimes, despite the clear presence of guilt or conflict, the underlying should is hard to ferret out. Then you can use a method called "laddering" to reach down to the basic value or rule. An example using the item "inner experience" will show how it works. A woman filling out the inventory noted that she felt extremely *guilty* regarding feelings of anger toward her son. She was irritated by his remoteness and emotional unavailability, but had trouble identifying the underlying should. She "laddered" down to her basic rule by asking this question: "What if I am angry at my son, what does that mean to me?" Her answer was that it meant that she was pulling back, letting go of him a little bit. She continued laddering by asking, "What if I am pulling back, what does that mean to me?" She was afraid it meant she didn't love or care for him enough. At this point she got in contact with the underlying should: that she should always *feel* love for a child. Because anger and withdrawal seemed to interrupt the *feeling* of love, they must be wrong.

A second example of laddering can be found in a young man's response to the item "church activities." He felt guilt and avoidance about not responding to an invitation to join the lay ministry. He asked himself, "What if I don't join, what would that mean to me?" It meant that he wasn't being generous with his time and energy. Again he asked himself, "What if I don't choose to be generous, what would that mean?" It meant that he would disappoint people who liked and thought well of him. It was then that he understood the should: "never disappoint someone who likes you."

So laddering is very simple. Whenever you notice an area of guilt, conflict, obligation, or avoidance, but are having trouble identifying your shoulds, ask yourself, "What if I _____ , what does that mean to me?" Then try to honestly decide what is implied by your behavior, what it says about who you are. Keep asking the question until you've gotten down to what feels like a core statement, something that implies a clear value or personal rule.

Avoid these two dead ends: first, don't answer with a simple judgment like "I'm bad" or "I'm screwing up." Try instead to state the *basis* of the judgment, the value from which the judgment springs. For example, rather than answering "It means I'm a jerk," a more specific answer would be "It means I'm not protecting someone in pain." The second thing you shouldn't do is answer with a feeling. For example, answering "It means I'm going to feel afraid" will lead you nowhere. The object is to get at your beliefs, not your feelings.

Right now, get out a piece of paper and write down the shoulds that pertain to each item on the inventory. Naturally, some items will yield no shoulds, because you simply don't have areas of guilt, conflict, obligation, or avoidance. Other items will be extremely fruitful. Write as many shoulds as you can.

Shoulds Inventory

1. Relationships
   - spouse or lover
   - children
   - parents
   - siblings
   - friends
   - people in need
   - teachers, students, or clients
2. Activities in the home
   - maintenance
   - cleaning
   - decorating
   - straightening
3. Recreational and social activities

4. Work activities
   - efficiency
   - co-worker relationships
   - initiative
   - reliability
   - achievement and working toward goals
5. Creative activities
6. Self-improvement activities
   - education
   - growth experiences
   - self-help projects
7. Sexual activities
8. Political and community activities
9. Religious and church activities
10. Money and finances
    - spending habits
    - savings
    - working toward financial goals
    - earning ability
11. Self-care
    - appearance
    - dress
    - exercise
    - smoking
    - alcohol
    - drugs
    - prevention
12. Food and eating
13. Ways of expressing and dealing with feelings
    - anger
    - fear
    - sadness
    - physical pain
    - joy
    - sexual attraction
    - love
14. Inner experience
    - unexpressed feelings
    - unexpressed thoughts
    - unexpressed wishes or desires

Challenging and Revising Your Shoulds

By now you have uncovered a number of shoulds that describe how you ought to behave. Some of these shoulds function as healthy guides.

Some of them are psychological bludgeons that the critic uses to destroy your self-esteem.

Right now, review your list of shoulds and mark the ones that your critic has used as the basis for attacks. You are now in a position to evaluate these rules to determine if they are healthy and useful. For each should your critic uses, do the following three things:

1. Examine your language. Is the should built on absolutes and overgeneralizations such as *all, always, never, totally, perfect,* and so on? Use "I'd prefer" or "I'd rather" or "I want to" instead of "I should." The specific situation where you're applying the should may turn out to be an exception to the rule. Acknowledge that possibility by using language that is flexible.

2. Forget concepts of right and wrong. Instead, determine the consequences of applying the rule to the specific situation. What are the short- and long-term effects on you and the people involved? Does the rule make sense, given who will be hurt and who will be helped?

3. Ask yourself if the rule fits the person you really are. Does it take into account your temperament, limitations, enduring traits, ways of protecting yourself, fears, problems, and things that you are not likely to change? Does it allow for your important needs and dreams and the pleasures that sustain you? Does the rule really make sense, given who you are and will likely remain?

Rebecca's case is a good example of how these steps will help you deal with your shoulds. Her list included a should that her pathological critic used almost daily. The critic said she should weigh no more than 120 pounds, while Rebecca, in fact, weighed 135–140 pounds.

The first thing Rebecca did was to examine her language. The phrase "no more than 120" gave the should an absolute quality. Rebecca rewrote her rule more flexibly—"I'd prefer to weigh in the neighborhood of 120 pounds." Next, she examined the probable consequences of applying her should. Here is her list of positive and negative outcomes.

Positive	*Negative*
1. Look slimmer.	1. Have to weigh my food.
2. Fit into some of my smaller clothes	2. Constantly have to think about what I eat.
3. Feel more attractive.	3. Constantly worry about gaining weight.
4. Like my body more.	4. Have to go back to Weightwatchers.
	5. Really have to eat out less.
	6. Most of my clothes will no longer fit.

Liking her body and feeling more attractive were a big lure for Rebecca, but the negative consequences were much greater than she had realized.

She had never put down in black-and-white before all the problems that dieting created for her.

Finally, Rebecca asked herself whether the "120 rule" fit the person she really was. She had to admit that her natural weight seemed to fluctuate between 135–140, and only with arduous dieting was she able to get into the 125 range. Soon enough her weight would start to climb and she would feel a sense of failure and a drop in self-esteem. Furthermore, much of her social life revolved around restaurants and shared meals. A diet meant curtailing her main way of being with friends. Rebecca's lover was clearly attracted to her as she was, and so there was little to gain in the way of emotional or sexual intimacy from weight loss.

With great reluctance, Rebecca began to accept that the "120 rule" didn't fit her and seemed to be costing more than it was worth.

Arthur is a high school composition teacher who suffers a continuous sense of guilt about his inability to "really teach writing." His critic attacked him with a rule he'd learned from a beloved professor: to write decently, students must write daily. At the very least, Arthur felt that they should complete several assignments per week. But in Arthur's large classes, he rarely gave more than two writing assignments per month. Here's how he dealt with his should.

First he rewrote the rule in more flexible language: "I'd like my students, if possible, to have two writing assignments per week." Then he examined the consequences.

Positive	*Negative*
1. Students get more feedback.	1. With five classes averaging thirty students each, I'd have 300 essays to read per week.
2. Students learn faster.	
3. I feel successful because I see more progress.	2. I'd lose most of my weekend correcting papers.
4. My students score higher on the state achievement tests.	3. It would severely limit time with my family.
	4. I'd never get to go rock climbing.
	5. It would take a lot of my physical energy.

Negative outcomes more than outweighed the positive, and it was clear to Arthur why he gave so few writing assignments.

At last, Arthur examined the question of whether the rule really fit him. His answer was a qualified yes. He still believed in the value of frequent assignments. But he now had an answer to his critic. Applying the rule in his crowded school would simply cost him too much both physically and emotionally.

Jamie's critic was clever. Her critic used two contradictory shoulds so that she remained in a permanent no-win conflict. Jamie is a painter who has a good local reputation. She is also the mother of a ten-month-old boy. On the one hand, the critic told her that she should give all her available time to her son. On the other, the critic demanded that she continue to paint at the same level of productivity she had before the baby was born.

Jamie's shoulds damaged her self-esteem in two ways. The "give everything to your son rule" made her reluctant to arrange any child care. As a result, she felt depressed and listless during the day because there was no time for painting or recreation. These feelings led her to kick herself for being a lazy, bad mother. Jamie's self-esteem also took a beating from the "keep painting rule." In the evening, when she felt too tired to face an empty canvas, she kicked herself for wasting her talent and being "uncommitted" to her art.

Here's how she dealt with her shoulds. First she rewrote them using flexible language: "I want to give most of my time to my son, but I want to keep painting as much as possible." Then she examined the consequences of each should.

A. Give most of my time to my son.

Positive
1. Don't have to feel anxious or guilty about turning him over to someone else.
2. He's safer with me than anyone else.
3. He gets more attention and love from me than anyone else.
4. The baby cries when I leave him.
5. I worry about his separation anxiety.

Negative
1. No energy to paint.
2. Seem to get depressed during day.
3. Miss painting and feeling involved in a canvas.
4. Feel stuck in the house.
5. Miss involvement with the artistic community.

B. Keep painting as much as possible.

Positive
1. The pleasure of painting.
2. A sense of meaning.
3. A break from the baby.
4. Maintain connection to art world.

Negative
1. Without child care, painting would exhaust me.
2. If I got dependable child care, it would cost $50 a week.
3. I would have to cope with anxiety and guilt about leaving the baby.

4. The baby gets less attention and love while I'm away.
5. I feel that the baby's less safe while I'm away.

Jamie asked herself whether her should made sense for the person she was. It was clear that her needs for artistic expression, meaningful activity, and time off from the baby were being denied by the "give everything to your son rule." She was trying to do without one of the sustaining pleasures in her life and it was costing her in the form of low self-esteem, low energy, and depression. After several weeks of ambivalence, Jamie finally decided to get a baby sitter for two five-hour periods—with the thought that she would later expand to fifteen hours if she felt comfortable.

Cutting Off the Should

When you have decided that a should is undermining your self-esteem, either as a general rule or in a particular situation, you need to cut it out of your internal self-talk. This means aggressively fighting back when the critic tries to hit you with your should. The best way to fight back is to prepare a one or two sentence "mantra" that you can memorize and use whenever you feel wrong for not living up to the should. You can say the mantra over and over, as many times as necessary, until the critic shuts up and leaves you alone. A mantra to combat your should would ideally include the following elements.

1. A reminder of the original need that created your should. For this you have to determine why you acquired the should in the first place. Was it to feel loved by your dad? To gain approval from a particular friend? To feel closer to a lover? To feel better about yourself? Less anxious? Safer?
2. The main reason your should doesn't fit you or the situation. You might remind yourself, for example, how your should demands that you be or do or feel something that is simply not you. You might also remind yourself that the negative consequences of following your should outweigh the positive.

Here's how mantras sound when condensed into a few simple statements.

Should: You should go back to school and make something of your life.

Mantra: School was my father's idea and I wanted to please him. But that life doesn't fit me. I'd only drop out again from the boredom and pressure.

Should: You shouldn't make mistakes.
Mantra: Not making mistakes was important to my father. But I'm just learning this job. I can only learn by trying. If I worry about mistakes, I'll freeze up and stop learning.

Should: You should be a witty, fascinating conversationalist.
Mantra: I thought that being a clever talker would help me fit in at school. But it's too much work and not me. I like to ask questions and get to know the other person.

Should: You should always take care with your appearance.
Mantra: I feel I need to look good in order to please my wife. But I'm happier in jeans and sweatshirts. That's what fits me!

Should: You should diet and stay thin.
Mantra: Mom always told me she liked me thin. But I'd rather weigh what I do than live with the tyranny of diets and scales.

Should: You should have a better job.
Mantra: A status job is my father's rule. But this job is safe and low-stress. When I want stress and uncertainty, I'll go somewhere else.

Now it's time to generate your own mantras. In the beginning, reserve them for your most deadly shoulds. Then, as those rules lose their power to create guilt, write mantras for your other shoulds. Having the mantra isn't enough. You must commit yourself to using it *every time* the critic attacks with an unhealthy should. The critic will give up only if you consistently answer back. Remember that silence is assent. If you fail to reply when the critic attacks, your silence means that you are believing and accepting everything he says.

Atonement—When Shoulds Make Sense

Some of your shoulds will turn out to be legitimate values, rules to live by that you need to follow to the best of your ability. When shoulds make sense, they don't usually interfere with your self-esteem.

The only time sensible shoulds interfere with your self-esteem is when you violate them. Then your critic jumps all over you for having done wrong. If, after examination, the rule you violated feels healthy to you, the only way to stop your critic is to initiate the process of atonement. Very simply, you have to make up for what you've done. Without atonement, you'll be saddled with a critic whose function is to make sure you pay and pay and pay.

Here are four guidelines to help you choose an appropriate atonement.

1. It's important to acknowledge the wrongness of what you did *to the person you hurt*. This makes it clear that you are accepting responsibility for your behavior.
2. You should atone directly to the person you wronged. Donating money to a charity, becoming a big brother, or joining the Peace Corps will atone less effectively than directly helping the one you hurt.
3. The atonement should be real, rather than symbolic. Lighting candles or writing a poem will not rid you of the critic. What you do to atone has to cost you something in time, money, effort, or even anxiety. And it has to be tangible enough so that it has an impact on your relationship with the person who is hurt.
4. Your atonement should be commensurate with the wrong done. If your offense was a moment of irritability, then a brief apology should do the trick. But if you've been cold and remote for the past six months, then you'll have to do a little better than "I'm sorry."

8

Handling Mistakes

In an ideal world, where perfect parents raised perfect children, there would be no connection at all between mistakes and self-esteem. But your parents probably weren't perfect. As a child, you were necessarily corrected when you did something your parents considered a mistake. You might have pulled up some flowers instead of pulling weeds. If the message "you're bad" came along with your mother's correction, then you were started along a deadly path. This path leads to the conclusion that making mistakes always means you're bad.

As you grew up, you internalized these parental corrections and blame. You took over the job of criticizing yourself for making mistakes. In short, you created your pathological critic. To this day, when you uproot a flower while weeding, your critic says, "Nice move, stupid. Why don't you just plow the whole garden under while you're at it?"

The contradictory values of our society helped you in creating your critic. You found that to be a good member of society you must be equal *and* superior, generous *and* thrifty, spontaneous *and* controlled, and so on. This lose-lose system of mutually exclusive values allows your critic to find some evidence of error in any action and blow it up, way out of proportion.

You may grow up defensive, rationalizing all mistakes. You may join the group whose members are so afraid of the slightest mistake that they can admit to none. Or you may follow the more common route of chronic depression over all your mistakes.

In extreme cases, paralysis sets in. You ruminate over past mistakes and constrict your activities and relationships to avoid any chance of future mistakes. Afraid of doing something wrong, you try to do the bare minimum perfectly. But even this little is impossible because change and mistakes are inevitable. You're trapped.

The fact of the matter is that self-esteem has nothing to do with being perfect. Self-esteem has nothing to do with avoiding mistakes. Self-esteem is rooted in your unconditional acceptance of yourself as an innately worthy being, regardless of mistakes. Feeling good about yourself is not something you do *after* all mistakes have been corrected —it's something you do *in spite of* mistakes. The only really serious mistake is agreeing with your pathological critic when he says that mistakes are evidence of worthlessness.

Reframing Mistakes

Reframing means changing your interpretation or point of view. You put a new frame around a picture or an event to change the way you look at it and thus change its meaning for you. For example, when you wake up from a nightmare your heart is pounding. You are genuinely frightened, convinced that you are falling or being pursued. Then you realize that you were just dreaming, and you feel a wave of relief. Your heart stops pounding and you calm down. Your mind has "reframed" the experience, changing the meaning from "I'm in danger" to "it was just a dream." Your body and your whole mood follow your mind's lead. Reframing mistakes means learning to think about them in ways that remove their nightmare qualities. Instead, you view your mistakes as a natural, and even valuable component of your life. This new view in turn allows you to respond more flexibly when you do make mistakes, to learn from them and move on.

Mistakes as Teachers

Mistakes are a function of growth and changing awareness. They are an absolute prerequisite for any learning process. Last year you bought the cheap paint, thinking it would do. This year you are a different person, grown older by a year and wiser by watching the paint fade. You are different by virtue of information you didn't have a year ago. It will solve nothing to damage your self-esteem now by castigating yourself for not having been able to see into the future then. Chalk it up to experience and go out and buy some decent paint. Pay for your lesson once, but only once. Attacking yourself is like paying twice: once for the new paint and once in the form of a mugging from your critic.

There is no way you can learn any task or skill without errors. This process is called successive approximation: getting closer and closer to successful performance through the feedback provided by mistakes. Every error tells you what you need to correct, every error brings you incrementally nearer to the behavioral sequence that works best for completion of the task. Rather than fearing mistakes, you need to welcome them during the learning process. People who can't stand making mistakes have trouble learning. They are scared to get a new job because they would be faced with new procedures and challenges. They're afraid to try a new sport because of all the errors they'll have to make before their body learns the subtle adjustments necessary to swing a racket or use a sand wedge. They won't buy a word processor or try rebuilding their carburetor because the inevitable mistakes in doing something new are just too painful.

Framing mistakes as necessary feedback for the learning process frees you to relax and focus on your gradual mastery of the new task. Mistakes are information about what works and what doesn't. They have nothing to do with your worth or intelligence. They are merely steps to a goal.

Mistakes as Warnings

The dream of perfection turns mistakes from warnings into sins. Mistakes can function like the bell on your typewriter that keeps you from going off the page, or the buzzer that warns you to put on the seat belt in a car. If you have a minor traffic accident, it can serve as a warning that you need to concentrate on your driving more closely. If you receive a D in a course in school, it can be a warning that your study habits need improvement. When you and your mate have a big fight over a small issue, it can be a warning that you aren't communicating about some other, underlying issue. But perfectionism changes the warning to an indictment. And you become so busy defending yourself from the attacks of your pathological critic that you have no opportunity to heed the lesson of the mistake. You can fight perfectionism by focusing on the warning rather than on your culpability.

Mistakes: Prerequisite for Spontaneity

The fear of mistakes kills your right to self-expression. It makes you afraid to be your spontaneous self, to say what you think and feel. If you are never allowed to say the wrong thing, you may never feel free enough to say the right thing—to say that you love someone or that you hurt or want to give comfort. The dream of perfection makes you stifle all of that because you have no right to a faux pas or excessive sentiment.

The willingness to make mistakes means that it's OK to disappoint people, to have a moment of awkwardness, to have the conversation take an uncomfortable turn. Consider the case of Andrea. She hangs out with the same two people at work because any new relationship would be too unpredictable. Suppose the new person didn't like her jokes or thought that some of her remarks were stupid. She'd have to watch everything she said. Andrea's situation illustrates how the fear of mistakes can (1) isolate you because you're afraid of the judgments of someone new and (2) choke off spontaneity because you have to vigilantly watch what you express.

Mistakes: The Necessary Quota

Allow a quota for mistakes. Some people have the pathological attitude that all mistakes can be avoided, that competent, intelligent, worthwhile people don't make them. This is paralyzing hogwash that can leave you afraid to take any chance in life. The healthier position is that everyone deserves a quota for mistakes. You should be allowed a certain number of social gaffes, work mistakes, poor decisions, blown chances, even failed relationships. This is a good time to start thinking in terms of reasonable error quotas, rather than the hopeless dream of perfection. A rule of thumb for most people is that between one and three decisions in every ten are dead wrong. And several others may be in a doubtful gray area. For mechanical, overlearned processes like typing or driving, the quota goes down. You don't expect to have an accident every tenth time you get in the car. But sooner or later you will have one, hopefully only a fender-bender, and you will need to chalk that one up as a mistake that you are entitled to under your error quota.

Mistakes as Nonexistent in the Present

To understand this concept, it will be helpful to first examine the most common categories of mistakes.

1. *Errors of fact.* You hear "highway 45" on the phone, write down "highway 49," and get lost.
2. *Failure to reach a goal.* Summer arrives and you are still too fat to get into your bathing suit.
3. *Wasted effort.* You gather 300 signatures on a recall petition that fails.

4. *Errors of judgment.* You decide to get the cheaper paint, and it fades.
5. *Missed opportunities.* The stock you decided not to buy at $5 is now at $30.
6. *Forgetfulness.* You get all the way to the potluck and realize that your salad dressing is still at home in the refrigerator.
7. *Overindulgence in legitimate pleasures.* The party was fun, but you have a hangover.
8. *Inappropriate emotional outbursts.* You yell at your spouse and feel awful about it later.
9. *Procrastination.* You never got around to fixing the roof, and now the dining room wallpaper is ruined.
10. *Impatience.* You try a bigger wrench on the nut and the bolt breaks.
11. *Violation of your moral code.* You tell a white lie: "I'll be out of town this weekend." On Saturday, you run into the person you're avoiding.

This list could go on and on. Classifying the ways to go wrong has been a popular human pastime since Moses came down from the mountain with the ten commandments.

There is a common thread running through these examples that will help in understanding mistakes. *A mistake is anything you do that you later, upon reflection, wish you had done differently.* This applies also to things you *didn't do* that you later, upon reflection, wish you *had done.*

The key word here is "later." Later may be a split second or a decade after the act. When you apply too much force to the nut and the bolt breaks, "later" is very soon indeed. It seems like "immediately," but it's not. There is a lag between the action and the regret. It is this lag time, short or long, that is the key to freeing yourself from the tyranny of mistakes.

At the exact moment of action, you are doing what seems reasonable. It is your later interpretation that turns the action into a mistake. "Mistake" is a label you always apply in retrospect, when you realize you could have done something *more* reasonable.

The Problem of Awareness

You *always* choose the action that seems most likely to meet your needs. This is the essence of motivation: wanting to do something more than any other thing.

Motivation comes down to consciously or unconsciously choosing the most desirable alternative for meeting the needs at hand. The potential benefits of the action you choose seem, at least at the time, to outweigh the foreseeable disadvantages.

Obviously, the action that seems best at the time will depend on your awareness. Awareness is the degree of clarity with which you perceive and understand, consciously or unconsciously, all the factors relating to the need at hand. At any given moment, your awareness is the automatic product of your innate intelligence, your intuition, and your total life experience up to that point, including your current emotional and physical state.

"Mistake" is a label that you apply to your behavior at a later time when your awareness has changed. At this later time you know the consequences of your action, and you may decide that you should have acted differently.

Since you always do your best (or choose what seems most likely to meet your needs) at any given time, and since "mistakes" are the result of a later interpretation, it follows logically that making mistakes should not lower your self-esteem.

"But," you say, "sometimes I know better than to do something, and I do it anyway. I know I shouldn't have dessert if I want to lose weight, but I go ahead and have that bowl of ice cream anyway. I feel awful afterwards, and I *should* feel awful because I let myself down."

If this is your line of reasoning, you're missing a crucial point about motivation. To "know better" is not sufficient to "do better" if your *awareness* at the time is focused on a stronger and opposing motivation. At the time, your desire for the ice cream was stronger than your desire to lose weight, so the "best" thing—indeed, the only thing—you could do was eat the ice cream.

If you label the choice you make "good" or "bad," you end up unjustly punishing yourself for actions you couldn't help performing. More relevant labels would be "wise" or "unwise" and "effective" or "ineffective," since these terms make the more compassionate and accurate judgment that your actions were made out of a limited awareness. In any event, a firm commitment to expanding your awareness will work much better than a grim resolve never to make the same mistake again. Because you *will* make the same mistake again, until you expand your awareness.

Responsibility

All this talk about always doing your best may sound like you are not *responsible* for your actions. Not so. You are definitely responsible for your actions.

Responsibility means accepting the consequences of your actions. Consequences always come home to roost. For every action there is a cost to be paid. If you are highly aware of the costs and willing to pay, you will choose relatively "wise" actions, have fewer occasions to label your actions later as mistakes, and feel better about yourself.

If you have a limited awareness of the costs incurred by your actions and aren't willing to pay when the costs come due, you may choose unwise actions, label them as mistakes later, and suffer blows to your self-esteem.

But in either case, you are responsible for your actions in that you will inevitably pay the price—willing or not, conscious or not. Becoming a more responsible person means increasing your awareness of the price you pay for your actions. And it's worth the effort, because low awareness means you are later surprised and dismayed at the cost of some of your decisions.

The Limits of Awareness

Your awareness of the probable consequences of your acts is limited by five important factors.

1. Ignorance. Many times you have no valid way of predicting consequences because you have *never* been faced with similar circumstances before. In effect you are flying blind. If you've never spray-painted before, you might have no way of knowing that holding the nozzle too close causes the paint to run. If you don't know how to fold the egg whites for your first soufflé, it may not rise properly.

2. Forgetting. There is no way to remember every consequence of every act you have ever performed. Many events are lost to awareness because they are not sufficiently painful or important. As a result, you frequently repeat mistakes because you simply can't recall how things turned out the last time. One of the authors, who had not been camping for several years, forgot how much he suffered from mosquitoes. As a result, he again neglected to bring repellant on last summer's trip.

3. Denial. People deny and disregard the consequences of previous mistakes for one of two reasons: fear or need. Sometimes they are so afraid of change or of doing things differently that they deny or minimize the negative consequences of their mistakes. Faced with the same choice again, they repeat a painful error because all the alternatives seem too threatening.

An example is the man who goes on dates and bores women to death with long recitations of his achievements. He suspects it might turn some people off but denies the consequences of his bragging: few repeat dates, no relationships. He clings to denial because he is so afraid of real communication, of letting his hair down and talking about his authentic feelings.

Overwhelming need creates the same kind of denial. If you really need something, you tend to deny the negative consequences of getting it. Consider the woman who keeps leaving and then going back to an abusive, alcoholic husband. At the moment she decides to go back she is most in contact with her feelings of love and dependency. Meanwhile she has to deny or minimize the inevitably painful consequences in order to have what she needs so much.

4. No alternatives. Many mistakes get repeated because people are simply unaware of any better way to act. They lack the skills, ability, or experience to generate new strategies and solutions. Consider the case of the woman who kept blowing job interviews because she stared at the floor, made brief, one-sentence answers, and couldn't sell herself.

5. Habits. Some habits, ingrained for a lifetime, prevent you from evaluating or having the slightest awareness of your choices. You don't think about the consequences because you don't know you're making a decision. A classic example is the habit of choosing a short-range benefit while ignoring a long-range disaster. A woman went from one dead-end relationship to another. She chronically made the mistake of gravitating toward men who reminded her of her father. Their apparent strength and authority attracted her, but in the long run their coldness and emotional shallowness destroyed the relationship. Another example is a law school graduate who consistently chose the short-term pleasure of smoking marijuana and spending whole weekends in a daze instead of studying for his bar exam.

Your awareness is mitigated by all of these factors. For many of your decisions, forgetting, denial, habit, and so on prevent you from making use of your experience. What you know and what has happened to you before is simply unavailable at the moment you decide to act. You cannot be blamed for this. Your awareness, however limited, was all you had to go on when you made the mistake.

But just because you aren't to blame, doesn't mean you can't do something about it. You can. The next section will show you how.

The Habit of Awareness

The *habit of awareness* is very simple. It is a commitment to predict the likely consequences, both short and long term, of any significant act or decision. Here are the questions you should ask yourself to increase awareness at the point of decision.

- Have I ever experienced this situation before?
- What negative consequences came or might be expected to come from the decision I plan to make? (Be sure to consider both short- and long-term consequences.)
- Are the consequences worth it, given what I expect to gain?
- Do I know any alternative with less negative consequences?

The main requirement for developing the habit of awareness is to make a promise to yourself. You commit to examining the probable consequences of every significant thing that you do. This shouldn't take the form of neurotic worry. Rather, it is the stance of the questioning mind: you use your experience to develop likely outcome scenarios from each decision. If you are able to make this commitment to awareness, you will make fewer major mistakes.

Chronic mistakes. Everyone has one or more areas where similar mistakes are repeated over and over. To increase awareness in these areas you should do two things after each reoccurrence of the error.

1. Write down in detail the negative consequences of the mistake. The very act of writing, whether you keep the notes or not, is an important memory aid.
2. Determine your priorities. What was the main thing you got or hoped to get from your erroneous decision? Were you seeking a short-term pleasure, were you trying to feel safe, trying to be liked by others, avoiding loneliness? Is this priority a theme in your life? Is it the basis of other poor decisions? If the same priority chronically sucks you into mistakes, then you must include this factor in your awareness. The priority may be important, but it is also dangerous. Any critical new decision should be examined to see if it is motivated by that priority. If so, that's a red flag. You may be headed toward a repeat of the old mistake. Ask the four questions listed above. Slow down and really examine your choices.

Raising Your Mistake Consciousness

Here are some exercises you can do to raise your mistake consciousness.

1. Realize that everyone makes mistakes. Even good guys and heroes. Political leaders, financial moguls, screen stars, great philanthropists, scientists, and healers all make mistakes. In fact, it's often true that the greater the person, the greater his or her mistakes. The Wright brothers failed many times before their plane finally flew at Kittyhawk. Salk struggled for years before he developed the polio vaccine. Mistakes are the inescapable by-product of learning or trying anything new.

Make a list of historical or public figures who have made significant mistakes. Only include those people for whom you have some appreciation and respect.

Make a second list of people you know personally and admire. List their mistakes. Even your beloved teacher may have lost his temper over a small mishap, the captain of your high-school football team may have been caught cheating on exams, and the top salesman at work may have bungled an easy sale.

Why is it that even good and admirable people make mistakes? The answer is that they didn't recognize their decision as a mistake at the time. They didn't fully anticipate the consequences of an act. Like every other human being that has walked this planet, they had an imperfect awareness—they could not predict with complete accuracy the rippling effects of a current decision on future experience.

Brilliant, creative, and powerful people all make errors because the future is hidden. It can only be guessed at. No amount of intelligence or understanding can generate a perfect forecast of what is to come.

2. Realize that even you make mistakes. Make another list of your own mistakes. Take some time at this, since you'll need this list for later exercises. If you seem to be always making mistakes and it feels like your list could go on indefinitely, edit your list down to your ten biggest mistakes.

Now comes the hard part. For the first item on your list, go back in time, back to the moment when the decision was made. Try to remember your thoughts and feelings just before the act. Did you know what would happen, or did you hope for some happier consequence? Did you have any idea of the pain that you or others would feel? If you were aware of the possibility of pain, try to recall how you weighed that against the image of some desirable outcome. Notice which factor seemed bigger at the time. Now try to remember the need or needs that pushed you to the decision. Recall the strength of those needs and how they influenced your choice. Did any alternative action seem more attractive to you? Here is the most important question: If you were to return to that time, with the *same* needs, perceptions, and predictions of future outcomes, would you act differently?

Go ahead and repeat this process with each mistake on your list. Naturally, you should skip items where your memory is too hazy to really answer these questions.

3. Forgiving yourself. You deserve forgiveness for your mistakes, no matter how painful the consequences, for three reasons.

(1) You made the only decision you could make, given your needs and awareness at the moment you made it. If you worked seriously at the previous exercise, you may have become clearer that you cannot act differently than your awareness allows *at a particular point in time.* You simply did the best you could.

(2) You have already paid for your mistake. Your error lead to painful consequences. You have endured those consequences and felt that pain. Unless your mistake hurt others and you need in some way to atone, you have already paid the price of being human.

(3) Mistakes are unavoidable. You come into this world knowing nothing. Everything you have learned, from standing upright to running a word processor, has been accomplished at the price of literally thousands of mistakes. You fell hundreds of times before you walked,

and you have probably "lost your files" more than once. The learning process goes on your entire life. And so do the mistakes. It makes no sense to kick yourself for something you can only avoid in the cemetery.

Visualization. To gain practice in viewing mistakes as a function of limited awareness, try this exercise, which combines relaxation, visualization, and affirmation.

Sit in a comfortable chair or lie down on your back. Uncross your arms and legs. Close your eyes. Take several slow, deep breaths. Feel yourself becoming more relaxed with each breath.

Starting at you feet, scan various parts of your body for tension and relax them. As you breathe in, notice any tension in your feet, then let it flow away when you breathe out. Keep your breaths slow and regular. Now notice any tension in your calves as you breathe in, and let the tension flow out as you exhale. Move up to your thighs for the next breath, then your buttocks and pelvis, then your stomach and lower back area, then your chest and upper back.

Now move your attention out to your hands. Inhale and feel any tightness, exhale and let it go. Do the same for your forearms, your biceps, your shoulders, and your neck. Dwell on these areas for several breaths if you need to.

Notice any tension in your jaw muscles, and let it go as you exhale. Next concentrate on your eyes, then forehead, then scalp.

Continue to breathe, slowly and deeply, sinking further into relaxation. Now begin forming a picture of yourself. See yourself as you were after a recent mistake (perhaps one of the mistakes on your list). See where you are, see your face, see the position of your body. Be aware that you did your best, given your awareness at that moment. Say the following affirmations to yourself. Just let them drift into your mind:

I am a unique and valuable human being.
I always do the best I can.
I love (or like) myself, mistakes and all.

Repeat these affirmations three or four times, changing the wording to suit yourself.

Now visualize yourself moving through your daily routine. See what you will be doing the rest of today or tomorrow. See that you are unique, that you are valuable, that you are trying to live the best you can. Watch how you always do what seems best at the moment you do it.

Finish with this affirmation: "Today I like myself more than yesterday. Tomorrow I will like myself even more."

When you are ready, open your eyes and get up slowly. As you go about your day, repeat the affirmations whenever they come to mind. Do the full relaxation exercise twice a day. In the morning before you get up, and in bed before falling asleep are good times, since you are already relaxed and in a receptive frame of mind.

The exercise will work better for you if you make up your own affirmations. The affirmations that work best are short, simple, and positive. Complex affirmations don't seem to get through to your subconscious. Affirmations that contain negatives, such as "I will not criticize myself," seem to be understood by your subconscious as if the negatives had been dropped out: "I *will* criticize myself." Compose affirmations that are positive: "I will speak well of myself."

To help you compose your own self-esteem affirmations, here are some examples that have worked for others.

I'm basically all right as I am.

I have worth because I struggle to survive.

I have legitimate needs.

It's all right to meet my needs as I see fit.

I am responsible for my life.

I accept the consequences of my actions.

I feel warm and loving toward myself.

I invariably do the best I am capable of at the moment.

"Mistakes" is a label I add later.

I am free to make mistakes.

Everything I do is an attempt to meet legitimate needs.

I am expanding my awareness to make wiser choices.

I am letting go of unwise choices in the past.

I can do anything I want, but what I want is determined by my awareness.

Everything I do involves a price to pay.

Shoulds, oughts, and musts are irrelevant.

In the moment of choice, I do only what my awareness permits.

It's foolish to resent others' actions—they also do only what their awareness permits.

Since everyone is doing his or her best, I can easily feel compassion and empathy.

My basic job in life is expanding my awareness.

No one is any more or less worthy than I.

My mere existence proves my worth.

I can learn from my mistakes without guilt and worry.

Everyone's awareness is different, so comparisons are worthless.

When I feel unsure about what to do, I can examine the consequences.

I can invent new ways to satisfy a need and wisely choose the best option.

9

Responding to Criticism

You're painting your bedroom, feeling good about getting the job done. The room looks like new. Somebody comes in and says, "It looks pretty good. Is that the color it will be when it dries? Did you really want it that bright? Uh oh, look at all the splatters on the floor. You'll never get that enamel off if you let it dry."

Your mood is ruined. The room that looked so fresh and sparkling now looks garish and sloppy. Your self-esteem withers under the criticism.

The negative opinions of other people can be deadly to self-esteem. They say or imply that you are not worthy in some way, and you can feel your own opinion of yourself plummet. Criticism is such a powerful deflator of weak self-esteem because it arouses your own internal pathological critic and supplies him with ammunition. The critic inside senses an ally in the critic outside, and they join forces to gang up on you.

There are many types of criticism. Some is even constructive, as it is when the critic is motivated by a desire to help and couches the criticism in terms of good suggestions for change. Other times, criticism is just nagging, a pointless, habitual recitation of your failings. Often your critic is engaging in one-upmanship, trying to appear smarter, better, or righter than you. Or perhaps your critic is being manipulative, criticizing what you're doing in an attempt to get you to do something else.

Whatever the critic's motive, all criticism shares one characteristic: it is unwelcome. You don't want to hear it, and you need ways to cut it short and prevent it from eroding your self-esteem.

Actually, criticism has nothing to do with true self-esteem. True self-esteem is innate, undeniable, and independent of anyone's opinion. It can be neither diminished by criticism nor increased by praise. You just have it. The trick to handling criticism is not to let it make you forget your self-esteem.

Most of this chapter will deal with the arbitrary, distorted nature of criticism. Once you understand and have practiced the skills of discounting criticism, you will go on to effective ways to respond to critics.

The Myth of Reality

You rely on your senses. Water is wet. Fire is hot. Air is good to breathe. The earth feels solid. You have found so often that things are exactly what they seem to be that you have come to trust your senses. You believe what they tell you about the world.

So far so good, as long as you stick to your sense impressions of simple inanimate objects. But when people enter the picture, it gets more complicated. What you *expect* to see and what you have seen before start to affect what you thought you saw. For example, you see a tall blond man grab a woman's purse and jump into a tan two-door sedan and roar away down the street. The police come and take your statement, and you tell them exactly what you saw. But the woman who lost her purse insists it was a dark-haired, short guy. Another bystander says the car was gray, not tan. Yet another person is sure it was a 1982 station wagon, not a sedan. Three people claim to have noted the license, and by cross-checking their stories the police think it was LGH399 or LGH393, or maybe LCH399.

The point is that in the heat of the moment you can't trust your senses. Nobody can. We all select, alter, and distort what we see.

A TV Screen in Every Head

The example above shows that you rarely perceive reality with 100 percent accuracy and objectivity. Most often you filter and edit, as if your eyes and ears were a TV camera and you were seeing reality on a screen in your head. Sometimes the screen is not in focus. Sometimes it zooms in on certain details and omits others. Sometimes it magnifies or minimizes. Sometimes the colors are off or the picture shifts to black and white. Sometimes when you are remembering the past, the screen shows you old film clips and you see no "live" reality at all.

Your screen is not usually a bad thing. Essentially it reflects the way your senses and your mind are wired together. Without the ability to manipulate images on your mental screen, you could never cope with the flood of information assailing you from the outside world. You could never organize and use past experience. You could never learn or remember. As suggested by the illustration on the next page, your screen is a fabulous machine, with lots of buttons and levers to play with.

Here are some important rules about screens:

1. Everybody has one. It's how human beings are wired up.
2. You can only see your screen, not reality directly. Scientists train rigourously to become as perfectly objective as they can. The scientific method is a very precise way to make sure that what researchers are looking at is really there and is really what they think it is. Nevertheless, the history of science is rife with examples of sincere scientists who have been betrayed by their hopes, fears, and ambitions into propounding false theories. They mistook their screens for reality.
3. You can't fully know what is on someone else's screen. You would have to become that person or possess telepathic powers.
4. You can't fully communicate what's on your screen. Some of what affects your screen is unconscious material. And the messages on your screen come and go much faster than you can talk about them.
5. You can't automatically believe what's on your screen. A little skepticism is a healthy thing. Check things out. Ask around. You may be able to become 99 percent sure about what's on your screen, but you can never be 100 percent sure. On the other hand, you shouldn't be so suspicious that you don't believe anything you see or hear. That is the road to alienation, conspiracy theories, and all-out paranoia.
6. Your internal self-talk is a voice-over commentary on what you see on the screen. Your self-talk can contain the destructive comments of your internal pathological critic, or your healthy refutations of the critic. The voice-over interprets and can distort what you see. Sometimes you are aware of the voice-over, but often you are not.
7. The more distorted your screen becomes, the more certain you will be that what you see there is accurate. There is no one so sure as someone totally deluded.

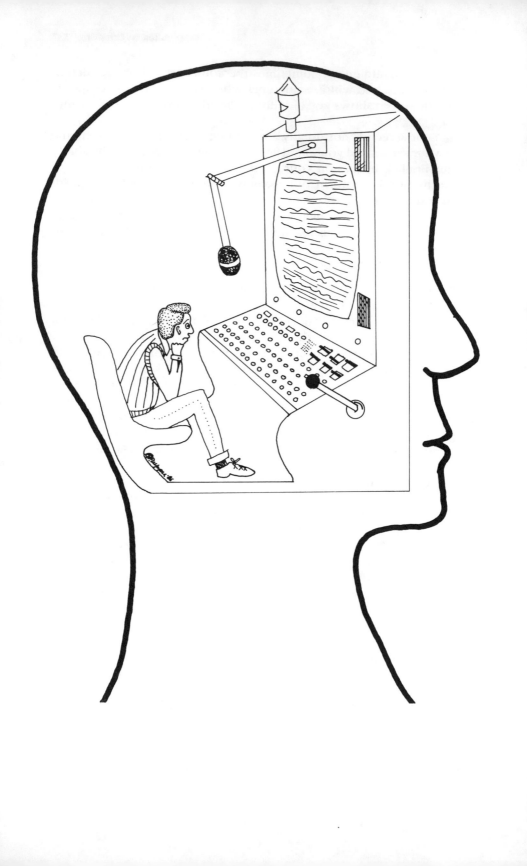

8. You can control some of what you see on your screen all the
    time. Just close your eyes or clap your hands.
9. You can control all of what you see on your screen some of
    the time. For example, meditation can take you to a place
    where you are intensely aware of only one thing. Hypnosis
    can narrow your focus down to one thought or past event.
    But outside of these special states, total control is rare.
10. You can't control all of what you see all of the time.
11. You can improve the quality of the picture on your screen,
    but you can't get rid of the screen. Reading a self-help book
    like this one is a way to improve the accuracy of what you
    see on your screen. So is studying physics, painting a still life,
    asking questions, trying new experiences, or getting to know
    someone better. As good as your screen gets, though, you're
    stuck with it. Only dead people don't have screens.
12. Critics don't criticize you. They only criticize what they see on
    their screens. They may claim to see you clearly, better than
    you can see yourself. But they are never seeing the real you,
    only their screen portrait. Remember, the more adamant a
    critic is about the accuracy of his or her observation, the greater
    the chance that his or her screen image of you is distorted.
13. Your perception of reality is only one of the inputs to your
    screen. These perceptions are colored by your inborn abilities
    and characteristics. Your perceptions can be influenced by
    your physiological or emotional state at the time. Your view
    of reality can be distorted or impaired by memories of similar
    scenes from your past, by your beliefs, or by your needs.

Let's examine this last rule in more detail. There are many input jacks,
as it were, through which images may reach your screen. Only five
of them have anything to do with reality—sight, sound, touch, taste,
and smell. And these five can be influenced or overridden by many
other inputs.

For example, you see a gray-haired man with wrinkles on his face
get out of a car and walk into a bank. This is what your senses tell
you. Your innate constitution will determine how quickly and intensely
you react to your sense impressions. If you have just had a hard time
finding a parking place and you're worried about being late for an appointment, you will be irritable and likely to make a negative judgment
of everything you see. Your past experience of gray-haired, wrinkled
men tells you that he is about fifty years old. Your knowledge of cars
tells you that his is an expensive Mercedes. His solemn expression reminds you of your Uncle Max, who has an ulcer, so you think that this
man probably has an ulcer. Your past experience of banks and men's
fashions tells you that he probably has money. Your beliefs and prej-

udices tell you that this guy is a rich, hard-driving businessman who wrings money out of those who need it more than he does. He is probably possession-proud, since he drives an expensive Mercedes, and he's probably unable to fully express his feelings, just like your Uncle Max. Your need to feel kinder, more noble, and caring than others leads you to rank this stranger below yourself in these important categories. You don't like him. You feel quite critical. Given the opportunity, you might express your criticism of this unfortunate man to him. And if he suffers from extraordinarily weak self-esteem, he might agree with your snap judgment of him. And the whole exchange would be a waste of your time and his, because it would have little to do with reality. It would be a result of the mishmash of observations, feelings, memories, beliefs, and needs that you had on your screen at a given moment.

Screen Inputs

In this section we will examine some of the powerful inputs, besides unadulterated reality, that can determine what you see on your screen.

1. Innate constitution. Certain things about everyone are genetically determined. Not just hair color, eye color, and the like, but certain behavioral tendencies appear to be established from birth. Some people are just more excitable than others. They react sooner and more vigorously to all sorts of stimuli. Some people are more nervous or more quiet than others. Some people seem to require frequent social contact, while others prefer solitary pursuits. Some people are smarter or have quicker reflexes. Others are more intuitive or sensitive to fine shades of meaning or feeling. Some people adapt easily to new things, while others shun change or innovation, preferring the traditional, familiar ways. Some people are morning people and some are night people. Some people can get along with little sleep and others can't function without their eight hours every night. Some people just seem naturally friendly, while others keep their distance.

These innate personality traits can easily color what people see on their screens. Night people may see a dim, gloomy world in the morning, and they are more likely at that time to be critical of others than at night, when they feel energized and ready to boogie. Loners see social functions as something to be endured, while party people see a quiet evening at home as a dreary prospect.

If someone criticizes you for being too shy and retiring, perhaps that person is innately gregarious and just can't see that the way you present yourself is OK. Or a critic who blows up at you over little things may have been born with an irritable temper, and his outbursts may have little or nothing to do with the few small mistakes you might make.

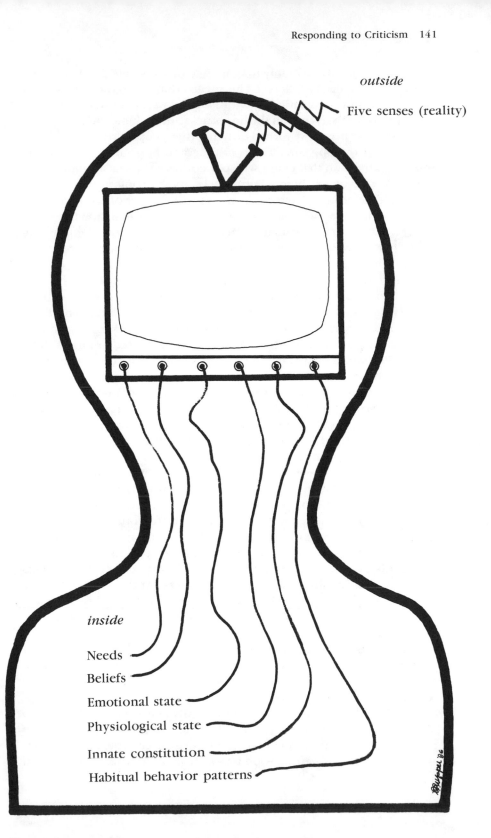

People vary considerably in how they process outside stimulation. Some are naturally "levelers." This means that when they see or hear something, they automatically, without thinking about it, damp down the sensation. It's as though the brightness and volume knobs on their screens are permanently turned down. Other people are "sharpeners" who do just the opposite. Their volume and brightness controls are turned up high, so that every whisper comes across as a shout, every firecracker is a cherry bomb. Fortunately, most people are somewhere in the middle ground. Extreme levelers are in danger of becoming psychopaths, because they need increasingly intense stimulation to exceed their threshold of excitement. Extreme sharpeners often become neurotic after years of being bombarded with stimuli that seem too intense and overwhelming.

In short, no matter how balanced, intelligent, or perceptive you are, you have innate, constitutional tendencies that prevent you from perceiving reality with perfect objectivity. And so no one can be a perfectly objective critic. You can only criticize what is on your screen, and that picture is not reliable. It is always a little distorted or incomplete.

2. Physiological state. What you see on your screen can be influenced by fatigue, headache, fever, stomachache, drugs, blood-sugar level, or any one of a hundred physiological events. You may or may not be aware of your physiological state. Even if you are aware of it, you may not notice what it is doing to your perception. And even if you do know what it is doing to your perception, you still may not be able to do anything about it.

For example, a man with an undiagnosed thyroid condition was suffering from fatigue, depression, and occasional anxiety attacks. He was alternately unresponsive and irritable with his family. At first he didn't notice that he felt or was acting any differently than usual. His physiological state was affecting what he saw on his screen without his knowledge. When his condition was diagnosed and stabilized with medication, his critical behavior lessened. But if he forgot to take his medication, he could get very listless or jittery. At these times, he was aware of his physiological state and how it was affecting his behavior, but he couldn't do anything about it until the medication took hold once more.

If someone often nags you, the problem could be an ulcer or a migraine, and not you at all. Your critic's unpleasant attitude may be a result of consuming a dubious chili dog, not a result of your failure to pick up the living room.

3. Emotional state. When you're really angry, you see the world through a red haze. When you are in love, the glasses change to the rose-colored variety. Depressed screens are tinted blue, and there's a whole genre of music for a soundtrack. If you are what you eat, then you see what you feel.

How many times have you seen this on TV? The hero works himself up into a rage, finally tells off his domineering boss or his unfaithful girlfriend, and then stomps out of the room. On the way out he encounters the office boy or the dog, to whom he screams, "And that goes for you, too!" Big laugh and dissolve to next scene.

This happens in real life too, but unfortunately without the painless dissolve to the next scene. Often you take the brunt of anger or rejection that has nothing to do with you. You are as uninvolved as the office boy or the dog. Your only fault was to be unlucky enough to encounter the critic who was still emotional about some earlier experience.

Sometimes critics are in a state of general arousal. They're feeling tense or worried or stressed by life in general. Then you cross them in some minor or even imagined way, and they blow up. Their state of arousal is expressed as anger, and their tension is released for a while.

For example, your boss chews you out for wasting money. You bought some necessary office supplies and furniture, nothing very extravagant, and you got good prices, too. If your self-esteem is fragile, you might conclude that you lack judgment and that you will never be a success in your job. However, you might learn later that your boss had just received a financial setback and was feeling particularly paranoid about keeping expenses down. There was nothing wrong with your judgment—the blowup was caused by your boss's free-floating state of arousal, and you became a chance opportunity for release.

4. Habitual behavior patterns. Everyone has coping strategies that have worked in the past and that will probably work in the future. These strategies tend to be applied automatically, regardless of the situation. For example, a child of violent parents may learn to avoid notice by not speaking up, by hiding needs, and by trying to anticipate what others want without actually asking them. These strategies will be carried over into adulthood, where they will not work very well for achieving a satisfying relationship with another adult.

Another example would be a woman who grew up in a family where an ironic, sarcastic style of humor was the norm. Outside her family circle, she often turns people off. Her habitual behavior pattern of satirizing and parodying those around her is taken as a critical, negative attitude.

Often when you feel criticized or slighted by someone, you find out later from the critic's friends that "he's always like that." What they mean is that his habitual behavior patterns lead him to be critical or negative with some kinds of people in some situations, regardless of the objective reality at the time.

Everyone drags an enormous baggage of old behavior patterns around all the time. More often than not people are reaching into their bag of tricks for a familiar way of reacting, instead of basing their reaction on a fresh, accurate assessment of the situation and your role in it. They are watching old tapes on their screen instead of concentrating on the live action reported by their senses.

5. Beliefs. Values, prejudices, interpretations, theories, and specific conclusions about an ongoing interaction can all influence what people see on their screens. People who value neatness may exaggerate all the sloppiness they see in the world. Those who are prejudiced against blacks or Jews or southerners cannot trust what they see on their screens concerning the groups they hate. If a man believes strongly in independence, he will tend to interpret cooperation as weakness. If a woman has a theory that all traumatic weaning causes weight problems in later life, then she will see obese people in light of her theory, not in the clear light of objective reality. If you lean back in your chair and cross your arms while talking to an insurance salesman, he may interpret that gesture as resistance to his sales pitch and redouble his efforts. His view of you on his screen will be determined by this interpretation, right or wrong. You may have leaned back because your muscles are stiff or because you wanted to get a view of the clock.

Beliefs are tied very strongly to past experience of what life is like, what works, what hurts, and what helps. The bank officer who rejects your loan application is probably not rejecting you personally. She is responding to her past experiences of people in similar financial situations who either did or didn't pay back their loans. The same goes for the woman who turns you down for a date. She is very likely operating out of her beliefs based on experience. She may believe that tall men are not for her, or that she must never date a Pisces, or that she must not get serious with anyone over a certain age. She is rejecting who she believes you are, not who you really are. The real you isn't on her screen at all.

6. Needs. Everybody you meet is trying to get needs met all the time. This imperative affects what people see on their screens. A hungry man has a keen eye for food on the table, but might not notice a roaring fire in the fireplace or the magazines on the coffee table. A cold woman entering the room will go straight for the fire and not notice the food or the magazines. A bored person waiting in the room would seize immediately on the magazines as a source of diversion. A thirsty person would find nothing in the room to satisfy that need and hold a lower opinion of the surroundings than the other three.

Emotional needs work the same way to distort screens and bring on criticism that has nothing to do with the actual situation. A man who wants to impress his date in a restaurant might be quite critical about the food and complain about the service, when in fact both are excellent. A less obvious case is that of the guy who is quite belligerent about asking you for your help because he has a strong need to be in control of every situation. Another subtle example is an acquaintance who is often very catty about other people's appearance as a result of her own need to be constantly reassured about her own physical attractiveness.

Criticism that is out of proportion to the occasion is often motivated by some hidden agenda. The critic shames you into doing something that you wouldn't do if you knew the real reason behind it. For example, let's say that your boss asks you to stay overtime or work on the weekend and then becomes very critical when you turn him down. His request and reaction make no sense to you—there just isn't enough work to do to justify the inconvenience. The real situation may be that your boss is just trying to impress his boss by saying that he had staff in over the weekend. Or that he needs you there to receive an important phone call and he's too lazy to come in and wait for it himself. There could be several hidden agendas, none of them having anything to do with your job or your performance.

Sometimes critics are fully aware of the emotional needs or hidden agendas that motivate them, and sometimes they're not. But since you're the person on the receiving end of the criticism, their awareness doesn't matter to you. All that matters to you is recognizing that needs distort a critic's perception of reality, and therefore no criticism can be taken at face value.

> *Exercise.* Go around for the rest of the day or all day tomorrow imagining that your eyes are a camera. Your ears are microphones. Be the director of a documentary. Consciously compose a voice-over commentary on what you see and hear. Shift your attention to emphasize the negative or positive aspects of a scene. When someone says something to you, pretend that both of you are characters in a soap opera. Imagine several possible responses besides the one you would normally give. Imagine several possible motivations for what other people do besides the motives you assume are correct. Notice how this distancing exercise changes your awareness of reality. It should make you realize that there are many more possible ways to see reality than the one you usually use. It should also point up how automatic and limited your usual perception of the world is.

The Screen as Monster-Maker

The illustration on the next page shows a simple, everyday encounter. The reality is simple and blameless: two men meet at a party. The man in glasses asks a newcomer what he does for a living, trying to make conversation and put him at ease. The newcomer is here with his wife. These are his wife's friends, not his. He'd rather be at home watching the ball game or drinking beer with his buddies. He hates

this sort of party and didn't want to come in the first place. He thinks
most of his wife's friends from work are stuck-up wimps who don't
know how to have a good time. All this background and his current
arousal level affect what he sees on his screen, and he responds to the
distorted image with a thinly veiled insult.

INPUTS:

Reality: Short guy with glasses, tie, asks, "So, what do you do?"

+   *Innate constitution:* Warning, new encounter, be careful, ex-
    pect attack.

+   *Physiological state:* Short of breath from running up stairs,
    sweaty, heartrate high.

+   *Emotional state:* Aroused. Irritated at being late, angry at wife
    for making me come.

+   *Habitual behavior pattern:* Take the psychological high
    ground. Get in the first blow and establish dominance.

+   *Beliefs:* Here's another intellectual twerp in glasses and a tie.

These stuck-up eggheads are always looking for a chance to put a working man down.

+   *Needs:* To relieve tension of anger and anxiety. To appear powerful, tough, competent.

=   *Response:* Loud, chest out, leaning forward into the twerp's face—"I work for a living. What do you do?"

Mantra for Handling Criticism

The moment you hear a critical remark, ask yourself, "What's on this person's screen?" Immediately assume that there is at best a tenuous, indirect connection to reality. You will stand a far greater chance of being right than if you assume that all critical remarks arise from some shortcoming in yourself.

Remember that people can only criticize what's on their screens and that their screens are not reliable. It's very unlikely that any criticism is based on an accurate perception of you. It's much more likely that the critic is reacting to emotions, memories, and behavior patterns that have almost nothing to do with you. Thinking poorly about yourself because of such criticism is a mistake. It's like running scared from a little kid with a sheet over his head who pops out behind a bush and says, "Boo!" You may be startled at first and pull back, but then you laugh and think, "It's OK, it's nothing real." Just so with criticism. You may feel briefly taken aback when someone criticizes you, but then you smile and say to yourself, "Boy, I wonder what's on his screen to make him so critical of me?"

Responding to Criticism

Does all this seem a little unrealistic? Do you find yourself saying, "Wait a minute, some criticism is based on facts. Sometimes the critic is right on the money, and you have to acknowledge it. Or sometimes you need to defend yourself. You can't just secretly smile and keep mum!"

If this is what you're thinking, you're right. Often you have to respond in some way to criticism. The mantra "What's on his screen?" is just a brief, but essential, bit of first aid for your self-esteem. Remember that all criticism shares one characteristic: it is unwelcome. You didn't invite people to dump the distorted contents of their screen on you. You may feel that you owe some critics a response, but you never owe a critic your self-esteem.

Ineffective Response Styles

There are three basic ways to go wrong in responding to criticism: being aggressive, being passive, or both.

1. Aggressive style. The aggressive response to criticism is to counterattack. Your wife criticizes your TV viewing habits, and you counter with a cutting remark about her affection for soap operas. Your husband makes a snide remark about your weight, and you counterattack by mentioning his blood pressure.

This is the "Oh yeah?" theory of how to handle criticism. Every critic is met with a hostile "Oh yeah?" attitude, and a response that varies in intensity from "How dare you even think of criticizing me?" to "Well, I may not be much, but neither are you."

The aggressive style of responding to criticism has one advantage: you usually get people off your back right away. But this is a short-term benefit. If you have to deal again and again with the same people, they will come back at you with bigger and bigger guns. Their attacks and your counterattacks will escalate into all-out war. You will turn potentially constructive critics into destructive enemies.

Even if your aggressive counterattack succeeds in shutting a critic up for good, you have not necessarily won. If people have genuine grievances with you, they may go behind your back and use indirect means to get what they want from you. You will be the last to know what is going on.

Consistently responding to criticism aggressively is a symptom of low self-esteem. You lash out at critics because you secretly share their low opinion of you and violently resist any reminder of your shortcomings. You attack your critics to bring them down to your own level, to show that although you may not be very worthy, you are more worthy than they are.

Consistently counterattacking your critics is also a guarantee that your self-esteem will remain low. The process of attack, counterattack, and escalation means that you will soon be surrounded by critics who besiege you with evidence of your worthlessness. Even if you had some self-esteem to start with, it will be battered down in time. Furthermore, your bellicose style of relating to people who are even slightly critical of you will prevent you from forming any deep relationships.

2. Passive style. The passive style of responding to criticism is to agree, to apologize, and to surrender at the first sign of an attack. Your wife complains that you are getting a little overweight, and you cave in: "Yes, I know. I'm just becoming a fat slob. I don't know how you can stand to look at me." Your husband tells you you're following the car ahead of you too closely, and you immediately say that you're sorry, slow down, and promise never to do it again.

Silence can also be a passive response to criticism. You make no response to criticism that deserves a response. Your critic then continues to harass you until you provide some belated verbal reaction, usually an apology.

There are two possible advantages to the passive style of responding to criticism. First, some critics will leave you alone when they find that they arouse no fight in you. It's not enough sport for them. Second, if you don't make any response at all, it saves you the trouble of thinking up something to say.

Both these advantages are short-term ones. In the long term, you will find that many critics enjoy shooting fish in a barrel. They will return time and again to take potshots at you, just because they know that they can get an apology or an agreement. Your response lets them feel superior, and they don't care whether it's sporting at all. And even though you're saved the trouble of thinking up a verbal response, you'll still find that you are expending a lot of mental energy in thinking up purely mental retorts. You don't say them, but you think them.

The real disadvantage of the passive style is that surrendering to others' negative opinions of you is deadly to your self-esteem.

3. Passive-aggressive style. This style of responding to criticism combines some of the worst aspects of both the aggressive and the passive styles. When you are first criticized, you respond passively by apologizing or agreeing to change. Later you get even with your critic by forgetting something, failing to make the promised change, or some other covertly aggressive action.

For example, a man criticized his wife for not clearing out an accumulation of magazines and paperbacks. She promised to box them up for the Goodwill truck. After being reminded twice to do it, she actually did call the Goodwill and make the donation. While she was at it, she culled some old clothes from the closet, including a favorite old shirt of her husband's. When he got angry about her giving his favorite shirt away, she apologized again, saying that she didn't realize that it was so important to him, and if he was so fussy he could call Goodwill and handle it himself next time.

In this example, the woman was unconscious of any plot to get even. Passive aggression is often unconscious. You make understandable mistakes. Your intentions are good, but somehow you screw up one little detail. You prepare a special dinner to make amends with your girlfriend, but you forget that she hates cream sauces. You are late for an important date or buy the wrong size or put a dent in the car.

Passive aggression lowers your self-esteem twice. Your self-esteem suffers first because you have agreed with someone about your shortcomings. Then your self-esteem gets taken down another peg when you covertly strike back. You secretly hate yourself, either for being sneaky if you're conscious of the counterattack or for being fallible if the retaliation takes the form of an unconscious mistake.

A consistently passive-aggressive response style is hard to change because it's indirect. The vicious circle of criticism-apology-aggression is a covert guerrilla war fought deep in the underbrush. It's very hard to break out of the circle and achieve a level of honest, straightforward communication. The passive-aggressive person ends up too scared to risk open confrontation, and the other person has had all trust and confidence destroyed by repeated acts of sabotage.

Effective Response Styles

The effective way to respond to criticism is to use the assertive style. The assertive style of responding to criticism doesn't attack, surrender to, or sabotage the critic. It disarms the critic. When you respond assertively to a critic, you clear up misunderstandings, acknowledge what you consider accurate about the criticism, ignore the rest, and put an end to the unwelcome attack without sacrificing your self-esteem.

There are three techniques for responding assertively to criticism: acknowledgement, clouding, and probing.

Acknowledgement. Acknowledgement means simply agreeing with a critic. It's purpose is to stop criticism immediately, and it works very well.

When you acknowledge criticism, you say to the critic, "Yes, I have the same picture on my screen. We are watching the same channel."

When someone criticizes you, and the criticism is accurate, just follow these four simple steps:

1. Say "You're right."
2. Paraphrase the criticism so that the critic is sure you heard him or her correctly.
3. Thank the critic, if appropriate.
4. Explain yourself, if appropriate. Note that an explanation is not an apology. While you are working on raising your self-esteem, the best policy is never to apologize and seldom explain. Remember that criticism is uninvited and unwelcome. Most critics don't deserve either an apology or an explanation. They will have to be satisfied with being told they're right.

Here's an example of responding to criticism with a simple acknowledgement:

Criticism: I wish you'd be more careful with your things. I found your hammer lying in the wet grass.
Response: You're right, I should have put that hammer away when I was through using it. Thanks for finding it.

This is all that needs to be said. No explanation or apology or pledge to reform is needed. The respondent acknowledges a minor lapse, thanks the critic, and the case is closed. Here is another example of simple acknowledgement:

> *Criticism:* I almost ran out of gas on the way to work this morning. Why didn't you fill the tank yesterday? I don't see why I always have to be the one who does it.
> *Response:* You're right. I noticed we were low on gas and I should have got some. I'm really sorry.

In this example, the respondent has caused the critic some real inconvenience and adds a sincere apology. Here's another example of a case where some explanation is in order:

> *Criticism:* It's nine thirty. You should have been here half an hour ago.
> *Response:* You're right, I'm late. The bus I was on this morning broke down and they had to send out another one to pick us all up.

Advanced acknowledgement involves turning a critic into an ally. Here's an example:

> *Criticism:* Your office is a mess. How do you ever find anything in here?
> *Response:* You're right, my office *is* a mess, and I can never find what I want. How do you think I could reorganize my filing system?

Exercise. After each of the following criticisms, write your own response using the full "you're right, paraphrase, explain" formula.

> *Criticism:* This is the sloppiest report I've ever seen. What did you do, write it in your sleep?
> *Response:*

> *Criticism:* Your dog dug a giant hole under our fence. Why can't you keep it under control?
> *Response:*

> *Criticism:* When are you going to return those books to the library? I'm sick of asking you. You've promised to do it twice now, and they're still sitting on the hall table.
> *Response:*

Acknowledgement has several advantages. It is always the best strategy for quick and effective deflation of critics. Critics need your resistance in order to keep hassling you. They want to fully develop their theme, hitting you time after time with examples and restatements of your failings. When you agree with a critic, you go with the force of the blow, as in judo. The criticism is harmlessly expended on empty air. The critic is left with nothing more to say, since your refusal to argue has made further talk unnecessary. Very few critics will persist after acknowledgement. They get the satisfaction of being right, and that is worth being denied the luxury of raking you over the coals at length.

Acknowledgement has one big disadvantage: it doesn't protect your self-esteem if you acknowledge something that isn't true about yourself. Acknowledgement only works to protect your self-esteem when you can sincerely agree with what a critic is saying. When you can't agree fully, you are better off using the clouding technique.

Clouding. Clouding involves a token agreement with a critic. It is used when criticism is neither constructive nor accurate.

When you use clouding to deal with criticism, you are saying to the critic, "Yes, some of what is on your screen is also on my screen." But to yourself you add, "And some isn't." You "cloud" by agreeing in part, in probability, or in principle.

1. *Agreeing in part.* When you agree in part, you find just one part of what a critic is saying, and acknowledge that part. Here is an example:

Criticism: You're not reliable. You forget to pick up the kids, you let the bills pile up until we could lose the roof over our head, and I can't ever count on you to be there when I need you.

Response: You're certainly right that I did forget to pick up the kids last week after their swimming lesson.

In this example, the blanket statement "you're unreliable" is too global to agree to. The charge that they will lose the roof over their heads is an exaggeration, and the "I can't ever count on you" just isn't true. So the respondent picks one factual statement about not picking up the kids and acknowledges that.

Here is another example of clouding by agreeing in part:

Criticism: Miss, this is the worst coffee I've ever had. It's weak and watery and barely warm. I heard good things about this place—I hope the food is better than the coffee.

Response: Oh, you're right, it's cold. I'll get you another cup from a fresh pot right away.

In this example, the waitress finds one objective truth that she can agree with and ignores the other complaints.

2. *Agreeing in probability.* You agree in probability by saying, "It's possible you're right." Even though the chances may, in your mind, be a million to one against it, you can still honestly say that "it's possible." Here are a couple of examples.

Criticism: If you don't floss your teeth, you'll get gum disease and be sorry for the rest of your life.
Response: You may be right. I could get gum disease.

Criticism: Riding the clutch like that is terrible for the transmission. You'll need an overhaul twice as quick. You should just let it out and leave it alone.
Response: Yes, I may be doing the wrong thing here.

These examples show the essence of clouding. You are appearing to agree, and the critic can be satisfied with that. But the unspoken, self-esteem-preserving message is "Although you may be right, I don't really think that you are. I intend to exercise my right to my own opinion, and I'll continue to do just as I damn well please."

3. *Agreeing in principle.* This clouding technique acknowledges a critic's logic without necessarily endorsing all of a critic's assumptions. It uses a conditional "if . . . then" format:

Criticism: That's the wrong tool for the job. A chisel like that will slip and mess up the wood. You ought to have a gouge instead.
Response: You're right, if the chisel slips it will really mess up the wood.

The respondent is admitting the logical connection between tools slipping and damage to the work, but has not actually agreed that the chisel is the wrong tool. Here is another example:

Criticism: You're really taking a chance by claiming all these deductions you don't have receipts for. The IRS is really cracking down. You're just asking for an audit. It's stupid to try to save a few bucks and bring them down on you like a pack of bloodhounds.
Response: You're right, if I take the deductions, I'll be attracting more attention to myself. And if I get audited, it will be a real hassle.

This response agrees with the critic's logic without agreeing with the critic's assessment of the degree of risk.

Exercise. In the space after the following three critical statements, write your own responses. To each criticism, agree in part, in probability, and in principle.

Criticism: Your hair is a fright. It's dry and fly-away, and it must be a month since you had it cut. I hope you're not going out in public like that. If you do, people will be laughing behind your back. How can you expect people to take you seriously when you present youself to the world like that?

Agree in part:

Agree in probability:

Agree in principle:

Criticism: You spend all your money on appearances: your clothes, your apartment, your car. How things look is all that matters to you—keeping up a good front. How do you expect to handle any emergencies if you never save anything? Suppose you got sick, suppose you lost your job? It just makes me sick seeing you squandering every dime you make.

Agree in part:

Agree in probability:

Agree in principle:

Criticism: Is this the best you can do? I wanted an in-depth analysis, and this just hits the high points. This report should be twice as long, with discussion of all the points I raised in my memo. If we turn this in to the planning department, they'll just toss it back. You need to try it again, and put a little thought into it.

Agree in part:

Agree in probability:

Agree in principle:

The advantage of clouding in its various forms is that it quiets critics without sacrificing your self-esteem. The critics hear the magic message "you're right" and are satisfied with that. They don't notice or don't care that you have said that they are only partly right, probably right, or right in principle.

Sometimes it's hard to content yourself with a clouding response. You may feel compelled to give voice to your real, fully developed opinions and feelings on the subject. It's tempting to argue and attempt to win the critic over to your point of view. This is all right, if the criticism is constructive and the critic is amenable to a change of viewpoint. But most criticism with which you disagree isn't worth dignifying with an argument. You and your self-esteem are better off clouding the issue with a token agreement and then changing the subject.

You may feel guilty when you first try clouding. It may seem sneaky and manipulative. If that's the case, remember that you don't owe anything to a critic. Criticism is unwelcome and uninvited. Criticism is often a sign of critics' basic negativity and insecurity: they have to harp on what's wrong with life instead of enjoying the positive side. They have to tear you down in order to bolster themselves up. Most critics are manipulative themselves: rather than directly ask you to do something, they try to influence you indirectly by complaining about you. Especially when criticism is incorrect or not constructive, you are perfectly within your rights to be just as manipulative as the critic. Your self-esteem comes first.

The only disadvantage of clouding is that you may use the technique too soon. If you don't understand the critic's motives or message fully and you use clouding to cut the exchange short, you may miss hearing something beneficial. Before jumping in with your clouding response, make sure that you understand what is being said and determine if the critic is trying to be constructive. If you can't tell exactly what the critic means, use probing.

Probing. A lot of criticism is vague. You can't tell what the critic is driving at. You must use probing to clarify the critic's intent and meaning. When you have uncovered the full message, then you can decide if it is constructive, if you agree with all or part of it, and how you will respond.

By probing, you are saying to your critic, "Your screen's not clear to me. Could you adjust the focus, please?" You keep asking the critic to clarify until you have a good picture. Then you can say, "Oh yes, I have the same channel on my screen" or "Well, yes, some of what you have on your screen is also on mine (and some isn't)."

Key words for probing are "exactly," "specifically," and "for example." Here are some typical probes: "How exactly have I let you down?" "What specifically bothers you about the way I do the dishes?" "Can you give me an example of my carelessness?"

"Oh yeah?" "Prove it!" and "Says who?" are *not* examples of proper probing. You should keep your tone inquisitive and nonargumentative. You want further information, not a fight.

When you are probing a nagger, it's helpful to keep asking the nagger for examples of the behavior change he or she wants you to make. Insist that the complaint be put in the form of a request for a change in your behavior. Lead your critic away from abstract and pejorative terms such as *lazy, inconsiderate, sloppy, grouchy*, and so on. Here is an example of probing a nagger:

> *He:* You're lazy.
> *She*: Lazy how, exactly?
> *He*: You just sit around.
> *She*: What do you want me to do?
> *He*: Stop being such a slug.
> *She*: No, really, I want to know what you'd like me to do.
> *He*: Well, clean out the basement, for one thing.
> *She*: And what else?
> *He*: Stop staring at the tube all day.
> *She*: No, that's what you don't want me to. What actual things do you want me to do instead?

This approach forces the nagger away from name-calling and vague complaining toward some real requests that you can seriously consider. It directs the focus away from a recitation of past sins and toward the future, where the possibility of change exists.

Exercise. After each of the following three vague criticisms, write your own probing responses.

Criticism: You're not pulling your weight around here.
Probe:

Criticism: You're so cold and distant tonight.
Probe:

Criticism: Why do you have to be so stubborn? Why can't you give a little?
Probe:

The advantages of probing are obvious. You get the information you need to figure out how to respond to a critic. You may find out that what sounded like criticism at first was actually a reasonable suggestion, an expression of concern, or a cry for help. At its best, clarifying your critic's message can turn a casual complaint into a meaningful dialogue. At worst, probing a critic will confirm your suspicion that he or she is maliciously attacking you and therefore deserves your most adroit clouding tactics.

The only disadvantage of probing is that it is an interim tactic. It just clears up your understanding of the critic's intent and meaning. You still have to choose whether to acknowledge the criticism or to use one of the forms of clouding. The decision tree in the next section will help you review which responses to make based on your probing.

Putting It All Together

The first part of this chapter taught you what to do the moment you first suspect that you are hearing something critical: Apply your mantra, "What's on the screen?" Remind yourself that the critic is only being critical of the content of his or her screen, not of reality. It has nothing to do with you directly. Resist the automatic agreement of your own internal pathological critic. Tell yourself to take your self-esteem out of the circuit.

Once you have your self-esteem out of the circuit, you can concentrate on what the critic is actually saying. Listen first for the critic's intention. Hear the tone. Consider the situation and your relationship to the critic. Is the criticism constructive? Is the critic trying to help or hassle?

Look at the decision tree below. It shows all the possible appropriate, assertive, high self-esteem responses you can make to any criticism.

If you can't tell whether the critic means to help or hassle you, you need to use probing until the intention becomes clear. Once you have determined the intention, you ask yourself if the content of the message is accurate. Do you agree with it?

If you find that criticism is meant to be constructive, but is simply inaccurate, all you have to do is point out the critic's error, and the case is closed. If constructive criticism is accurate, all you have to do is acknowledge it, and again the case is closed. The same goes for criticism that is not constructive, but happens to be completely accurate: you just agree with it and spike the critic's guns.

The only case that is left is the one in which the critic is not constructive and not accurate. This critic not only is out to hassle you, but he or she has also got the facts wrong. This critic deserves a clouding response—agree in part, in probability, or in principle, and stop there.

Exercise. Use some example of criticism from this chapter or from your own life. Run them through the decision tree and see how you would respond, depending on what is constructive and what is accurate.

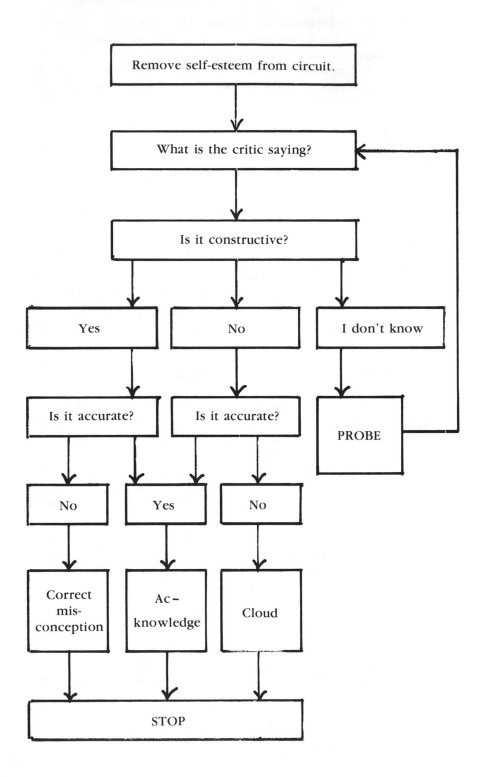

10

Asking for What You Want

The inability to ask others for what you want is a classic symptom of low self-esteem. It stems from your basic feeling of unworthiness. You feel that you don't deserve to get what you want. Your wants don't seem legitimate or important. Other people's wants seem much more valid and pressing than your own. You go around asking other people what *they* want and trying to get it for them.

You may be so afraid of rejection or so out of touch with your needs that you aren't even aware of what you want. You can't afford the risk of consciously wanting something from others.

For example, you may fantasize about a certain kind of lovemaking that particularly appeals to you, but never experience it because you never ask for it. In fact, you never even consciously admit to yourself that you want it. It's "just a fantasy." You don't acknowledge your want because if you did, you might actually ask for it. And if you asked for it, you might be rejected as "too kinky." Or your sexual partner might take your request as an implication that you find your sex life together inadequate.

This chapter will list and explain your legitimate needs, discuss the relationship between needs and wants, teach you how to raise your awareness of your wants, provide exercises to analyze and precisely define what you want, and give training and practice in asking for what you want.

Your Legitimate Needs

What follows is a list of legitimate needs—the environmental conditions, activities, and experiences important for physical and psychological health. The purpose of this list is to stimulate your thinking about the importance and variety of human needs. You may think that some of the needs don't apply to you, that some of them are redundant, that there are needs omitted, or that the list is not categorized properly. That's fine. In fact, feel free to add to, subtract from, combine, and reorganize the needs on this list. Doing so will be an excellent way to begin thinking about your own personal needs.

Physical needs. From the moment you're born, you need clean air to breathe. You won't survive long without pure water to drink and nutritious food to eat. To these you can add the need for some type of clothing and shelter adapted to the part of the planet you inhabit. Other obvious physical needs are the need to rest and sleep regularly. You also need to exercise your muscles, or they will atrophy. Finally, you need a certain level of security or safety to survive physically.

Emotional needs. Less obvious, but hardly less essential, are your emotional needs—to love and be loved, to have companionship, to feel that you are respected, and to respect others. You need sympathy and compassion from others, and you need to express your own sympathy and compassion for them. When you do well, you need recognition, appreciation, and congratulations. When you don't do so well, you need forgiveness and understanding. You need outlets for your sexual drive, a need that is physical on the hormonal level, but is a quest for intimacy and belonging on the emotional level.

Intellectual needs. Your mind needs information, stimulation, and the challenge of problems to solve. You have an innate need to comprehend and understand the people and events around you. You need variety, recreation, and play time. You have a drive to accomplish things. You need to grow and to change. You need the freedom to honestly express your thoughts, and you need authentic, consistent responses from others.

Social needs. You need to interact with others, and sometimes you need to be by yourself and not interact with others. You need useful employment—a role in society that helps define your identity and makes some kind of positive contribution to others. You need to feel that you belong to a group. On the other hand, you also need autonomy—to be self-determined and to make your own choices.

Spiritual, moral, and ethical needs. You have a need to seek meaning in your life. You want to know what the universe is for and why humans are in it. You need some way of putting a value on your own life. You need to believe—in God, in people, in love, or in some other higher value. You seek to figure out and live by your own standards of behavior.

Needs Versus Wants

The difference between needs and wants is one of degree. At one end of the spectrum are life-and-death needs like the need for food and water. If these needs aren't met, you will literally perish. At the other end of the spectrum are the most minor and whimsical wants. These are luxury items that contribute to your comfort, but are not essential to your survival. You may have a craving for pistachio ice cream with caramel sauce, but you won't die if you don't get it.

Somewhere in the middle of the spectrum is the dividing line between needs and wants. It is in this middle ground that people with low self-esteem get into trouble.

If you have low self-esteem, it's hard enough for you to pursue survival needs. But your less vital needs and wants seem unimportant, particularly if they conflict with someone else's. Moreover, you tend to identify essential needs as mere wants and neglect to satisfy them. You think that you're being a stoic and forgoing comfort for the sake of others; but actually you're an unwitting martyr to your low self-esteem. You're not merely uncomfortable, you're surrendering important emotional, social, intellectual, or spiritual needs for fear of hurting or offending someone.

For example, you might stay at home every night instead of enrolling in night school because you think that your absence in the evenings would be a hardship on your family. Although you'd really like to get a degree, you don't feel that you deserve to take so much time and energy away from your family. So you never ask. And you feel an increasing sense of entropy and stagnation. The fact is that you have a strong, genuine, and legitimate need to learn, change, and grow. You are stifling yourself and causing yourself real suffering by incorrectly labeling your genuine need as an unnecessary indulgence.

The dividing line between a need and a want varies within each person. Sometimes you absolutely *need* to talk to someone about a perplexing personal problem, while at other times the same problem seems less pressing, something you merely *want* to solve, but can postpone working on till later.

Likewise, you may have lower "need thresholds" in some areas than you have in others. For example, you may have very strong emotional needs, but relatively weak intellectual ones. You may feel compelled to get close to people in a large, nurturing circle of relatives and friends, but have very modest ambitions where your job is concerned. Or vice versa.

You are the only one who can judge the relative strength of your needs and wants. If you feel that something you want is important for you, then it *is* important and you have a right to ask for it. It doesn't matter if everyone else in the world thinks that what you want is a mere luxury item. For you, it's a critical need and you're not going to be happy until you ask for and get it.

For the purpose of this chapter, and the purpose of raising your self-esteem, from here on we will refer to all needs and wants as "wants" and assume that they are all important and legitimate. If you find yourself saying, "Well, I'd really like to have this, but I don't really *need* it," remind yourself of two things: (1) you have a *right* to ask regardless of whether you need or merely want something, and (2) as a sufferer from low self-esteem, you might not know an intense need if it bit you.

Wants Inventory

This inventory is designed to raise your awareness of your wants. Complete the following questionnaire. In column A, put a check mark next to the items that are applicable to you. In column B, rate the items you have checked from 1 to 3, as:

1. Mildly uncomfortable
2. Moderately uncomfortable
3. Extremely uncomfortable

A *Check here if the item applies to you.*

B *Rate from 1 to 3 for discomfort.*

WHAT
I have trouble asking for:

A	B	
____	____	approval from _____ .
____	____	approval for _____ .
____	____	help with certain tasks.
____	____	more attention or time with my mate.
____	____	someone to listen and understand.
____	____	attention to what I have to say.
____	____	dates with people I find attractive.
____	____	job interviews.
____	____	promotions or raises.
____	____	service from clerks or waiters.
____	____	respect.
____	____	time by myself.
____	____	satisfying sexual experiences.
____	____	time to play and have fun.
____	____	variety, something new and different.
____	____	time to rest.
____	____	forgiveness.

_____   _____   answers to some nagging questions.
_____   _____   companionship.
_____   _____   permission to make my own choices.
_____   _____   acceptance of who I am by others.
_____   _____   acceptance of my mistakes.
_____   _____   other: _____

WHO
I have trouble asking for what I want from:

_____   _____   my parents.
_____   _____   fellow workers.
_____   _____   classmates.
_____   _____   students/teachers.
_____   _____   clients.
_____   _____   clergy, religious authorities.
_____   _____   my spouse or mate.
_____   _____   strangers.
_____   _____   friends.
_____   _____   acquaintances.
_____   _____   civil servants.
_____   _____   my boss or superiors at work.
_____   _____   relatives.
_____   _____   employees.
_____   _____   children.
_____   _____   older people.
_____   _____   sales people and clerks.
_____   _____   lovers.
_____   _____   authority figures.
_____   _____   a group of more than two or three people.
_____   _____   a person of the opposite sex.
_____   _____   a person of the same sex.
_____   _____   other: _____

WHEN
I have trouble asking for what I want when:

_____   _____   I want help.
_____   _____   asking for service.
_____   _____   asking for a date.
_____   _____   making an appointment.
_____   _____   I need a favor.
_____   _____   asking for information.
_____   _____   I want to propose an idea.
_____   _____   I feel guilty.
_____   _____   I feel selfish.
_____   _____   asking for cooperation.

_____	_____	negotiating from a one-down position.
_____	_____	a lot of people are listening.
_____	_____	others' tempers are high.
_____	_____	I'm upset.
_____	_____	I'm afraid of looking stupid.
_____	_____	I'm afraid the answer will be no.
_____	_____	I might look weak.
_____	_____	other: _____

Evaluation. Look over your inventory and notice the sorts of things you want most, the people from whom you want them, and in what situations your needs are most acute. You will probably notice patterns—certain needs that you never ask anybody for, certain people from whom you can't ask for the simplest favor, or problematic situations in which your self-esteem and assertiveness desert you entirely.

Wants into Words

The most important skill in asking for what you want is formulating an assertive request. If asking for things is hard for you, it's wiser to prepare your request in advance, rather than to say what comes to mind spontaneously. Preparing an assertive request first involves getting the facts and then distilling them into a clear statement of your wants. Here are the facts you need:

From _____

> Write down the name of the person who can give you what you want. If there are several people from whom you want the same thing, write out separate requests for each of them.

I want _____

> Spell out what you want the other person to do. Stay away from abstractions like "show respect" or "be honest." Don't ask for a change of attitude or level of interest. Instead, specify exact behavior: "I want to have an equal vote in choosing a daycare provider" or "I want Joe to tell me the real reason he keeps postponing our wedding and where he gets all the money he throws around."

When _____

> Indicate the deadline for getting what you want, the exact time of day you want someone to do something, or the frequency with which you want something—any aspect of time that will help narrow down and refine your request. For example, you

might want help cleaning the house every week. Be specific and write, "Every Saturday morning right after breakfast."

Where _____

Write down the places where you want something—any aspect of location that will serve to precisely define what you want. If you want to be left alone when you are in your den, specify that place as your special place to be alone.

With _____

Specify any other people who have to do with your request. For example, if you want your husband to stop teasing you about your forgetfulness in front of his relatives, spell out all the relatives' names.

This outline is designed to help you specify *exactly* what it is you are requesting—the desired behavior, the time, the place, and the situation. When you clarify these facts in advance, your request will be so specific that negotiation will be easier and arguments less likely.

Holly had hoped that Al would help edit her article on pain management. Occasionally after dinner she would vaguely mention some of the problems she was having organizing the material. Al would listen while popping a videocassette into the VCR and adjusting the TV. He consistently failed to pick up on her hints. Here is Holly's outline of the facts regarding her request:

From: Al
I want: Help editing my article, going over the contents and the organization page by page.
When: After dinner on Thursday for three hours. And if we don't finish, again on Saturday morning.
Where: In the study, where all my materials are, and away from the TV.
With: Al alone.

Randy prepared his request to deal with his brother's caustic sense of humor. Jim had a tendency to make fun of Randy's clothes, his job, his shyness with women, and so on. This was a particular problem during family gatherings when their dad was present. Here is Randy's fact outline:

From: Jim
I want: No more jokes or remarks about my clothes, job, or social life. A real conversation about recent events in our lives.
When: Usually over dinner.
Where: Get-togethers at dad and mom's house.
With: Dad particularly.

Now it's time to make your own request outline. From your wants inventory, choose three things that you want from three different people. Be sure to choose items that you rated only mildly or moderately uncomfortable. Tougher, more anxiety-provoking confrontations on your list should be dealt with later. For each want, fill in the facts for your request outline:

From:
I want:
When:
Where:
With:

Distilling the Assertive Request

Now it's time to prepare assertive requests that condense the basic facts in your three outlines into a brief statement about your wants. Holly's assertive request turned out like this:

Al, I really need some help from you to edit my pain control article. I'd like to go over the content and organization with you on a page-by-page basis. Could we get together after dinner Thursday for a three-hour editing session in the study? And if we don't finish, polish if off Saturday morning?

Randy's assertive request took this form:

Jim, I'd really appreciate it if you could go easy on the jokes about my clothes and social life and such. It's particularly hard for me when we're with dad at family dinners. It would feel better if we could really talk a bit—about how we're doing and what's been going on lately for each of us.

Notice how specific Holly's and Randy's requests are. Every important fact in their request outlines has been included. There's no guesswork, no uncertainty for the other party. Because their wants are clear, there is a much greater chance for compliance or working out a compromise.

Write your own assertive requests before going on to the next section.

Whole Messages

Often it isn't enough just to say what you want. People need to know more of the background for your request. They need to know your perspective or understanding of the problem. It may also be helpful for them to know your feelings—how the situation or problem has affected you emotionally. When you offer your *thoughts* (how you perceive the situation), your *feelings*, and your *want* statement, this is called a "whole message."

Whole messages promote intimacy and mutual acceptance. People are less likely to ignore your wants when they are aware of your feelings and perspective on a situation. It's rather abrupt and possibly quite irritating to say to a friend, "I want to get out of here." It's better to deliver a whole message like this: "The party's packed wall-to-wall. I feel kind of claustrophobic. Mind if we leave?" This will get a much more sympathetic response.

When you leave your experience of a situation or your feelings out of a request, people may feel pressured to do something, but they won't know why. They're more likely to argue or use anger to push you and your wants away. That's why it's important, particularly in close relationships, to let people know where your wants are coming from—to give them a window on your full experience of a situation.

Your Thoughts

Your thoughts are your perceptions, your understanding of a situation. You explain your experience of what is happening and how you interpret it. Holly and Randy provide examples of how thoughts give background to requests:

Holly's thoughts: When you adjust the TV while I'm asking your advice, I wonder if you're really interested in helping me or whether it's too big a hassle.

Randy's thoughts: In your jokes I always end up seeming very stupid. And I imagine that's what you think of me.

Your Feelings

Feelings help the listener have empathy for your experience in a situation. The best way to express your feelings is in the form of "I messages." In "I messages" you take responsibility for your emotions. You say:

I felt hurt.
I was a little angry.
I felt left out.
I was saddened.
I was disappointed.
I felt mainly confused.

This is in contrast to "you messages," which are accusing and pejorative and dump all responsibility for your feelings on the other person:

You hurt me.
You made me angry.
You left me out.
What you did depressed me.
You disappointed me.
You confuse me.

Notice that "you messages" tend to make people defensive and hostile, while "I messages" seem less confrontive and tend to elicit concern.

Holly expressed her feelings toward Al like this: "I feel hurt when you don't seem interested." Randy's feelings toward his brother took this form: "I feel embarrassed in front of dad and a little angry."

Putting It Together

Whole messages are very compelling. It's time to generate whole messages of your own to complete your three assertive requests. The format is very simple:

I think (my understanding, perceptions, interpretations).
I feel ("I messages" only).
I want (distilled from your request outline).

Here is Holly's whole message:

When you adjust the TV while I'm asking your advice on the article, I wonder if you're really interested in helping me. Then I feel hurt. I really need your help with the editing. I'd like to go over the content and organization with you on a page-by-page basis. Could we get together after dinner Thursday for a three-hour editing session in the study? And if we don't finish, polish it off Saturday morning?

Here is Randy's whole message:

When you kid me about my clothes or my dates at family dinners, your jokes make me sound pretty stupid. And I imagine that's what you really think of me. I feel embarrassed in front of dad and a little angry. I'd really appreciate it if you'd go easy on the jokes. It would feel better if we could talk about how we're doing and what's been going on lately for each of us.

Here are some shorter examples of wants expressed in the form of whole messages:

I think I do more than my share of the work around here. I feel resentful when I'm working and you're reading the paper or watching TV. I want you to help me with setting the table and doing the dishes after meals.

I think George and I have a lot in common. I enjoy being out with him, and I'm getting to like him a lot. I want to invite him to dinner next week and have you help me make some lasagne.

I don't think your cousin is a very good mechanic. I feel obligated to take my car to him because he's family, but I get really pissed off when he can't fix things right the first time. The clutch is slipping again, and this time I want to take it to the shop downtown.

I think *Casablanca* is Bogart's best movie. I've always been attracted to his bittersweet, impossible love for Bergman. Let's go see it tonight.

When I tell you how hard my day was with the baby, you usually tell me that you had just as hard a day at work. Then sometimes I start to feel like you didn't hear me. I feel a little angry because I don't get to really tell you what's going on. When I complain about my day, it would feel really good if you heard me out for a while and then let me know that you understand how tough it is sometimes.

The case you're giving me is important, but I have three cases on my desk that are ready to go to trial. Frankly, I feel overwhelmed. I'm stressed to the limit. Can you possibly assign this to somebody else?

Rules for Requests

Work on your three requests until they are as clear, direct, and uncritical as possible. Then try them out on the people who can give you what you want. To help you in perfecting your requests, here are some rules for asking.

1. If possible, get the other person to agree on a convenient time and place for your conversation.
2. Keep your request small enough to avoid massive resistance.
3. Keep your request simple—just one or two specific actions for the other person to understand and remember.
4. Don't blame or attack the other person. Use "I messages" so that you will stick to your own thoughts and feelings. Try to be objective—stick to facts. Keep your tone of voice moderate.
5. Be specific. Give exact figures and times for what you want. Don't hedge. Don't make a lot of conditions. Describe what you want in terms of behavior, not a change in attitude.
6. Use assertive, high self-esteem body language: maintain eye contact, sit or stand erect, uncross your arms and legs, make sure that you're close enough. Speak clearly, audibly, and firmly,

without a whining or apologetic tone to your voice. Practice your requests in front of a mirror to correct problems in your body language. You can also listen to your request on tape to evaluate your voice tone and inflection.

7. Sometimes it's helpful to mention the positive consequences of giving you what you want. You could also mention the negative consequences of denying your request, but the positive approach works better. As the old adage has it, you're likely to catch more flies with honey than with vinegar.

When you have perfected your requests and practiced them in the mirror, go ahead and make them in real life. Taking that step will not be easy, but it will be very rewarding. Start with the least threatening person first. After you have made your prepared requests, go back to your list and prepare some others, still saving the most discomforting confrontations for last.

This is one area in which practice does make perfect and success builds upon success. As you work through your list of wants, you will soon find that you don't have to argue with yourself so much about whether a particular desire is reasonable or legitimate. You will need to spend less time rehearsing your requests. You will begin to see what you want more clearly and to ask for it spontaneously and directly.

You'll be surprised at how often people will simply say yes to a clear, nonjudmental request. You will reap double benefits by getting what you want and gaining more self-confidence as well.

11

Visualization

Visualization is a powerful, proven technique for refining your self-image and making important changes in your life. It involves relaxing your body, clearing your mind of distractions, and imagining positive scenes.

Whether or not you believe in the effectiveness of visualization doesn't matter. Faith in the technique may help you achieve results faster than a "nonbeliever," but faith isn't essential to the process. Your mind is structured in such a way that visualization works no matter what you believe. Skepticism may keep you from trying visualization, but it won't stop the technique from working once you do try it.

This chapter will teach you basic visualization techniques, give you practice in forming vivid mental impressions, and guide you in creating your own unique visualization exercises for improving your self-esteem.

Visualization raises your self-esteem in three ways: by improving your self-image, by changing the way you relate to others, and by helping you achieve specific goals.

Improving your self-image is the first and most important step. If you currently see yourself as weak and helpless, you will practice visualizing yourself as strong and resouceful. If you tend to think of yourself as unworthy and undeserving, you will create scenes in which you are obviously a valuable, worthy individual making an important contribution to your world. If you consider yourself sickly, accident-prone, and depressed, you will counter this belief with scenes of yourself as a healthy, careful, cheerful person.

The second step is to use visualization to change how you interact with others. You visualize scenes in which you are outgoing, assertive, friendly, and so on. You see yourself in satisfying relationships with your family, your mate, your friends, and your fellow workers. You imagine yourself forming new relationships with interesting, positive people who find you interesting and positive in your own right.

Third, you can use visualization to achieve specific goals. You imagine yourself getting that raise, finally earning that important degree, moving into that particular neighborhood, excelling in your favorite sport, making a real difference in your world—in short, being, doing, and having what you want in life.

Why Visualization Works

The chapter on handling criticism contains a metaphor that will help explain why visualization works. According to this metaphor, people experience reality indirectly, as if they were watching a TV screen in their heads. They don't experience the world as it really is—they can only see what's on their screens. And what's on their screen is determined to a large degree by the power of imagination. This means that your mind and body react in much the same way to imaginary experiences as to real experiences. In particular, your subconscious mind seems to make no distinction between "real" sensory data and the vivid sense impressions you conjure up during a visualization exercise.

For example, if you imagine yourself freely mixing at a party, you will get a boost of confidence nearly equal to actually going to the party and successfully interacting. And the imagining is easier, since you're totally in control and experiencing less anxiety.

The affirmations you will include in your visualizations serve as conscious, positive correction to the negative comments of your pathological critic. They form a "voice-over" component to your visualization, as if you were watching a documentary with a commentator explaining what you see on the screen.

Acquiring visualization skills is simply a matter of learning how to do consciously what you already do subconsciously. You already create, edit, and interpret what you see on your screen. If you have low self-esteem, you probably create scenes in which you are the underdog, edit out any compliments, and interpret much of what you see as evidence of your inadequacy.

You can replace much of this subconscious negative propaganda with visualized scenes in which you are the hero, you receive well-deserved compliments, and you perform competently. In the process of learning to form vivid mental images, you will also sharpen your ability to perceive reality accurately and observe yourself with more detachment and objectivity.

There's another way of understanding why visualization works so well to change your behavior and your image of yourself. Consider visualization as a method for reprogramming the way you make simple decisions. Every instant of every day you are faced with tiny, mostly unconscious decisions. Should you turn right or left? Have toast or a muffin? Call up Jan or put it off? Have another piece of pie or skip it? Wear your seat belt or ignore it? Run the yellow light or stop? Join the group by the water cooler or the people at the coffee machine?

Visualization reprograms your mind to recognize and choose the slightly more positive of any two choices. Over time, the sum of thousands of tiny positive choices is higher self-esteem and a lot more happiness.

This programming of your automatic decision making is nothing new. You do it already, but if you have low self-esteem, you do it in reverse. You visualize and subsequently choose the negative path. You see yourself as unworthy, and so you expect and choose to lose, to be rejected, to be disappointed, to be depressed, to be anxious, to be assailed by doubt and insecurity. You take the second piece of pie even though you are overweight. You are angry at yourself, so you don't wear your seatbelt and you try to beat the yellow light. You gravitate toward the negative people, the painful situations.

Visualization can change all this. You can use it to give a conscious, positive nudge to what has heretofore been an automatic, subconscious, and negative process. You can reprogram your choice-making apparatus so that you choose to win, to be accepted, to have your expectations met, to be positive, to be relaxed, to be bolstered by hope and confidence. You can reinforce your positive tendencies so that you turn down the fattening pie. You can appreciate yourself enough to wear the seatbelt and stop taking foolish chances. You can gravitate toward the positive people and emotionally healthy situations in which you have a chance to grow and succeed.

Imagine a school of fish, darting left and right, up and down at random. All exert the same energy to get nowhere in particular. If you could become a consciously programmed fish, you could get somewhere you want to go, without exerting any more energy than before.

Visualization Exercises

Step one in visualization is to get relaxed. The most effective visualizing happens while your brain is producing alpha waves, which can only happen when you are in a state of deep relaxation. The relaxed alpha state is one of heightened awareness and suggestibility.

Do your visualization exercises twice a day. The best times are just before falling asleep at night and upon awakening in the morning. You are particularly relaxed and in a suggestive frame of mind at these times.

First Session

Sit down in a chair that supports your head, or lie down on your back in a quiet place where you won't be disturbed. Make sure you're not too warm or too cold. Close your eyes.

Take a deep breath, letting the air slowly fill up your lungs so that your chest and stomach both extend. Let the air out slowly and completely. Continue to breathe like this, slowly and deeply.

Focus your attention on your feet. As you breathe in, notice any tension in your feet, and as you breathe out, imagine the tension flowing away. Your feet feel warm and relaxed.

Now focus on your calves, shins, and knees. As you breathe in slowly, notice any tightness in these areas. Let the tension ebb away as you slowly exhale, sinking into relaxation.

Move your attention up to your thighs. Breathe in and become aware of any tension in the large muscles of your upper legs. Exhale and let the tension flow away.

Now notice any tightness in your buttocks or pelvic area as you inhale. On the exhale, let this tightness loosen and dissolve.

Now notice as you inhale whether you are carrying any tension in your stomach muscles or your lower back. As you breathe out slowly, let any tension relax.

Breathe in slowly and notice any tightness in your chest or upper back. Exhale slowly and completely as the chest and back tension eases and flows away.

Now move your attention out to your hands. Breathe in and feel any tension in your fingers, palms, or wrists. Let this tension flow away as you exhale slowly.

Next move up to your forearms and focus on any tightness here as you inhale. Then exhale and let the tightness dissolve.

Inhale slowly and become aware of the tension in your upper arms. As you breathe out, let your biceps and other upper arm muscles become relaxed and heavy.

Now notice if you are holding tension in your shoulders. Breathe in and really focus on the tension. Breathe out and let the breath carry the tension away, out of your shoulders. Shrug your shoulders and take another breath if you need to to get the tension out of this area, which is often very tight.

Move up to your neck and feel all the tension there as you inhale. Exhale and let the tension flow out of your neck. If your neck still feels tight, roll your head around and take another full, deep breath to get your neck really loose.

Let your jaw hang open as you inhale and notice how you may be clenching your jaw. Move it around and let it relax as you exhale slowly and completely. Keep your jaw slightly open to make sure it stays relaxed.

Now focus on the muscles of your face as you breathe in: your tongue, mouth, cheeks, and forehead, and around your eyes. Let go of any squinting or frowning feelings as you exhale.

Finally, scan down your entire body. Notice any areas that are still a little tense, and let them relax fully as you continue to breathe slowly and deeply. At any time during your visualization you can come back to the relaxation phase and relax any areas that have become tense.

At first you may find that distracting thoughts pop into your mind when you try to visualize. That's normal. Just notice what the thoughts or images are and let them go. Resist the temptation to pursue enticing trains of thought and refocus your mind on the material you have planned to visualize.

1. In this first exercise you will concentrate on one sense at a time, imagining simple shapes and colors. This is similar to the way students of Tantric Yoga learn to meditate. Moslem and Sufi mystics use much the same approach to train their inner vision.

First you will exercise your interior sense of sight. Keep your eyes closed and imagine a black circle on a white background. Make the circle perfectly round, perfectly black. Make the background as bright and perfectly white as you can. Move your interior vision around the circle, seeing the perfect roundness of it, seeing the sharpness of the dividing line between the black and the white.

Now change the color of the circle to yellow. Make the yellow very bright, the clearest, most vivid primary yellow you can imagine. Keep the background bright and white.

Now let the yellow circle fade out and replace it with a green square. Make it a bright or a dark green, whichever you want. Keep the square perfect, not a rectangle or a parallelogram, but a true square.

Now erase the square and imagine a blue triangle. Make it a pure, primary blue, a blue like they had up on the wall of your first grade classroom to teach you the meaning of blue. Make the triangle an isosceles triangle with three sides of equal length.

Now erase the triangle and make a thin, red line. Make it a bright, fire-engine red. Check your background and make sure that it's still white.

Now let your imagination loose for a while and make a series of changing shapes in many different colors. Change the background as well as the foreground. Try to speed up your changes without losing the vividness or completeness or perfection of the images.

2. The next part of the exercise will concentrate on sound. Let your mental eye close. Make the shapes and colors go away. It may help to imagine that you are in a thick fog, where you can see nothing. Become "all ears."

First, hear a bell. Make it ring over and over. What kind of bell is it? Is it a church bell, a doorbell, a dinner bell, a ship's bell, a desk-captain's bell, a cowbell, or what?

Now hear a siren, far away, like a fire engine half a mile in the distance. Bring it closer, louder and louder, until you almost have to put your hands over your mental ears. Hear it scream past you. Hear the Doppler effect that makes it seem to get higher in pitch as it approaches, then drop in pitch as it passes you. Hear it fade away again in the distance until it can't be heard any longer.

Now hear the ocean crashing on a rocky beach. Hear the crash of the waves as they break far out. Hear the rumble and crunch as the white water piles up against the rocks. Hear the hiss and gurgle as the waves finally spend themselves on the sand and gravel of the shore. Throw in the cries of some seagulls. (If you've spent your life in a landlocked area, imagine the sounds of a creek swollen with spring rains, roaring, crashing, and tumbling down a rocky creekbed.)

Now hear the sound of the engine of a car. Start it up. Race it. Drive it up a steep hill and hear it labor. Hear it cough and sputter as you run out of gas.

Now listen carefully and hear your mother saying your name. Hear it with tones of love, and then tones of anger. Try it with exasperation, with happiness, with sadness. Do the same with your father's voice, your lover's voice, and the voices of others in your life.

3. The next part deals with the sense of touch. Imagine that your mental fog is thicker than ever. You can't see. And you have cotton stuffed in your ears so that you can't hear a thing. All you can do is feel. Imagine that you're sitting on a hard wooden chair. Feel the back and the bottom pressing against you. Imagine that there is a hard wooden tabletop in front of you. Reach out mentally and feel the hard, square edge and flat surface.

Now imagine that there are several objects on the table. Reach out and find the first one. It's a small sheet of coarse sandpaper, about three inches square. Feel the rough and the smooth sides. Run your fingers over them and really feel the grit on one side and the dry, smooth paper on the other. Flex the sheet in your hands and feel its resistance to bending. Keep folding until the paper buckles and folds in half.

Put the sandpaper down and pick up a same-sized piece of thick velvet. Feel how soft and plush it is. Raise it to your face and run it over your closed eyes, down over your cheeks and lips. Wad the velvet up and then smooth it out on the table.

Now let go of the velvet and pick up a smooth stone about the size of an egg. Feel how hard, smooth, cool, and heavy it is.

Now hold out your hand palm up and imagine that someone has put a dab of hand lotion into it. Mentally rub your hands together and smear the lotion all over them. Feel the slipperiness and coolness first, and then the warmth and comfort.

Continue to explore your sense of touch. Try plunging your hands into running warm water. Make the water hotter and cooler. Imagine touching warm, living human skin. Try stroking a cat or dog. Imagine the feel of your favorite tool or cooking utensil.

4. The next part of the exercise is focused on the sense of taste. Imagine that you still can't see or hear and now can't feel anything either. All you can do is taste. Imagine a few grains of salt on your tongue. Let the taste of salt flood your mouth, making you salivate and swallow.

Now change the salt to a few drops of lemon juice. Concentrate on the sensation of sourness. Feel your whole mouth pucker up.

Now touch the tip of your tongue to a very hot chili pepper. Feel the intense, spicy heat burning on your tongue.

Now cool the heat with a bite of vanilla ice cream: sweet, cold, smooth, and creamy. Really taste it.

Continue to taste a succession of your favorite foods. Eat a whole imaginary meal from soup to nuts.

5. Now you will concentrate on your sense of smell. Close off all your other senses and imagine the smell of Thanksgiving turkey. Reexperience the pleasure of coming into the kitchen or opening the oven door and smelling that rich, festive aroma.

Now do the same with your favorite perfume, cologne, or flower scent. Let the smell engulf your imaginary nostrils.

Continue with other smells you like, or even smells you don't like: pizza, wine, fresh bread, ocean air, new-mown hay, wet paint, hot tar, model glue, rotten eggs, and so on.

That's enough for now. Mentally recall where you are—the room, the furniture, and so on. Open your eyes when you are ready and reorient yourself before you get up. You may be a little dizzy if this has been a long or particularly vivid session for you.

Analyze your experience. Did one sense come easier than others? Most people's visual images are most intense, with sounds running second. It really doesn't matter which sense you find easier to imagine. Even though the word "visualization" implies that it is about the sense of vision, any sensory impressions you can form in your imagination will work. Capitalize on your strong point and emphasize whichever sense comes easiest to you.

All people can improve their ability to form imaginary sense impressions. As you practice forming sensory impressions in your mind, you will get better and better at it. The images and sounds and feelings will become stronger and more vivid. You will be able to add finer and finer details.

Improving your ability to imagine in one sensory modality will also improve your ability in the other modalities. If you started out only being able to see dim pictures and couldn't hear any sounds, keep practicing on the visual images. Your ability to see pictures will improve and generalize until you can also hear sounds. Feeling, taste, and smell will gradually become clearer as well.

Did you find it hard to concentrate on just one sense at a time? Perhaps when you were forming the blue triangle you got a flash of the sights, sounds, and smells of your first grade classroom. Perhaps you got a complete image of a fire engine when you tried to imagine "fire-engine red." Or while imagining the sounds of the ocean, you may also have smelled or tasted the salt air or felt the sand under your bare feet. This is a good sign. It shows that you have a knack for filling in the sensory details and including inputs from more than one sense system.

During the next few days, notice how your senses combine to form your experience. Notice how a meal at a restaurant is a complex blend of sense impressions: the sight of the food, the sound of the utensils and other diners, the taste and smell of the food, the feel of it in your mouth and as you swallow. The more you notice in the real world, the more vivid and enjoyable that world will become. Noticing your sense impressions and how they combine in your waking, conscious, walking-around state is also excellent practice for combining imaginary sense impressions to form vivid, effective visualizations.

Second Session

In this exercise you will practice creating a full, vivid experience containing impressions for all five senses. To begin, retire to your quiet spot and relax by using the relaxation procedure you learned in the first session.

Now you are going to build up a full experience of a red delicious apple. Start by visualizing the color red. Then shape the color into the outline of an apple—basically round, a little narrower at the bottom, bulging at the top. Now see the apple in three dimensions. Rotate the image in your mind so that you can see the little knobs underneath, the stem in the indentation in the top, and so on. If you haven't already done so, add shadings of color—from lighter red on one side to darker red on the other. Add the little white speckles that red delicious apples have all over them. See the shiny gleam. Let your image of the apple come to rest on an image of a plate.

Add some sounds now. Let the apple raise up an inch and drop with a thump onto the plate. Slide the plate across a wooden table. Now across a tablecloth. Hear the crunch of biting into an apple.

Now add the sense of touch. Pick up the apple in your hands and feel the cool, smooth, heavy weight of it. Slowly take a bite of the apple and feel the resistance as your front teeth break through the skin.

Now taste the first rush of sweet, slightly tart juice. Smell the sweet, fresh aroma.

Continue noticing one sense after another: the sight of the white flesh, the feel of the pulp as you chew, the taste of the skin and flesh, the smell, the cool, wet feeling, the heft and shape of the apple changing as you eat it. Keep going until you are done and have put the core back on the plate and wiped your lips and hands with a napkin.

End the exercise by coming back to the here and now. When you are ready, open your eyes and analyze the experience. Did you find that you imagined yourself in a particular room in your house? Did any images pop up from your childhood? Did you feel silly? Do you feel hungry for an apple? Did you feel full afterward?

Third Session

The first part of this session is an eyes-open exercise you can do any time. In a full-length or very large mirror, examine your face: hair color and style, forehead, eyebrows, eyes, nose, cheeks, smile and laugh lines, mouth, moles, marks, facial hair, pores, different colorings, ears, and so on. Practice smiling and looking serious. Become an expert on your own face. You'll be surprised at how many new things you notice in your own face.

Do the same for the rest of your body. Scan downward and study your neck, shoulders, arms, and hands. Check out your chest and stomach, your hips and legs. Turn around and see as much as you can of your back view. Notice your posture. Stand up straight and slowly slump down. Swing your arms around and march in place. Look at some old snapshots of yourself if you have them, to see how you have looked to other people. You need to get a clear, conscious idea of what you really look like to do the next step of the exercise.

Note that this should not be a critical appraisal. This is not the time to take an inventory of all the things you would like to change or wish were different.

When you have become an expert on your own appearance, you can go on to the second part of this exercise. Do this part in bed in the morning, as soon as you wake up. Keep your eyes closed and make sure you are still in a totally relaxed state.

Visualize yourself waking up in the morning. Feel the warm bed, see the dark of the inside of your eyelids. Hear the alarm clock. Feel the hard plastic of the clock button as you fumble to turn it off. Fall back into bed, sigh, groan, roll over and out of bed.

The floor is cold against your bare feet. Look around and observe your room: furniture, belongings, doors, and windows. Get your clothes and put them on, one at a time, feeling the fabric slide over your body. See the colors.

Do whatever grooming you usually do—combing hair, brushing teeth, and so on. Notice the smells of toothpaste, cosmetics, or whatever there is to smell. Notice any usual aches and pains in your body as you warm up and start moving. Make the scene as vivid and real as possible.

Now remind yourself that you are actually still lying in bed. Open your eyes and get up, performing all the actions that you have just visualized. Be very aware of the actual sensations as they compare with your visualization. Make careful note of the differences, of what you missed or got wrong.

Do this exercise every morning for a week, each time adding the details that you left out the day before to your visualization. You are developing your ability to image, in a way similar to a movie director learning to envision how a scene will look on camera before filming it.

A week of this kind of systematic practice will greatly increase the complexity and intensity of the imaginary scenes you create. This type of rehearsal is excellent preparation for creating your personal, self-esteem raising scenes.

The rules that follow will also help you form effective self-esteem visualizations.

Rules for Creating Effective Self-Esteem Visualizations

1. See yourself making small, positive steps each day toward your goal. Include the process as well as the product. If you want to stop being a wallflower, you can visualize yourself leading the band or doing a stand-up comedy routine at a big party. That's OK, but you should include some other, smaller steps. Hear yourself asking a familiar-looking stranger where you have met before. See yourself walking up to someone and asking for a dance. See yourself offering to pass out hors d'oeuvres at a party as a way to mingle and meet others.

2. Visualize overt behavior. Find images of yourself doing something, rather than just looking a certain way, possessing certain abstract qualities, or having certain things. Keep asking yourself, ''What does higher self-esteem mean to me in terms of behavior? What would I be doing if I had it? What would my behavior look like, sound like, feel like?'' For example, if you want to create an image of yourself feeling good about your abilities, you need more than an image of yourself smiling—that image could mean anything. Instead, see and hear yourself volunteering for a difficult but rewarding assignment. Hear some-

one complimenting you on a job well done, and hear yourself calmly acknowledging the compliment without any self-depreciation.

3. Include the positive consequences of higher self-esteem. See yourself successful at work, enjoying closer and more satisfying relationships, achieving goals.

4. Include assertive, high self-esteem body language: erect posture, leaning forward to people, smiling, arms and legs uncrossed, close to people rather than keeping your distance, nodding as someone else speaks, and touching others when appropriate.

5. See yourself struggling a bit at first, and then succeeding. This approach has been shown to be more effective than seeing yourself as successful from the first try.

6. See yourself liking you more, not just other people liking you more. The latter follows from the former, not the other way around.

7. See yourself as not only "better" in the future, but also as being basically OK right now.

8. Think of self-esteem as something you have, but are out of touch with. See yourself discovering your self-esteem like a treasure lost and found again. See dark clouds clearing away to reveal the sun that was always there. Hear beautiful music emerging from static as you tune into your self-love. Feel warmth and softness as you pull on a cashmere sweater you misplaced and have just found.

9. It's helpful to combine visualization with affirmations. Say a short affirmation during and at the end of each visualization scene. The affirmation will act like an hypnotic suggestion, reinforcing the visual, auditory, and tactile messages with a verbal message straight to your subconscious.

An affirmation is a *strong, positive, feeling-rich statement that something is already so.*

"Strong" means that an affirmation should be short, simple, and unqualified.

"Positive" means that it should not contain any negatives for your subconscious to misconstrue. Your subconscious tends to drop out the negatives, so that "I *do not* dwell on the past" is heard as "I *do* dwell on the past."

"Feeling-rich" means that an affirmation should put things in terms of emotions, not abstractions or theories. Say "I love myself" instead of "I acknowledge my innate value."

"Statement" means that an affirmation should be a declarative sentence, not a question, an order, or an exclamation.

"Already so" means that an affirmation should be in the present tense, since that's all your subconscious understands. Your unconscious mind is timeless, making no distinction between the past, the present, and the future—all is one big now.

Here are some examples of effective affirmations:

I love myself.
I am confident.
I am successful.
I do my best.
I am interested in life.
I am fine just the way I am.

The best affirmations for you will be the ones you compose to match your personality, circumstances, and goals. Affirmations that you have composed for exercises in other chapters can probably be adapted for use with your visualizations.

10. If you have deeply felt spiritual beliefs or theories about the cosmos, bring them into play in your visualization. Feel free to visualize God or Buddha or some symbol of universal love. You could see yourself treating yourself with respect and tender caring as a reflection of God's love for all humankind. You could visualize a universal love or energy streaming through the universe and picture your growth in self-esteem as a pulling away of screens that block that energy from reaching you. Use your beliefs in a creative way.

In general, it helps to see the universe as a place with sufficient emotional, physical, and spiritual nourishment for everybody—a benevolent universe that can potentially work for everyone. In such a universe, all humans are capable of change and improvement, all deserving of love, all with grounds for hope.

Self-Esteem Sessions

The sample sessions that follow are guidelines only. You will evolve your own personal, idiosyncratic versions, with the specific sensory details and affirmations that work best for you.

Self-Image Session

This is the first type of self-esteem visualization you should create for yourself. It is a general purpose session designed to correct the way you see yourself. You create scenes in which your behavior shows that you are worthy instead of unworthy, confident instead of doubtful, secure instead of anxious, cheerful instead of depressed, self-loving instead of self-hating, outgoing instead of shy, attractive instead of ugly, capable instead of helpless, good instead of bad, proud instead of guilty, and self-accepting instead of self-critical.

Prepare for the session by retiring to your quiet place and going through your relaxation routine. With your eyes closed, breathing slowly and deeply, imagine this first scene:

You are taking a shower. See the steam. Feel the warm, wet water hitting your back and running all over your body. Hear the sound of the running water. Smell the soap and shampoo.

You feel great: invigorated, warm, and loose. Luxuriate in the pure sensual pleasure. Tell yourself, "I deserve to enjoy this." Enjoy the sensation of getting clean all over, feeling new and refreshed.

Now you're out of the shower and dried off. You're getting dressed in your favorite clothes. See the colors of the clothes. Feel the textures as you slowly draw each article of clothing on over your clean, warm body. Tell yourself, "I deserve nice things. I deserve to feel good."

Go to the mirror. Admire your clothes. See how nice you look in them. Stand up straight and feel how clean and refreshed your skin feels under the clothes, how strong and resilient your muscles feel when you stand straight. Notice with pleasant surprise that your usual aches and pains are gone at this moment. Tell yourself, "I look fine."

Fix your hair the way you like it. Adjust your collar. Smile at yourself in the mirror. Actually feel the muscles in your face form the smile. Gaze at yourself smiling and notice how much more open and relaxed you look when you smile. When you see the parts of your appearance that you usually don't like, notice that they seem less dominant, less important. If a self-critical thought comes to mind, shrug your shoulders and let it pass. Tell yourself, "I'm actually OK just as I am."

Now go into the kitchen. See the kitchen in detail: the stove, the cupboards, and the sink just the way they are. Go to the refrigerator and open it. See it full of nutritious, appealing food: fresh fruits and vegetables, milk and juices, lean meats—whatever healthy foods you would like to eat. Look in the cupboards and see nutritious whole grains and beans, wholesome ingredients for the kinds of good food you'd like to prepare for yourself. Tell yourself, "I've got what I need."

Prepare a simple dish for yourself, something delicious and good for you. It could be a salad, some soup, or a nutritious sandwich. Take your time and enjoy the process of getting out the ingredients, slicing bread or vegetables, warming up the soup, arranging things attractively on the plate. Tell yourself, "I deserve to eat well."

See the colors, feel the temperatures and textures, smell the enticing aromas. Admire the dish you have made for yourself. Tell yourself, "I'm good at this."

Eat the dish, sitting down quietly at the table and taking your time. Linger over each bite, really tasting and savoring each bite of the delicious food you have made for yourself. When you're finished, feel how full and comfortable you feel, how nourished and at peace with life. Let a feeling of languorous contentment and well-being steal over you. Tell yourself, "I love myself. I take care of myself."

Clean up after yourself. As you are cleaning, drop a cup or a plate and break it. Tell yourself, "Oh well, it's no big deal." If derogatory labels pop into your mind like "stupid" or "clumsy" or "bad," cut them off and shrug your shoulders. Tell yourself, "I allow myself to make mistakes. I'm OK just as I am, mistakes and all."

Now get ready to leave your home. You are going for a leisurely walk. Go outside and stroll down the street. It's a sunny day, warm and pleasant. Enjoy the feel of your muscles moving, your lungs breathing the fresh, pure air, the warmth of the sun on your shoulders. Notice how your usual aches and pains seem to have disappeared at this moment. Notice how bright and crisp and clear everything looks. Hear the sounds of birds, a dog barking in the distance, cars going by, music playing on a radio somewhere. Tell yourself, "I can enjoy the simple things of life."

See someone walking toward you, a stranger or a neighbor you recognize but don't actually know. See the stranger catch your eye and smile at you. You nod and flick your gaze downward, breaking eye contact. Feel the little flutter in your chest, the little sinking feeling or chilling jolt of adrenalin that you usually feel and call shyness or reserve.

Now see another stranger approach. Again the stranger meets your eye and smiles. This time, maintain eye contact and give a small smile in return. Tell yourself, "I am willing to take risks."

Once more, see another stranger approach and smile at you. This time, maintain eye contact, smile widely, and say loudly and clearly, "Hi, how are you?" Continue walking down the sidewalk, smiling slightly to yourself. Tell yourself, "I am outgoing and confident."

Now get ready to end this session. Recall your surroundings. When you are ready, open your eyes and get up. As you go about your daily routine, recall this visualization and repeat your affirmations to yourself: "I deserve nice things. I deserve to feel good. I look fine. I am actually OK just the way I am. I've got what I need. I deserve to eat well. I'm good at doing things. I love myself. I take care of myself. I allow myself to make mistakes. I'm OK just as I am, mistakes and all. I can enjoy the simple things of life. I am willing to take risks. I am outgoing and confident."

Here are some further suggestions for self-image scenes: making a doctor's appointment for a checkup; receiving a compliment gracefully; shopping for new clothes or furnishings; buying vitamins, cosmetics, or exercise equipment; enjoying physical exercise or cultural activities; spending enjoyable quiet time alone; being successful at a sports activity; enjoying your favorite recreation. Choose these or other situations in which you tend to be hard on yourself or which would constitute evidence of higher self-esteem for you if you did them.

Make sure that you follow the rules about visualizing overt behavior, including positive body language, stressing self-acceptance first, and seeing yourself as basically OK in the present.

Relationships Session

This series of scenes focuses on how you feel about your dealings with others. The important issues are feeling comfortable in the company of others, expressing yourself adequately, asking for what you want, responding to criticism, and in general feeling that you can hold your own as an equal, worthy participant in your interactions with others.

The following visualization is just a guideline. Use it as a model for designing your own scenes that are appropriate to your personality and situation in life.

Prepare for the visualization by retiring to your quiet place and taking plenty of time to get completely relaxed. When you are relaxed and ready to begin, imagine the following:

You're having dinner in a good restaurant with someone you like. It can be someone you actually know now, someone you would like to know better, or someone you just make up. See the candlelight, smell the food, taste what you are eating, hear the muted clink of cutlery and hum of conversation. Look across the small, intimate table and see your friend. Smile and laugh at a witty remark. Hear your friend laughing with you. Say to your friend, "You know, this is fun. I really enjoy being with you." Your friend replies, "Well, thanks, what a nice thing to say. I always have a good time with you, too." Tell yourself, "I enjoy being with friends. My friends enjoy being with me."

Now imagine that you are at home talking to another person. You have planned to spend the evening together, and this other person is suggesting that you try a new Hungarian restaurant and then go to see a foreign film in the next town. See the other person clearly. Hear the tones of voice as he or she tries to persuade you.

Imagine that the other person is someone you want to please, someone with whom you would usually agree automatically. But this time, notice that you are tired and that your feet hurt. You'd really rather order a pizza and stay home and watch TV.

Watch yourself square your shoulders, take a deep breath, and admit: "Well, I'm real tired tonight, and what I'd rather do is order a pizza and stay home. We could watch TV and just relax. I don't feel up to a lot of driving and staying out late."

Listen as your friend expresses sympathy and agrees to stay home with you. Tell yourself, "I can ask for what I want."

Now imagine that you are in a classroom, a business meeting, a committee meeting, or some kind of discussion group. See the room, hear the voices of the other people, notice what you are wearing, the decor of the room, the clock on the wall. Take some time to make the scene real for yourself.

As you listen to the discussion, you realize that the group is try-ing to come to a unanimous agreement, and that they will never all agree. You get the idea that you should all vote and accept the deci-sion of the majority.

Watch and listen to yourself as you sit up straighter in your chair, clear your throat, take a deep breath, and interrupt the squabbling by saying, "Wait a minute." When you have everyone's attention, say: "I think we could discuss this all night and still not agree. I suggest that we put it to a vote and abide by majority rule. There are other, more important issues we need to move on to."

See the other people smile and nod their heads. Listen as the leader of the group thanks you and proceeds to take a vote. Tell yourself, "I have valuable opinions. I can speak up in a group."

For the next scene, imagine that you are talking to your mother or father or someone else who knows you well and has strong opin-ions about your life. Scan this person's facial features and listen care-fully to the tone of voice as you hear the critical comment "I don't know why you don't move out of that neighborhood. It's turning into a slum. Surely you could do better."

As this criticism registers with you, notice how you lean back from the attack just slightly. Notice how your posture becomes more de-fensive—perhaps you fold your arms or turn your head away.

Then see yourself rally to respond to the criticism assertively. Ac-tually feel your arms uncrossing, your head lifting, and your gaze meeting your critic's eyes. Hear yourself responding in a calm, reason-able tone: "Yes, you're probably right. This neighborhood is getting pretty run-down." Notice that you don't apologize or defend or ex-plain or argue. Tell yourself, "I can acknowledge criticism and keep my self-respect."

Now prepare to end the visualization. Become aware of your sur-roundings and slowly open your eyes and reorient yourself. As you run into people in your everyday life, recall your interpersonal visuali-zations and bring to mind the appropriate affirmations: "I enjoy be-ing with friends. My friends enjoy being with me. I can ask for what I want. I have valuable opinions. I can speak up in a group. I can acknowledge criticism and keep my self-respect."

Here are some other situations you could try: asking for a date, enjoying new people, successfully handling a complaint or a socially awkward situation, returning some unwanted merchandise, saying "I love you" to someone and meaning it as a compliment, asking for a raise, applying for a job, or saying no to someone who wants you to do something that you don't want to do. Pick situations in which you usually feel insecure and one-down.

When creating interpersonal scenes, the important rules to re-member are the ones about including a certain amount of initial struggle, assertive body language, and positive consequences, and stressing how self-acceptance comes before acceptance by others.

Goals Session

Setting and achieving goals can give a big boost to your self-esteem. Visualization is one of the most effective tools for clarifying your goals and creating an expectation of success.

Start small, with simple, short-term goals. Pick the kind of everyday goals that you tend to beat yourself up about: getting to work on time, exercising a certain amount every week, finishing school assignments, writing important letters, getting your teeth looked at, and so on. When you're just starting to use visualization, it won't help very much to visualize grandiose accomplishments or valuable possessions twenty years down the line.

The visualizations that follow give several examples of how to envision simple goals. Use them as a model for creating your own images of what you want to accomplish.

Sit or lie down in a quiet place and do your favorite relaxation exercise. When you are relaxed and in a suggestible frame of mind, imagine the following scenes:

First, visualize getting to work or class on time. Hear the alarm clock. See yourself waking up, shutting off the alarm, and getting right out of bed. Continue with your routine of showering, dressing, eating, and leaving with plenty of time to get where you need to be on time. Add the kind of multisensory details that you have used before to make your visualization vivid and convincing.

Throughout this scene, add details that show you are relaxed, unhurried, and efficient. You find your keys and your papers right where you set them out the night before. You have busfare or gas in your car or a babysitter lined up—whatever you need to have in place in order to be on time. Say to yourself, "I'm organized and punctual."

Invent a few obstacles, such as hearing the phone ring or your battery being dead. See yourself calmly cutting the phone call short or getting a jump from your neighbor's car. Tell yourself, "I can stay relaxed and focused on my timetable."

Visualize the positive benefits of arriving on time. You are relaxed and ready to start your day. Your boss or teacher or the other people there are pleased with you. You are off to a good start. Tell yourself, "I am managing my time well."

Before leaving this scene, tell yourself, "Right after dinner tonight, before turning on the TV, I will make sure I have everything I need for the morning."

Now imagine another scene. Imagine that you have been putting off working on your dissertation, your tax forms, or an important application that you have to fill out. The deadline is approaching. See yourself going into your office or the library. Set out all the materials you need: paper, pens, files, books, receipts. Notice how you organize your work into logical steps and calmly, persistently work your way through them. Tell yourself, "One step at a time wins the race."

Include some difficulties. Feel yourself getting tired, impatient, and discouraged. Your eyes are burning, your stomach is sour, your mind wants to switch off. Get up and stretch, take a walk around the room, and then get back down to it. See yourself getting a second wind, figuring your way past a confusing part. Tell yourself, "I can handle this."

See and hear and feel what it's like to type the final page of the dissertation, sign the bottom of your tax form, or stuff the application into an envelope and mail it. Say to yourself, "I'm finished in plenty of time."

See the positive results of meeting your deadline: the pleased smile of your chairperson when you deliver your completed dissertation, the new VCR you buy with your tax refund, the notification that your application has been accepted. Tell yourself, "I deserve this reward."

Before leaving this scene, tell yourself, "I will gather up the material I need first thing in the morning."

Now move on to the next scene. Imagine that you have been wanting to get outdoors more, get some exercise, and grow some of your own food. Imagine and fill out with sensory details each of the logical steps you will have to take.

See yourself getting your landlord's permission to plant a vegetable garden. Imagine the sights, sounds, and smells of going to the nursery to pick out tomato plants, radish and lettuce seeds, onion bulbs, and cucumber plants. Tell yourself, "It's easy when I take just one step at a time."

Really feel the earth in your hands, the hard wooden handle of the borrowed spade, the sun on your bare shoulders as you turn over the soil in your planting beds and rake it smooth. Tell yourself, "I'm good at this."

Imagine the careful planting, the straight rows, the watering, the first sprouts, the weeding and watching. Finally, see yourself harvesting your own vegetables, washing them, and fixing a big, bountiful salad. Tell yourself, "I'm nurturing myself as I nurture my garden."

Include the positive consequences: your tan, your muscle tone, how pleasant and productive the backyard looks. See yourself with several friends at dinner; you tell them, "Everything in the salad is from my garden." Tell yourself, "I take care of myself."

Just before you leave this scene, tell yourself, "I will take the first step and talk to the landlord tomorrow after work."

Now get ready to come out of the scene. Remember where you are, and open your eyes when you are ready. Remind yourself of your final affirmation about performing the first step by a certain time and resolve once more to do it.

When you create your own visualizations, stick to one goal at a time, not three separate ones as in the above sample session. Remember to keep your goals simple and short-term at first. The self-esteem boost that you get from achieving small goals will give you the confidence you need to set and accomplish bigger, more long-term goals later.

The most important rules for forming effective goal visualizations are to break things down into small steps, concentrate on observable behavior, see yourself struggling at first, include the positive consequences of accomplishing your goal, and end with an affirmation spelling out the first step and when you will perform it.

Special Considerations

If a visualization session isn't going easily, stop and return to it later. Effective visualization is pleasant and nearly effortless. It depends on a state of relaxed receptivity. If you are too tense or preoccupied, you're better off doing something else and saving the visualization for a more peaceful time.

Some results will come right away. Others will appear erratically or take a long time to show up. Other results will be unexpected. Take what you get, be patient, and try not to get discouraged. Your subconscious may be working out some big changes, while your conscious mind, especially your pathological critic, is telling you that nothing is happening and the whole technique is a waste of time. Do the exercises faithfully for at least a month before you make any decision about quitting or trying some other technique.

The best results come when you aren't trying too hard or expecting too much. It's a paradox: you have to let go of what you want before you can get it. View your visualization exercises as pleasant and relaxing in and of themselves, whether they "work" eventually or not.

12

Hypnosis for Self-Acceptance

Hypnosis is a powerful tool for change. It can alter how you think and feel at the deepest levels. For years, hypnotherapists have been helping clients increase feelings of self-acceptance and worth by using the highly suggestible trance state to change past negative programming. But you don't need a hypnotherapist to receive the benefits of hypnotic suggestion. You can do it yourself by learning the simple techniques outlined in this chapter.

Why Hypnosis?

You begin forming your sense of self at a very early age. By age two, you are able to differentiate yourself from others. You are aware of when your parents approve and disapprove of you. As you begin to grasp the subtleties of language, you get very specific feedback about your behavior and its effect on others. You accumulate a sense of self from thousands of small interactions during which parents communicate some judgment about you, the person. While your conscious mind has forgotten nearly all the times your father called you stupid or your mother fumed that you were selfish, your subconscious has recorded every word. Every negative attack is retained in your subconscious, exactly as you heard it. Every look of irritation or disgust is there. Every time you felt blamed, every time you were not comforted is recorded there.

Your picture of yourself, your sense of who you are is really a summation of all the material held in the storehouse of your subconscious mind. And that's why improving self-esteem is such hard work: it's very difficult to argue with all those thousands of judgments. In your conscious mind, you may assert that you are a good and worthy person. But your subconscious is saying, "Yeah, but what about the time you lost the keys to your father's car? And what about your father hating you so much he just moved out? And when your mother told you you did sloppy work? And what about her hitting you for lying about breaking the St. Francis statue?" It's like boxing with a phantom. These memories are locked away, silently influencing you. You can't refute or reframe them because your conscious mind has forgotten most of the specifics of what happened. Enter hypnosis. Hypnosis has the power to speak directly to your subconscious mind.

Changing Negative Programming

Because subconscious memories and beliefs are difficult to influence with the "logic" of your conscious mind, you need to learn the language of the subconscious, the language of images and suggestion. During the trance state, you can communicate directly and effectively with your subconscious and begin to challenge some of your deeply held negative beliefs. You can begin to replace your old programming (based on childhood experiences) with an accurate self-assessment (based on an adult recognition of your strengths). You can literally erase old negative labels and learn forgiveness for your mistakes. You can start to let go of some of the old rules about who you should have been, how you should act, and what you should feel. Instead, you can tell your subconcious that you have always done your best, that you have legitimate needs, and that you are worthwhile because you feel and live.

The basic task of hypnosis is to soften the judging parental voice (the pathological critic). Gradually, affirmations repeated in the trance state begin to take root. You feel a growing sense of compassion for the person you are. You must recognize, however, that the judging voice won't disappear in a few days or even a few weeks. It took years and thousands of negative interactions to plant that voice in your subconscious. Even in the trance state, where you are tremendously open to suggestion and change, it will take many, many repetitions of self-accepting affirmations before your old programming lets go.

Hypnosis as a Memory Tool

The key affirmations and mantras in this book are not always easy to recall. Reading them once or twice will do you absolutely no good unless you remember them. And remembering them requires repetition. Hypnosis has enormous potential for enhancing your memory because (1) it repeats positive messages while you are highly suggestible, (2) it implants these messages into your subconscious mind, and (3) it can direct you to use these messages at appropriate times (for example, when the critic is kicking you). If you use the hypnotic induction in this chapter, it is guaranteed that you will at least remember the basic affirmations you need to raise your level of self-esteem. You will also be more likely to *use* the affirmations when feeling depressed and vulnerable to the voice that says, "Look at those stupid mistakes at work! Look how you've raised your kid! Look how you waste your money!"

You don't have to believe the affirmations in the hypnotic induction for them to work. Because you are in a very special state of relaxation and openness, they will take root on their own. Hypnosis helps you let go of the frustrations and defeats in a day. You drift to a special place of calmness and peace. In that place you are more accepting, you listen. And belief comes gradually, like a shoreline that at first seems distant, a faint shadow on the horizon. But slowly it grows more distinct, more real as you approach the beach.

Hypnosis as a Learning Tool

Your old cognitive style used global labeling, mind reading, and self-blame to slap you down. In chapter five on "Cognitive Distortion," you learned healthier, more realistic ways of thinking. Hypnosis will reinforce a new way of thinking that doesn't use labels, doesn't blame, and doesn't assume negative judgments in the minds of others. You can learn more effectively with hypnosis because it bypasses your conscious mind. It talks to your subconscious, where hypnosis not only teaches, but also *motivates* you to think differently.

What Is Hypnosis?

First and foremost, hypnosis is a state that's *natural* for all humans and many animals. One form of hypnosis is shock, the response to trauma that cools skin temperature and minimizes bleeding while decreasing movement and breathing. But you don't need to have been in shock to understand hypnosis. You have already been in a trance state many times! You have entered hypnosis while daydreaming, driving long distances on the freeway, remembering sequential events,

watching TV, and so on. In fact, nearly any automatic activity can induce a trance. You may have noticed that after a strong emotion, particularly anger or grief, you enter a period of emotional numbness.
You feel shut down, "out of it." When that happens, you have entered
hypnosis. This state allows you a few moments of tranquillity to lower
your stress levels and begin to heal.

Self-hypnosis is *absolutely safe.* No case of harm from self-hypnosis has ever been reported. You are in complete control. You will
go no deeper than you feel comfortable and you can terminate the
trance whenever you wish. (One caution: if you record your induction on tape, never play that tape while driving or operating machinery.
The best place to play your tape is while sitting comfortably in a chair
or lying in bed.)

Some people have real misconceptions about the nature of hypnosis. One belief is that you have not entered hypnosis if you can still
hear and feel the world around you. This is not true. At a moderate
trance level (which is all you could expect to achieve with the induction in this chapter), you are very aware of sounds and sensations. In
fact, the ticking clock may sound much louder, the itching on your
leg seems more intense. Another belief is that people under hypnosis
might not be able to "come out" or move if they needed to. The truth
is that you are in a state of hyper-relaxation and suggestibility, not coma
or paralysis. You can open your eyes, make decisions, and move any
time you need to. A third misconception is that self-hypnosis might
induce nightmare images or visions for some people. The truth is that
it won't—unless you happen to have taken LSD before playing your
tape. During the trance you will see yourself relaxing in a special,
peaceful place. That's about it.

Here is what you can expect during a trance:

1. *Economy of action and relaxation.* You will experience a
   reduction of muscular activity and energy output. Subjectively
   you feel languorous and lazy.
2. *Limb catalepsy* (a kind of rigidity in the muscles of your arms
   and legs). Your limbs will tend to stay in any position in which
   they are placed, almost as if they had become heavy lead
   pipes.
3. *Taking words at their literal meaning.* If you asked a hypnotized person, "Would you tell me your wife's name?" he would
   merely reply, "Yes." If you asked him, "Do you know how
   to get to the zoo from here?" he would say yes or no, but
   wouldn't give you the directions.
4. *Exclusion of negatives.* Hypnotized people often don't hear
   the negatives in a sentence. If you said to a hypnotized person, "You do not like to smoke," it could be heard as "You

like to smoke." If you said, "You do not want to listen to your critic," it would very possibly be heard as "You want to listen to your critic." Using negatives during hypnosis creates the risk of reaping the exact opposite of the result you planned.

5. *Narrowing of attention.* All you seem to care about is the voice on the tape or your own suggestions. You hear other things, you feel sensations, but they don't seem to matter. It's as if your mind had become incredibly lazy. You get very focused because it's too much work to think about anything else.

6. *Increased suggestibility.* You feel like doing what your voice on the tape says. You feel like taking your own suggestions. It seems right. You feel open to anything, it's all fine with you. Imagery especially intensifies the suggestions. For example, if you see your legs as heavy lead pipes, they really do feel much heavier. If you imagine your eyes glued shut, it seems much harder to open them. If you imagine yourself walking tall with a confident smile, then the suggestion that you are feeling stronger and more capable has more weight.

Elements of the Self-Esteem Induction

The best way to understand hypnosis is to examine the anatomy of an induction. What follows is a step-by-step description of the self-esteem induction, with examples of the suggestions that typify each step.

Step 1. Preparing to relax.
Let your eyes begin to close . . . and as they close take a deep breath . . . a deep breath all the way down into your abdomen. Now you can begin to relax every muscle in your body.

This step helps you to focus attention inside your body. As your eyes close, you begin to think about your breathing and your inner sensations. Your awareness of the outer world decreases somewhat as you start to relax.

Step 2. Systematic relaxation of your body.
Let your legs begin to feel heavy . . . heavier and heavier as they relax . . . heavier and heavier as they let go of the last bit of muscular tension. Your legs are becoming more and more heavy and relaxed . . . like heavy lead pipes. Imagine them as heavy lead pipes . . . so heavy and relaxed.

You relax your legs, arms, face, neck, shoulders, chest, and abdomen in order. As you relax every muscle in your body, you become more and more internally focused. You also become more mentally relaxed as the physiological tension eases.

Step 3. Using imagery to deepen relaxation.
You feel that you are drifting and drifting . . . floating and drift-
ing down, down, down into total relaxation . . . feeling almost
drowsy, feeling peaceful and calm.

The imagery suggests that you are going deeper, which facilitates the
narrowing of attention. The drifting implies a weightlessness, a lighten-
ing of burdens.

Step 4. Deepening the trance.
And now you see a staircase . . . a staircase going down to a
lovely, peaceful place. In a moment you'll go down the stairs,
and with each step you will relax. You will relax more deeply
with each step. You will count backward from ten to zero, count-
ing each step as you become more and more deeply relaxed . . .
drifting down each step . . . relaxing more and more deeply.
Ten . . . nine . . . eight . . . seven . . . six . . . five . . . four . . . three
. . . two . . . one . . . zero.

The staircase going down is standard imagery for deepening hypnosis.
The count is very important, because the process of following this sequence frequently acts as the trigger for entering trance. If you are uncomfortable with the staircase image, don't be afraid to substitute. Use
an elevator or escalator or a path going "down, down, deep into a
redwood forest."

Step 5. Entering your special place.
And now you come to a special place . . . your special place where
you feel safe and calm . . . calm and peaceful. You feel totally
relaxed in your special place. You look around, you notice the
shapes and colors in your special place. You listen for the sounds
of your special place. You notice how your body feels in this
special place.

The special place is where you go for total peace and relaxation. It
could be a place you've actually been, or a completely made-up place.
It could be your room as a child or a dappled glade full of tall grass
and wild flowers. It doesn't matter. What's important is that it works
for you. The image has to evoke the desired state of calm. Take some
time right now to choose your special place. Close your eyes and try
to get a picture of it. See the shapes and colors. Is anyone with you,
or are you alone? Now listen for sounds. If you're at the beach, hear
the waves crashing, the hiss of foam as they recede, hear the seagulls
calling overhead. Now notice how your body feels in the special place.
Are you warm, can you feel the sun? Can you feel the ground beneath
you? The more complete your image, the more sense modalities you
use to construct it (sight, sound, feel, smell), the more relaxed you will
become.

Step 6. Erasing negative programming.

Now see a blackboard with the old negative labels you have been given in the past. See them on the blackboard. But you are a good person . . . a good person . . . you are a good person . . . you are fine . . . you are fine the way you are and you have always done the best you can. See those labels on the blackboard and now see an eraser in your hand. You have an eraser and you erase those labels from the board. You erase each one. They are gone. They are without meaning for you now. And now you write something on the board. You write your affirmation for today. You see yourself writing your positive affirmation.

The blackboard image is extremely powerful. You get to literally erase the old labels that critical parents assigned to you and replace them with healthy affirmations. You get to assert your worth so that your subconscious mind can gradually evolve a more positive self-portrait. "Your affirmation for today" refers back to chapter four on "Accurate Self-Assessment," where an exercise asked you to develop a new affirmation each day from your list of strengths. So at this point in the introduction you simply visualize yourself writing that brief sentence on the blackboard.

You see your affirmation on the board and now you add three of your important strengths that make you feel good . . . feel good . . . feel good. You write three of your strengths and you feel good writing them.

Again this refers to the exercises in chapter four. Choose three strengths from your list of positive qualities before listening to the induction. Preferably, these should be one-word descriptions. When you hear the suggestion to add three strengths to the blackboard, see yourself writing your preselected items.

Step 7. Disarming the critic.

And now you know you can let go of your critic. You no longer need the critic. The critic always lies and you reject him. You reject your critic. The critic has cost you too much. And now you see what he has cost you.

This segment of the induction refers back to the chapter three on "Disarming the Critic." It encourages your subconscious to push away the voice of the critic, to disown him. It reminds you that you have other ways to meet the needs your critic meets—you no longer need him. "The critic has cost you too much" refers to the exercise where you listed the toll your critic takes on work, relationships, and your level of well-being. "See what he has cost you" is your cue to remember one of the items from that list. As with other "inserts," it helps to select this item in advance.

Step 8. Letting go of shoulds.
You are letting go of your unhealthy shoulds. You are letting go of rules that no longer fit you. You are letting go of the rules that hurt you.

This harkens back to chapter seven on "shoulds." The basic message to your subconscious is that your shoulds must fit the unique person you are; the rules you live by must enhance your life, they must be good for you, and they must lead to positive outcomes. You are letting go of shoulds that don't fit, you reject them.

Step 9. Creating compassion.
You are kind to yourself. You are a good person . . . a good person. You are worthwhile because you live and feel. You are a unique and valuable human being because you live and feel. And you feel warm and loving toward yourself.

The message here comes from chapter six on "Compassion." Your worth does not depend on what you do, on your behavior. Your worth comes from being alive. You are aware and you feel and that is enough to make you valuable. It would be very hard to convince your subconscious of this message with rational argument. You have years of programming that makes your subconscious believe the opposite. However, by repeating this message in a trance state, you can *directly* influence your subconscious toward a different sense of self.

Step 10. Revising old projections.
People see you as a good person, a worthwhile person. Those who fail to see your worth have something on their screen that keeps them from seeing the good person you are. When people really see you, they see you as a good person.

One of the ways you've suffered in the past is to mind-read that others are reacting negatively to you. You project that they are judging you as stupid, selfish, ugly, and so on. You imagine that everyone is your critic, seeing you in the same harsh light. The suggestions in step 10 remind your subconscious that you are a good person and that other people see you that way. Refer to the metaphor of the TV screen introduced in chapter nine to reframe any rejection you suffer as a perceptual failure on the other person's part.

Step 11. Accepting mistakes.
You know now that you are free to make mistakes, it is fine to make mistakes. You do the best you can. You always do the best you can within the limits of your awareness. Within the limits of what you know at any given time you do the best you can. You love yourself, mistakes and all. You are a good person. You learn from your mistakes and you are free to make them.

One of the main issues raised in chapter eight on "Handling Mistakes" is that everyone does his or her best at any given moment in time. You make the best decision you can based on what you know, what you need, your history, the strategies you've learned to solve the problem. If your awareness were different, you might make a very different decision. But with your current awareness, you always make the best available choice. The suggestions in this step also implant in your subconscious the affirmation that you accept mistakes, that you do not expect perfection. This is enormously important, because perfectionism and the fear of error are major impediments to improving self-esteem.

Step 12. Posthypnotic suggestions.

Today you like yourself more than yesterday, and tomorrow you will like yourself more than today. And tomorrow you will feel able to believe more of the positive about yourself. You will remember more and more of the positive about yourself.

The object of a posthypnotic suggestion is to accelerate positive change in the future. You are already in a suggestible state; this is the perfect time to suggest ways you will continue to feel better about yourself *after* the trance is over.

Step 13. Coming-up suggestions.

In a few moments you will count back up from one to ten. You will come all the way up feeling alert, refreshed, and wide awake.

The purpose of the suggestions "alert, refreshed, and wide awake" is to make sure you don't come out of the trance feeling a little dopey and half-asleep. Hypnosis should make you feel like you've had a good, restful nap, ready for the rest of the day.

Step 14. Coming up count.

You're starting to come up . . . one . . . two . . . coming up . . . three . . . four . . . feeling more and more alert . . . five . . . feeling refreshed . . . six . . . coming up to full consciousness . . . seven . . . alert and more and more awake . . . eight . . . opening your eyes . . . nine . . . ten . . . fully alert, refreshed and wide awake.

This is the end of the trance. When you record this part, you should let your voice get louder, with more emphasis. You should give yourself a moment to get used to the room and make the transition back to full consciousness.

Recording Your Induction

Recording your induction is an option, not a must. It is quite possible to memorize the basic outline and main affirmations. You will then

simply close your eyes and make all the suggestions internally. Shift
the induction to the first person ("My eyes are beginning to close . . .
and as they close I take a deep breath") if that feels more comfortable.

If you have had no previous experience with hypnosis, it will probably be easier to record your induction. Here's what you should do
to prepare for the recording:

1. Preselect your daily affirmation and three strengths from your
   strengths list. You also need to preselect one item from the
   list of what your critic has cost you.
2. Select your special place and practice imaging it until the
   scene truly has a relaxing effect. Decide whether you want
   to use the "special place segment" of the induction or rewrite it as a specific description of your particular special place
   (using sight, sound, touch, and perhaps even smell sense modalities).
3. Read the induction aloud several times to get familiar with it.
   Record yourself practicing so you can hear how it sounds. Read
   slowly and keep your voice level.
4. Use a good quality 60-minute cassette (30 minutes per side).
5. Select a quiet place where you will not be interrupted.
6. Get comfortable. If you end up shifting around or feeling uncomfortable, your movements will affect the quality of your
   recording.
7. Prepare yourself mentally to be relaxed. If you don't sound
   relaxed, the recording will bring very limited results.

The Hypnotic Voice

There are basically two voice styles you can use for an induction.
The easiest for the beginner is the *monotone voice.* This voice is without inflection. There is no change in pitch or volume. You drone the
phrases of the induction, pausing between each phrase where you see
three dots, pausing a little longer when you come to a period at the
end of a sentence. Try not to vary the tempo, and speak each word
with an even beat.

The *rhythmic voice* sounds very different. Here you have a definite
cadence of stressed and unstressed syllables. "You are slipping *deep*er
and *deep*er, *drift*ing and *drift*ing into *to*tal relax*a*tion." "Now you are
letting *go,* letting *go* of the last bit of *ten*sion." "And you ac*cept* your
*feel*ings because they are *part* of you and you are a good *person.*" It
doesn't matter which syllables you stress, but the overall effect must
be relaxing. It has to work. If it doesn't, stick with the monotone voice.

You may wish to emphasize certain words or phrases in your induction. There are three ways to do this:

1. Distort the word. For example, "You are going doooown, doooown, doooown." You might stretch out the words "heavy" or "good" or "kind."
2. Momentarily raise the pitch of your voice. You might say, "You *love* yourself, mistakes and *all*," with raised pitch for special emphasis. "You are *kind* to yourself" might also deserve a pitch change for emphasis.
3. Silent pause. You can give special meaning to a word or phrase by pausing momentarily afterward. A brief silence often lends more weight or significance to a suggestion.

The Self-Esteem Induction

Let your eyes begin to close . . . and as they close take a deep breath. A deep breath all the way down into your abdomen. Now you can begin to relax every muscle in your body. Let your legs begin to relax . . . let your legs begin to feel heavy . . . heavier and heavier as they relax . . . heavier and heavier as they let go of the last bit of muscular tension. Your legs are becoming more and more heavy and they relax . . . like heavy lead pipes. Imagine them as heavy lead pipes . . . so heavy and relaxed. Your arms too are becoming more and more heavy . . . heavier and heavier as if they had become heavy lead pipes. You feel gravity pulling them down. You feel your arms letting go of the last bit of muscular tension . . . letting go . . . letting go . . . letting go of tension as they get heavier and heavier, more and more deeply relaxed. Your arms and legs feel heavy, heavy, and relaxed. Your body is relaxing as your arms and legs let go of the last bit of muscular tension. They are totally relaxed. And now your face begins to relax . . . your face begins to let go, let go, let go of tension. Your forehead becomes smooth as silk, smooth as silk . . . your forehead feels smooth and relaxed, letting go of tension . . . letting go of all the tensions of the day . . . letting go of every worry and concern . . . becoming smooth and relaxed as you let go of any worries from the day. And your cheeks too are becoming relaxed, smooth and relaxed . . . your cheeks are relaxed and letting go of tension . . . your forehead and cheeks are totally relaxed and now you begin to relax your jaw . . . allowing your jaw to become looser and relaxed . . . loose and relaxed. Your jaw is letting go of tension as you feel the muscles relax and let go of any anger, any frustration from the day. Your jaw is letting go of anger and frustration as you feel your lips begin to part. Your lips will begin to part as you let go of the last bit of tension in your jaw . . . and as you let go of tension in your jaw your lips begin to part. And now you feel your tongue relax . . . your tongue is lolling in your mouth . . . and as your jaw relaxes you feel your neck and shoulders letting go of tension . . . you feel your neck becoming completely relaxed. There is no tension in your neck as you relax your neck and now your shoulders . . . your shoulders can begin to droop as you let go of all the anxiety and all concerns. Your shoulders droop and let go of the last bit of muscular tension . . . letting go, letting go, letting go of all the muscular tension. Your neck and shoulders are totally relaxed. And now you can relax your chest and abdomen by taking a deep breath . . . a deep breath all the way down into your abdomen . . . you take a deep breath and it fills your abdomen . . . and as you let go the tension goes out of your body with the old air. And now you can take another deep breath into your abdomen . . . filling your abdomen as you relax your chest and stomach. And as you let go of the old air all the tension goes out of your body and you feel more and more deeply relaxed . . . your body feels deeply relaxed . . . your arms and legs heavy and relaxed . . . your face smooth and relaxed . . . your jaw loose and relaxed . . . your neck relaxed, your shoulders drooping . . . your body feeling totally relaxed. And you begin to feel that you are drifting and drifting . . . floating and drifting down, down, down into total relaxation. You feel almost drowsy, feeling peaceful and calm. You are drifting deeper and deeper, deeper and deeper into total relaxation. You are floating and drifting, you are feeling drowsy, peaceful and calm. Drifting and drowsy . . . drifting and drifting down, down, down into total relaxation. And now you see a staircase . . . a staircase going down to a lovely peaceful place. In a moment you'll go down the stairs, and with each step you will relax . . . you will relax more deeply with each step. You will count backward from ten to zero, counting each step as you become more and more deeply relaxed. Counting down each step . . . relaxing more and more deeply . . . ten . . . nine . . . eight . . . seven . . . six . . . five . . . four . . . three . . . two . . . one . . . zero. You are drifting toward a peaceful lovely place . . . drifting deeper and deeper into total relaxation . . . drifting down, down, down . . . drowsy and drifting. And now you will go down one more flight of stairs and with each step you will become more and more deeply relaxed . . . ten . . . nine . . . eight . . . drifting deeper and deeper . . . seven . . . six . . . five . . . four . . . more and more drowsy, peaceful and calm . . . three . . . two . . . one . . . zero. And now you come to a special place. [You may write in your own description of your special place or use the more general suggestions in this induction.] *Your special place where you feel safe and calm . . . calm and peaceful. You feel totally relaxed in your special place . . . you look around, notice the shapes and colors in your special place . . . you listen for the sounds of your special place . . . you notice how your body feels in this special place. This is your place to come and relax any time you want. You come here as a refuge, as a haven any time you want to feel totally relaxed. And this is a place where you feel strong and confident. You look strong and confident . . . and you feel your value . . . you feel accepting of yourself. You imagine yourself in your special place wearing a confident smile, proud of who you are. You feel confident and proud of who you are. And you imagine yourself here in your special place and feel that sense of peace floating through you . . . you feel calm and full of well-being. Nothing can disturb you and you know this feeling of peacefulness and calm will last for a long time. You feel so relaxed that you drift deeper and deeper, deeper and deeper, drifting and drowsy . . . you feel so drowsy and relaxed in your special place . . . drowsy and floating . . . and you feel positive feelings flowing through every part of your body. And now you see a blackboard with the old negative labels you have been given in the past . . . you see them on the blackboard. But you are a good person . . . a good person . . . you are a good person. You are fine . . . you are fine the way you are and you have always done the best you can. See those labels on the blackboard and now see an eraser in your hand . . . you have an eraser and you erase those labels from the board . . . you erase each one . . . they are gone . . . they are without meaning for you now. And now you write something on the board . . . you write your affirmation for today . . . you see yourself writing your positive affirmation . . . you see the words forming in chalk as you write your affirmation on the board. [Pause.] And you understand the meaning of your affirmation . . . you see your affirmation on the board and now you add three of your important strengths that make you feel good . . . feel good . . . feel good. You write three of your strengths and you feel good writing them. [Pause.] You appreciate these strengths because they are yours, they describe you and you see them on the board. More and more you are feeling strong and good . . . and now you can let go of your critic . . . you let go of any need for your critic. The critic always lies and you reject him . . . you reject your critic. The critic has cost you too much . . . and now you see what he has cost you . . . you remember one of the many things he has cost you . . . and you are aware that you no longer need your critic, you can forget your critic. And because your critic is becoming more and more silent . . . more and more silent, you are letting go of your unhealthy shoulds . . . you are letting go of rules that no longer fit you . . . you are letting go of the rules that hurt you. You feel good because you no longer need the rules that hurt you. You think about the consequences of your acts, you try to understand the consequences of your acts and you are letting go of rules that hurt you. And more and more you are kind to yourself . . . you are a good person . . . a good person. You are worthwhile because you live and feel . . . you are a unique and valuable human being because you live and feel . . . and you feel warm and loving towards yourself . . . you love yourself because you are a good person. You have legitimate needs and wants . . . you accept your feelings . . . you accept your feelings because they are a part of you and you are a good person . . . a good person . . . you feel kind and loving toward yourself. People see you as a good person, a worthwhile person. Those who fail to see your worth have something on their screen that keeps them from seeing the good person you are. When people really see you they see you as a good person. And you know now that you are free to make mistakes, it is fine to make mistakes . . . you do the best you can . . . you always do the best you can within the limits of your awareness. Within the limits of what you know at any given time you do the best you can. You love yourself, mistakes and all . . . you are a good person. You learn from your mistakes and are free to make them. You feel accepting of yourself, you feel positive feelings flowing throughout your entire body. Today you like yourself more than yesterday and tomorrow you will like yourself more than today. And tomorrow you will be able to believe more of the positive about yourself . . . you will remember more and more the positive about yourself. And these positive feelings will stay with you and grow stronger and stronger . . . the positive feelings will grow stronger tomorrow and the day after tomorrow. You feel very relaxed, very peaceful. And in a few moments you will come back to full conscious awareness feeling stronger and more positive . . . feeling confident and strong . . . feeling more accepting of yourself. And in a few moments you will come back up from one to ten. You will come all the way up feeling alert, refreshed and wide awake . . . you will feel completely alert and awake . . . you will feel relaxed and renewed when you come all the way up. And you are starting to come up . . . one . . . two . . . coming up . . . three . . . four . . . feeling more and more alert . . . five . . . feeling refreshed . . . six . . . coming up to full consciousness . . . seven . . . alert and more and more awake . . . eight . . . opening your eyes . . . nine . . . ten . . . fully alert, refreshed and wide awake.*

Listening to Your Induction

Probably the best way to listen to your recorded induction is to play it in bed before you go to sleep at night. Make sure that you're in a situation where you won't be interrupted and you feel safe and comfortable. If you fall asleep during the induction, don't worry about it. The message is still getting through to your subconscious. You are absorbing continuous nourishment for your self-esteem.

Try to listen to your induction once a day for four weeks. Thereafter you should drop to every second or third day. After you feel a significant improvement, use the induction only as needed.

Realistically, your first recorded induction will not be perfect. Certain cadences may bother you, a particular suggestion may not seem quite right; perhaps you would like to reverse the relaxation sequence and start with your face. This is be be expected. Modify and rerecord your induction as many times as you wish. Each time that you revise and correct your induction it will become that much more effective.

After a while any induction, no matter how well done, begins to lose some of its power. The impact of some of the imagery begins to fade. At that time you can experiment with redesigning the induction so that it becomes new again. You can write your own suggestions, using material from your strengths list. Or you can build in your current successes and accomplishments. For example, "You see all the love you have for your son . . . and the love in your heart helps you appreciate your worth." The beauty of writing your own suggestions is that they can be tailored exactly for you, crafted from the experiences of your own life.

Here are a few simple rules for creating hypnotic suggestions:

1. Keep suggestions simple and concise.
2. Repeat your suggestions at least three times using similar words and phrases.
3. Suggestions should be positive. Avoid using negatives such as "I feel no stress."
4. If possible, attach a visual image to a suggestion. "You feel confident . . . you see yourself smiling, your body relaxed."
5. Make suggestions that give you time to change. For example, "You are feeling more and more confident at work . . . each day you feel more comfortable with co-workers . . . each day your confidence grows . . . tomorrow you will be more confident than today."

13

I'm Still Not OK

Sheila, a 29-year-old waitress, had been fighting hard to control her critic. But she remained convinced that her low self-esteem had far more to do with a basic feeling of worthlessness than with her criticizing inner voice. She put it this way to her therapist:

> It's a feeling that I'm bad, screwed up. Just a gut feeling. Like I'm unworthy . . . like I don't deserve anything. The critic comes from the feeling. When I attack myself I'm just putting words to a feeling that's already there. Even if I strangled the critic, wiped him out, I'm sure this self-hate would still be there, sticking to me like the tar baby.

Shelia has a point. The feeling of being "bad" that she talked about had much to do with her alcoholic mother, who had always demanded that Sheila take care of her. Even at the age of three, Sheila knew that she had to be "very sweet to mom or else there would be an explosion." Being sweet meant telling her mom that she was pretty, brushing her hair, listening to her complain, and later reading to her in bed. If Sheila wanted to play instead of wait attendance on her mother, if she wanted to complain or get support, her mother became quite upset: Sheila was selfish, Sheila didn't care about anyone. Or worse, Sheila got the silent treatment—a day in which her mother was courteous, even kind, but never uttered a word. Sheila's feeling of badness is a summation of literally thousands of such painful interactions. Many of these experiences occurred before she fully understood language. She learned she was "not OK" at a very deep level of awareness. She knew it—just like she knew that lemon tastes bitter or the night is dark.

For people like Sheila, the feeling of worthlessness is a deeply held belief. An overactive critic is only a part of the problem. Beneath the critic lies a reservoir of hurt and guilt. (There are also feelings of anger, resentment, and revenge, but they are less relevant to this discussion.)

The feeling of badness can be generated in many ways. Here are some examples:

1. A primary care-giver is frequently absent or unavailable for nourishment. The child experiences this lack as abandonment, and on some level decides that he or she is unworthy of love. The emotional logic goes like this: "If they loved me, they wouldn't leave me; and if they don't love me, then I'm unlovable."

2. A child experiences enough deprivation and abuse to feel rage at his or her parents. But then comes the guilt. The emotional logic says: "I should love my parents; so if I hate them, then I'm bad."

3. Following a divorce, the child loses contact with the noncustodial parent. The emotional logic: "I drove him away; he left us because he hates me; I'm bad."

4. A child is the victim of sexual abuse. The emotional logic: "I do secret, bad things that I should never talk about; _____ wants me to do those bad things; I must be bad."

5. A child is the victim of extreme or capricious punishments. The emotional logic: "I must be very wrong for them to hurt me like this."

6. A child is criticized severely for a broad range of behaviors or aspects of appearance. "Dad always says I'm too fat; I must be ugly." "Mom says I'm lazy; lazy people are worthless."

7. A child is forced to support a highly depressed or narcissistic parent. Anything that the child does to meet his or her own needs or to function independently triggers an extreme rejection. The child learns: "My needs are bad, my feelings are selfish."

The most significant contributor to an early feeling of wrongness is the sense that one has somehow been abandoned. There are many ways a child can get this message, but once received it has enormously destructive impact on a sense of self. Abandonment—either physical or emotional—feels life-threatening to a child. It's terrifying. And for this awful thing to happen, something must be wrong. Few children are able to see that the fault does not lie with them. Abandonment is experienced as a staggering punishment for an unspeakable crime.

A Special Vulnerability

People who have grown up in family situations like the ones described above have a special vulnerability. Those early experiences have a lasting resonance that can intensify any current trauma. The old feeling of badness has the effect of amplifying even mild hurts into a devastation. For example, if someone gets angry at you, you have the automatic response that you're dead wrong. For an instant, you have a sinking feeling of worthlessness. You have to quickly shut the feeling off by denying it or by getting angry yourself. Almost any painful event can trigger the "I'm not OK" feeling: the loss of a relationship, being criticized, or feeling pushed away or ignored. A small mistake or failure can be blown up to the size of Everest. Sometimes the feeling of being controlled or discounted can hook into the "I'm bad" belief. Loneliness or even simple boredom may confirm your basic wrongness. On some level, you may feel that you deserve pain. And having it proves how bad your crimes have been.

It's as if you're carrying an awful secret: the knowledge that beneath your social mask is a person so psychologically disfigured that no one could stand seeing the real you. But you live in constant fear that they *will* see you, that through some mistake or lack of adroitness on your part they will catch a glimpse of the worthless person inside. If someone gets angry, criticizes, or pushes you away, you sense it is because they have seen the person inside and are rejecting him or her. And that new hurt is intensified by all the early ones. No matter how small the current trauma, it is a reminder of the times as a child when you felt rejected or abandoned and came to believe you were to blame for it all.

Protecting Against the Pain

A basic feeling of wrongness puts you in the constant danger of feeling a great deal of pain. One harsh word can do it, one look of annoyance, one noticeable error. You need protection. The problem is that minor defenses such as putting it out of your mind or arguing back to the critic don't always work. The pain is simply too great. You try reasoning it through, telling yourself it's a small thing, telling yourself that everybody gets annoyed once in a while. But the reasonable voice gets drowned out in a flood of wrongness. Underneath everything is that empty, lonely place where you feel worthless. And you are afraid of falling into it. The fear gives you an intense need to save yourself, to protect yourself from those feelings in any possible way. Enormous pain requires massive defense: the psychological equivalent of the Maginot Line. There are three major kinds of defenses:

1. Running away. This defense includes drugs and alcohol, various forms of avoidance, and emotional isolation.
2. Attacking others. You block the feeling of being bad with outer-directed rage.
3. Attacking yourself. You block the feeling of being bad with inner-directed rage.

The first two defenses are obvious ones, but the last one seems outwardly absurd. How can attacking yourself block a feeling of worthlessness? The answer is that you attack yourself in the hope of achieving perfection. The underlying belief is that if you just beat yourself up enough you will finally correct your flaws and atone for your sins. The whole self-attack is an exercise in denial—denying the terrible fear that you will always feel as worthless as you do now. While you rage at yourself, you are maintaining a kind of omnipotent fantasy that everything you hate in yourself can be fixed—and that when you have literally beaten yourself into shape, the feeling of wrongness will finally be gone.

This self-flagellation actually relieves pain. You're so focused on identifying faults and zealously mobilizing yourself for a psychological overhaul that the deep feeling of not being OK gets masked for a while.

Addicted to Your Defenses

You can become addicted to psychological defenses in the same way that people become addicted to alcohol. Initially the defense helps to anesthetize some of the deeper levels of anxiety and hurt. Because it works and you can count on it, you return again and again to the same coping strategy. After a time, you are willing to tolerate very little of the original anxiety or hurt before resorting to your defense. In the same way that an alcoholic turns again to the bottle, over and over you run away, attack others, or attack yourself at the first sign of that feeling of wrongness.

The remainder of this chapter will focus primarily on the defense of self-attack. This is because self-attack has a more directly toxic effect on your self-esteem than the defenses of running away or attacking others. While running away and attacking others damage your relationships to family, friends, and co-workers, attacking yourself damages your basic identity.

One of the most basic human problems is the unwillingness to face certain kinds of pain. This is quite understandable. But in the end, the defense proves more painful than the original feelings you ran away from. Addiction takes it's toll. The short-term pain relief creates destructive patterns that undermine your relationships and your self-esteem. The alcoholic feels better after a drink. But production falls off at work, he loses energy for his kids, and his wife grows tired of watching him pass out. It's the same with self-attacks. You feel better while your acute sense of badness is paradoxically obscured by a witch hunt for your flaws. Over time, however, you are further destroying your self-worth. And when you fail to be more perfect, when the worm does not become a butterfly, it seems to prove all the negative things you always believed about yourself.

The Addict Faces Reality

You cannot recover from an addiction without facing the truth. At A.A. meetings, men and women stand up to talk. They begin by admitting, "I'm an alcoholic." You are addicted to your defenses. You are addicted to self-attack. You must admit this before anything can change.

Hoping or expecting to fix what's wrong with you is part of your system of denial. Every time you try to beat yourself into being better you are running away from reality. You are pretending that it's possible to live up to your perfect standards. You are creating a fantasy in which you finally carve yourself into your personal ideal. It's as if your psyche was an insensitive block of wood and you were going to chisel, gouge, and cut a sculptured masterpiece. Or worse, you see yourself as a willful child whom you must slap and beat to steer toward the path of good.

This addiction denies reality in two ways. First, you deny what it means to be human by insisting that it is possible or even desirable to pursue perfection. You forget about your needs, about your hunger and your longing for things. You forget what it feels like not to get them, how you try and certain dreams remain out of reach, how you then must find a substitute, some strategy of partial fulfillment. Your psychological and physical survival depends on this basic struggle. The stakes are high and you fail a lot, and yet you have to keep trying, to try even painful or destructive approaches as long as they contain some small hope of meeting your needs. This is what being human is about. This is how people are made—always questing for nourishment. Expecting perfection is an attempt to ignore this basic human struggle.

The second way you deny reality is to think that you can hack and cut at yourself and still produce more good than harm. By attacking yourself, you are helping to destroy the number one requirement for healthy change—a sense of worth. When you feel good about yourself, you feel motivated rather than depressed, you feel more attractive and socially competent, and you feel strong enough to take risks and try new things. Self-attack actually reduces your capacity for change, for trying, for reaching out. Far from pushing you to do better, it exacerbates your sense of helplessness.

Seeing the Consequences

Like the alcoholic, you have to face what your defense is costing you. In the chapter "Disarming the Critic," you explored the price you pay for listening to your critic. You'll find it helpful now to review your list of negative effects from self-attacks.

When you judge yourself harshly, nearly every aspect of life becomes more difficult. Here are some examples:

- You expect that others see your flaws and are as disgusted by them as you are. So you must be constantly vigilant to prepare for their inevitable rejection.
- It's hard to be open or revealing with people because you expect them to reject "the real you."
- You get very angry or depressed when criticized.
- You avoid social situations where there is a chance of criticism or rejection. You don't take risks, you don't meet new people, and you endure loneliness rather than reach out.
- You fear mistakes, and so you don't like to do new things. It's hard to learn anything because the inevitable errors throw you off. You have to work extremely hard so that no one will ever find fault with what you do.
- You avoid challenges because you expect to fail.
- You avoid disciplining your children because you are afraid of their anger.
- It's hard to say no or set limits in relationships because you would feel wrong if the other person got upset.
- You are afraid to ask for things because a refusal would mean that you're an unworthy person.
- You choose sexual partners who are flawed and who you imagine will put up with you. It's hard to pursue someone really attractive because you can't conceive that such a person would want to be with someone like you.
- You give too much and sometimes let people use you because you can't imagine why else they would hang around you.
- You are so focused on your flaws that you often feel depressed or disgusted with yourself. Much of what you do seems wrong or stupid or incompetent.
- You avoid people who admire or really love you because they must be either deluded or worse off than you are.

Not all of these examples will apply to you, but each one that does tends to diminish and restrict your life. It's harder to get your needs met, to do things that excite you, or to be with people who are really nourishing.

You may have grown up in a family where you felt wrong and

cut off from love. Those feelings are very hard to face. But you must understand this: your defense of self-attack is only making the damage worse, only making you more vulnerable. In the end, your self-attacks will be more destructive than the original hurts.

Learning Abstinence

For the true alcoholic, there is only one answer: abstinence. It's the same for anyone addicted to self-attack. You must literally go cold turkey on all forms of pathological judgment.

Pathological judgments are based on the belief that things are intrinsically good or bad. You evaluate yourself and others as *being* good or bad, right or wrong. *Healthy* judgment, by contrast, is the awareness that something *feels* better or worse, or that it affects you in such a way that you feel good or bad. To put it simply, pathological judgment would say that something *is* bad, healthy judgment would say that it *feels* bad (meaning painful). Here are some specific kinds of judgments that you must abstain from:

1. Judging anyone's behavior as good or bad. Hard as it sounds, you must give up moral opinions about the actions of others. Cultivate instead the attitude that they have made the best choice available, given their awareness and needs at the time. Be clear that while their behavior may not feel or be good *for you*, it is not bad.
2. Evaluating as good or bad or right or wrong things you read, see on TV, or observe on the street. This includes assaults, terrorist bombings, political corruptions, and so on.
3. Comparing people on any dimension where one person is judged to be better and the other person is judged worse. This includes speculating about who is more intelligent, more generous, more competent, and so on.
4. Using negative global labels of any kind (*stupid, selfish, crazy, ugly, fat, phoney, inane,* and the like).
5. Expecting that people should be any different than they are. It is critical that you accept people as doing exactly what they have to be doing (given their current needs and awareness). It may be unpleasant or painful for you that they act the way they do, but you must accept that their behavior is *exactly* what it should be at this moment.
6. Blaming anyone for your pain. The pain exists, but to blame anyone is to say they should be different than they are.
7. Judging yourself as good or bad in any way. This includes your thoughts, feelings, motivations, hopes, cravings, fantasies, or behavior.

Your judgments are poison. They are like a double shot of whiskey for someone with cirrhosis or candy for a diabetic. You can't afford judgments about yourself or anyone. Every time you make a value judgment about another person, you are priming your critic to level the same judgment at you. Every "should" you apply to your friends, your lover, or someone you read about in the paper will always come back to haunt you. The paradox is that while the rules you make for others seldom influence them, the rules always affect and diminish *you*.

Judgment has a spiritually contracting effect. It builds fences and limits inside you. It's OK to feel this but not that, to say this but not that, to want this but not that. Your inner life becomes an obstacle course where you continually dodge the wrong, bad, and unworthy thoughts, feelings, and impulses. You lose spontaneity and openness. You reject yourself because it is impossible to follow all of the rules all of the time. Judgments take the joy, the expansiveness out of life. You contract from the fear of being judged and become vulnerable to depression.

How does a person addicted to self-attack stop judging? It takes a great deal of will power and commitment. It takes constant vigilance to stop the little voice that wants to say, "He's a jerk . . . she's lazy . . . he's corrupt . . . I'm selfish . . . the neighbors are slobs. . . ." That little voice is spewing its poison much of the time. You have to find a way to quiet it. The concept of abstinence is key here. Just as the alcoholic must abstain from even one drink, you must abstain from even one judgment. Nothing is worthy of judgment. Nothing is good, nothing is bad. Events occur. They may be pleasurable, painful, or neutral. You may regret some and wish to repeat others. Just as you avoid certain people and wish to seek out others. There is no right or wrong in any of it.

Abstaining from judgment doesn't mean that you have to spend time with people you don't enjoy or let yourself be abused or taken advantage of. You remain free to do what you think best to nurture and protect yourself. It's fine to have preferences, to enjoy Buddy Holly but not Brahms. But these choices are based on your particular needs and tastes, not on any sense of moral oughtness. You may choose fidelity to your spouse, but you must make no judgment about those who do not. You may recoil from violence, but you must still recognize that the violent are making the best choice available (given their needs and awareness at the time).

Remember: one judgment leads to another. Even a small slip—such as thinking how poorly someone is dressed—makes you more vulnerable to judgments about your own attire. Thinking how incompetently a meeting was run makes you more vulnerable the next time you organize anything. And it's extraordinarily easy to slide back into a world view that fosters judgment:

1. You see people making choices to do "evil" things. You believe that they could have done otherwise, but chose "the easy way." You see people hurting each other and imagine that they have chosen to inflict pain because they've succumbed to "temptation" and *let* themselves go bad.
2. You see people doing "foolish" things, bringing pain to themselves and others, and imagine that they have deliberately chosen the foolish path.
3. You believe that people "give in" to weakness and commit sins, that they can choose not to love or care for others, that they allow themselves to sink into selfishness, corruption, greed, and so on.
4. You imagine that your personal rules are universal and should be applied to everyone.

It's sometimes very satisfying to see things this way. There's a feeling of righteousness, even superiority. The world seems to make more sense when you can divide the players into good and bad. Your anger feels justified when you can see the other person as culpable and wrong. And it's easier to reject *yourself* when you feel that you have *deliberately* chosen to do the wrong or foolish thing.

There are many painful things in the world, and it's comforting to label them evil and reject them. When you make something painful into something bad, you are distancing and protecting yourself. That's perfectly natural. But judging in this way depends on the illusion that people are totally free to do anything they wish. And when they make mistakes that bring pain to themselves or others, it can only be because they were too lazy or selfish to do the right thing.

How do you escape this world view? You can escape by developing the awareness that everyone chooses the highest perceived good. Plato said it first: man *always* chooses the highest good. The rub is that your highest good depends on which of your needs has preeminence at the moment. If you feel sexually aroused, your highest good may be to have sex—unless a greater competing need is to protect yourself from emotional harm (as when you're attracted to someone other than your spouse and know that he or she would be hurt and angry). Another competing need might be to protect your self-esteem ("He won't think much of me if I sleep with him on the first date" or "I'm so nervous I might not be able to perform").

Consider this example. Suppose your daughter comes in while you're watching TV and asks for help with her homework. You have several competing needs:

1. To continue to enjoy the show
2. To help her get through her assignments

In addition, you have certain beliefs and awareness:

1. Your daughter often asks you to do work that she is capable of doing on her own.
2. You believe that she should learn to be more self-reliant and solve some of her own problems.
3. You also believe that a parent should always be ready to help a child.

Your highest good will depend on which of these needs and awarenesses is most powerful. In the end, your need to enjoy the show and your belief that your daughter should be more self-reliant may prove strongest. It's irrelevant whether your beliefs and awarenesses are true or false, or how your decision will affect your daughter in the long run. You can only act on the prevailing needs and awareness you have at that moment in time. Three months later, when your daughter brings home a ghastly report card, you may decide that you were mistaken to withhold help. But what happens later cannot be known while you are making your decision.

Here's another example. Suppose you and a friend are at a party. Nearly everyone else is a stranger to you, and you feel the need for more support and attention from your friend. But you have a problem. You are afraid to ask directly for things. Your family had a very indirect style of communicating, and you literally don't know how to talk about your needs. You need attention, and you start sorting through your repertoire of strategies to get it. Here again, your decision depends entirely on your current awareness. If all you know how to do is to be cold and irritable and hope that your friend will notice your distress, that will be your strategy. Six months later, after taking an assertiveness course, you might do something different. But as of this moment, you will make a choice based on the awareness available to you.

What does it mean that people choose the highest good? It means that you are doing the best you can at any given time. It means that people always act according to their prevailing awareness, needs, and values. Even the terrorist planting bombs to hurt the innocent is making a decision based on his or her highest good. It means you cannot blame people for what they do. Nor can you blame yourself. No matter how distorted or mistaken a person's awareness is, he or she is innocent and blameless. That's because no one can act differently than his or her current awareness permits, and you can change only when your awareness changes.

Exercises

The following exercises will help you integrate an attitude of non-judging into your life.

1. Practice reading the newspaper without making a single judgment about any of the behavior reported in any story. Take the position (even if you don't fully believe it) that each person is choosing the highest good based on his current awareness.

2. When you see people driving dangerously or failing to observe highway courtesies, accept the behavior without judgment. How they drive is a direct reflection of their current needs and awareness. The speeding teenager needs to show off to his girlfriend or act out his anger or display his maleness more than he needs to drive safely. When he loses faith in his young reflexes, becomes more aware of danger and death, then his driving will change. He will change when his awareness changes.

3. When you see people wearing unattractive clothes or hair styles, or whose physical appearance is not to your taste, practice this mantra: he or she is blameless for any choices that created his or her appearance.

4. Think of the politician you like the least. Imagine, for a moment, the things that really turn you off. Now take the position that his or her beliefs, values, and actions are the only ones possible given the limitations of his or her current awareness and ambitions.

5. Get a mental image of the person you most dislike. See that person sitting in a chair in front of you in every detail: hear the tone of voice, notice the mannerisms, observe the facial expressions. Remember a past incident when this person really made you angry. Now try a nonjudmental attitude. Remind yourself that he or she isn't choosing to be bad. This man is doing the best he can, given his needs and awareness. You find this woman's behavior painful, but she cannot be blamed for that. Like everyone else, she is trying to survive by pursuing her highest good at this moment. This person cannot *be* anything else than what he or she is—until his or her awareness changes.

6. Spend a few moments chatting with your least favorite person at work. Notice his or her annoying mannerisms, style, opinions, and so on. But do so without judgment. Take the position that this person has been shaped by and adapted to a unique set of circumstances. He or she has made the best choices available.

7. Call up a family member whom you dislike. During the conversation, practice your nonjudging attitude. Nothing the person says should be evaluated as good or bad, right or wrong.

8. This exercise requires spending some time in the past. Recall several scenes where you either felt very disapproving of others, or felt very disapproved of and wrong yourself. Relive

these scenes step by step. See the action unfolding. But this time experience the events without judgment. Remind yourself that everyone chooses the highest good, everyone makes the best choice available. Try to understand how the person's needs and awareness shaped his or her choices. Strive for a compassionate view of your own needs and choices.

9. When friends gossip about and judge others, resist the temptation to join in. Mildly suggest that "so-and-so isn't so bad" and excuse yourself from the group.

Facing the Pain

When you abstain from judging, you will notice some important emotional changes. For a while you will be more consciously aware of that basic feeling of "wrongness." Judging is your defense against the fear of falling into the pit—that empty, worthless place inside. Without judgment, you cannot use anger at yourself or others to obscure these feelings.

Just as the alcoholic has to learn to stop using his habit to run away from his feelings, you are learning to stop escaping the feeling of wrongness with judgments. But it means having to face the pain. Obviously this is easy to say and very hard to do. The pain can be enormous. But the only alternative to facing pain is avoiding it, and that strategy has already cost you too much.

Facing pain is a skill. If you know how pain works and how to cope with it, your actual encounters with it will be less overwhelming. When you're in a lot of pain—whether it's a toothache or the worthless feeling—the pain dominates your attention and becomes the only thing that matters. It's hard to remember a time when the pain wasn't there. And hard to imagine being OK again. It's as if pain erases both the past and the future. All you care about is now, and now seems unbearable.

This peculiar ability of pain to dominate your attention masks its true nature. Pain is never static or unremitting. *Pain comes in waves.*

Perhaps the best illustration of the oscillating nature of pain is grief. A sense of loss whelms up, a feeling so intense that one cannot imagine an end to it. But then, after a time, a numbness comes, a period of calm and relief. Soon numbness is replaced by another wave of loss. And so it continues: waves of loss, calmness, loss, calmness.

This is the natural cycle of pain. As soon as you reach an overload, your emotions shut off, you literally stop feeling for a little while. These waves continue, with smaller amplitudes and longer rest periods, until the hurt finally eases.

The body reacts to physical pain in exactly the same way. One man who had severely burned his hand described his reaction in this way: "The pain was so intense I wanted to scream. But after a while I noticed this strange thing. The pain would shut off at times—maybe for ten or twenty seconds. And then it would start again. It got very regular, so that I could look forward to when it shut off. Then I could rest. I found I could tolerate the pain because I knew there were these little breaks."

Both your body and mind have natural mechanisms that dampen pain for periods so that you get a chance to catch your breath. Understanding pain means that you anticipate these rest periods and use them to take breaks from the pain.

Your not-OK feeling has exactly the same oscillations as any other kind of pain. It comes on so intensely that all you care about is escape. But if you face the pain, you'll notice that soon enough the wave passes. In between waves, you can remind yourself of your coping mantras. You can remember that you've endured this feeling before and that eventually it passes. You don't have to attack yourself or anyone else, because soon the worst of it will be over.

The important thing is not to be fooled by the immediacy of pain. Don't get caught in thinking:

- It will last forever.
- I can't stand it.

Use, instead, the coping thoughts:

- It will pass.
- I *know* I can wait till the wave passes.
- This feeling comes from early hurts, it has nothing to do with my true worth.
- I can *feel* like I'm bad and still *be* good.

Floating Past the Pain

Facing the pain means not defending yourself with judgments. But it doesn't mean that you can't protect yourself in other ways. Aside from accepting the waves and waiting for the rest periods, your best protection against pain is *distancing*. You put space between yourself and the pain (using either images or words) and float past the hurt.

A well-known ride in Disneyland provides a concrete illustration of "floating past." A riverboat slowly navigates around an island. Various scenes come into view. One scene depicts an Indian massacre. The log cabin is burning. A pioneer family lies grotesquely murdered in the yard. Nothing moves. Slowly the boat floats around a bend and the death scene passes out of sight.

This is how you can float past pain. You know it will be over in a while. You merely have to wait it out. Slowly, inexorably, you are moving past the hurt, the wrongness. Here are some ways to get distance while you float past.

- Visualize the pain. Give it a shape, a color. Make it as ugly or weird as you like. Take some deep breaths. With each breath, see it move further away. You are floating past and it is further and further behind you. Keep focusing on your breathing as the pain slowly disappears.
- In your imagination, step outside of yourself. You can see how bad you feel. You can see how you struggle with the pain. See your face, see the position of your body. Imagine the pain like a red glow in your body. It will fade in a while. Take deep breaths as you watch the red glow diminishing. Imagine that the hurt is passing as the glow gradually fades. When you are ready, go back inside yourself.
- Breathe deeply. Focus on your breath, on the rhythm, the sensation of clean air coming into your lungs. Notice how your body feels at this exact moment. Experience where the tension lies and relax any areas of tightness in your body. Do not listen to negative thoughts that may get triggered by negative feelings. Think only of relaxation and breathing until the painful feelings pass.
- See a mental picture of yourself days or even years from now when this pain is long since over. See yourself looking confident and relaxed.
- Say to yourself: "These are old feelings, they come whenever this situation happens. I will survive them. I'll float by till the worst of it passes."

Anchoring to the Good Times

As you have already discovered, talking back to the deeply held not-OK feeling isn't easy. That's because your not-OK feelings are anchored to the memory of many, many negative interactions with your parents and other significant people in your life. When you try to talk back to the feelings, the struggle comes down to words against images. And in that contest, images ofen win. The answer is to use anchoring to your own advantage. You can combat the not-OK feelings with a technique that helps you reexperience times when you felt confident and good about yourself.

The term "anchoring" comes from Neuro-Linguistic Programming, a communication model developed by Richard Bandler, John Grinder, Leslie Cameron Bandler, Judith DeLozier, and others. They consider an anchor to be any stimulus that consistently evokes the same response. If you think of your Uncle Albert every time you see a Hawaiian shirt, then Hawaiian shirts are an anchor for you. The shirt is the stimulus, and your memory of your uncle is your consistent response.

Most of your anchors are involuntary, the result of sensory associations formed automatically as you live from day to day. But you can form voluntary anchors, conscious associations that you can use to improve your self-esteem. The key to using anchors to foster self-esteem is to choose a simple stimulus and an intense response. In the anchoring exercise that follows, the stimulus is a touch on the wrist that you can administer to yourself at any time. The response is a feeling of confidence and self-acceptance based on a memory or a fantasy. Take a moment right now to sample this easy but very powerful exercise.

1. Sit in a comfortable position, in a place where you won't be interrupted. Rest your hands in your lap, but keep them slightly separated. Close your eyes and take a moment to relax your body. Scan your body from head to toe and consciously relax any tight places you feel.

2. Keep your eyes closed and go back in time. Go back and picture a time when you felt successful or especially confident. Find a time when you felt very good about yourself. When you see that time, take a deep breath. Notice everything about that time: the sights, the sounds, the tastes and smells and feelings. See how you looked, how others looked. Hear the confidence in your voice, hear the praise from others. Let yourself *feel* the confidence and self-acceptance.

   If you have difficulty finding a memory that produces strong feelings of confidence, create fantasy images that have the same effect. See yourself at some future time looking and feeling confident and worthwhile. Don't worry if the fantasy seems unlikely or unrealistic. It's the *feeling* of confidence you're after.

3. When your images are clear enough to make you feel confident, touch your left wrist with your right hand. Touch it firmly, in a particular spot that you can easily remember. You are anchoring your feeling of confidence to this touch on your wrist, and you want to be able to exactly duplicate that touch later on.

4. Repeat this sequence with four other memories or fantasy scenes. When your mental scene has created a strong feeling of self-worth, touch your wrist in precisely the same way.

Here's how a barber named Jack used anchoring to combat his feelings of worthlessness. He searched his memory for some good time when he felt confident and worthwhile. He remembered that once his fifth grade teacher had pinned his drawing of a desert scene up above the blackboard, as an example of good artwork to guide the rest of the class. He concentrated on the look and sound and smell of that classroom until he felt the same warm glow in his chest and the same feeling of pride and accomplishment that he had felt at age eleven. At that moment, he touched the inside of his left wrist to anchor the memory.

Next Jack recalled his first leave home from the Navy, when he dropped in on his old high school girlfriend, wearing his uniform, fit and tanned after basic training. He remembered how she had fussed over him and how strong and grown-up he had felt, a man of the world going off to fight for his country. When these feelings were at their height, he again touched the inside of his left wrist to anchor them.

For his next scene, Jack brought back the experience of building a model of the U.S.S. *Constitution*. It was an expensive, complicated model that he put together during summer vacation when he was sixteen. He remembered a particular day when he was painting the hull, simulating the look of tarnished copper plates, while listening to his collection of Broadway musical soundtracks on his mom's record player. His mom was at the doctor's, his brother was at camp, and his dad was at work. He had the house to himself and was totally enjoying himself. Jack remembered thinking that he was good with his hands. There wasn't anything he couldn't make or learn to make. He sang along with the records, admiring his own voice and his memory for song lyrics. When this feeling of contentment and liking himself was intense, Jack touched his wrist to anchor the good time.

Jack couldn't think of another strong memory, so he chose a fantasy scene. He saw himself opening his own shop: total hair care for men and women, in an elegant downtown location. He saw himself working at the first chair, with five other operators ranked behind him, looking to him for leadership, depending on his style sense and business acumen. He saw himself counting the till at the end of the day, sharing out the tip kitty and throwing in fifty dollars as a bonus to the staff. He saw the admiration and appreciation in the other hairdressers' faces and heard their thanks. When the feeling of success and competence was strongest, he touched himself on the wrist to anchor the feeling.

When Jack caught the bus to work the next day, he felt the familiar feeling of "being a nobody" creeping over him. But he remembered that he now had some firmly anchored resources with which to fight back. While riding the bus, he touched his wrist and was pleased to notice that the bad feeling retreated. He didn't laboriously run through all the scenes all over again. He just got a mental glimpse of crayons, his old Navy uniform, a tiny bottle of copper paint, and the hum of electric hair clippers. More important, he had some contact with the feelings of pride, strength, competence, and success.

After you have anchored to your own personal good times, you can touch your wrist whenever you need to fight the not-OK feeling. Your positive memories or fantasies are resources that you can call up any time you need them. You need only touch your left wrist with your right hand and they will help you neutralize that feeling of wrongness. Now you have more than words to fight with. You can combat negative feelings and images with a touch that anchors you to positive feelings and images.

The Option of Therapy

Sometimes the "not OK" feeling proves extremely difficult to overcome. If you have tried many of the techniques in this book and the feeling remains, do not think that your situation is beyond hope. Self-help books are not the answer for everyone. Many people require the help of a trained psychotherapist to change these long-standing negative feelings.

Research indicates that psychotherapy is extremely effective with problems of self-esteem. A relationship with a therapist who sees your strengths and who accepts your less than perfect qualities can make enormous changes over time. Do not be afraid to seek help. Sometimes it is essential that you get the support of another person who cares and has the knowledge to guide you through a change process.

14

Building Self-Esteem in Children

By Judith McKay, R.N.

You want the best for your kids. You want them to be good people, successful, happy, and capable in the world. You want them to be able to make friends, use their talents, and make the world work for them.

Helping your children grow up with strong self-esteem is the most important task of parenthood. The child with good self-esteem has the best chance of being a happy and successful adult. Self-esteem is the armor that protects kids from the dragons of life: drugs, alcohol, unhealthy relationships, and delinquency.

The Power of Parents

No matter who you are, your parents (or the people who raised you) remain the most important people in your life. That's because they exert the strongest influence on how you feel about yourself. Your own struggle to achieve good self-esteem has shown you how many of the condemning, judging voices you carry inside are the voices you heard in childhood. The fears, limits, and feelings of helplessness you struggle with today have been with you from your earliest years.

It is your parents who led you to see yourself as competent or incompetent, stupid or smart, effective or helpless, worthless or lovable. And it is your parents whom you wanted to please. The need for their approval is so strong that the drive for parental acceptance may continue long after they are dead.

Try to remember what you wanted from your own parents. Did you want their forgiveness, recognition, admiration? What would it mean to you today to have your parents appreciate what you really are: your limits, your special abilities, your dreams?

Maybe you will never get this appreciation from your parents, and you will have to learn to give to yourself the gift of acceptance. But you can give this gift to your children. When you give them the gift of acceptance, when you really see, value, and appreciate them, you provide your children a psychological armor that will protect them for a lifetime.

Parents as Mirrors

You are the whole world to a baby—the source of all comfort and security, the banisher of fears and pain. Every waking hour he or she learns about himself or herself from you. You are the mirror that shows this new person who he or she is.

From your smile a baby learns that he or she is delightful, from your touch a baby learns that he or she is safe. From your responsiveness to his or her crying, a baby learns that he or she is effective and important. These are the first lessons about his or her worth and the building blocks of self-esteem.

Babies who are not comforted, who are not held, spoken to, rocked, and loved, learn other lessons about their worth. They learn that their cries of distress don't bring relief. They learn helplessness. They learn that they are not important. These are the first lessons in poor self-esteem.

As they grow older, children will have other mirrors that show them who they are. Teachers, friends, and sitters will all perform this role, but a child will return to the reflection in the mirror that his or her parents held for this sense of goodness, importance, and basic worth.

Providing a positive mirror for your children does not mean that you approve of everything that they do or that you let them run the family. There is a way to raise socialized, reasonable children with strong self-esteem. It requires that you look at your child, look at yourself, and look at your patterns of communication.

Look at Your Child

It's not easy to really *see* your child. Your vision is clouded by your hopes and fears. Your son might remind you of yourself or your mate or another child. You have opinions about how your daughter ought to be, and how you hope she will be. It's a challenge, but when you are able to see your child accurately you will be rewarded with a relationship that is more enjoyable, with more reasonable expectations and less conflict. And you will be contributing to your child's self-esteem.

Accurately seeing your children builds self-esteem in four ways.

First, you are able to recognize their unique abilities and talents—to reinforce them, nurture them, and help them recognize what is special about themselves.

Second, you are able to understand their behavior in the context of who they are—you don't misinterpret a natural shyness as being unfriendly, or a need for privacy as rejection. Seen in context, even negative behavior is more understandable and predictable.

Third, seeing your children accurately helps you focus on changing only the behavior that is important to change—behavior that's harmful to them, behavior that isolates them socially, or behavior that is disruptive to the family.

Fourth, children who feel that they are really seen and understood by their parents can afford to be authentic. Such children don't have to hide parts of themselves because they fear being rejected. If you can accept all of your child, the good and the bad, your child can accept himself or herself. This is the cornerstone of good self esteem.

Exercise: Who Is Your Child?

This exercise will help you look at your child and make sense of what you discover.

1. Over the course of a week, write a description of your child. Pretend you are writing it to someone who has never met him or her (such as to an old school friend or a distant relative). Be sure to describe your child in every way: physically, socially, intellectually, emotionally. How does your daughter act in school? What does she enjoy doing when she is alone? What makes your son angry, happy, challenged? What is he best at? Worst at? How does your child get his or her needs met—needs for security, attention, affection? What is it about him or her that is hardest for you? How is your son like you? How is he different? Does your daughter do best with structure or freedom? Does she prefer order or chaos? Does she enjoy music, sports, drawing, books, or math?

Write as detailed a description as you can and add to it during the week. You will find yourself thinking about your child and looking at him or her more carefully than you have since his or her birth. You might discover qualities that you never notice or revise a previously held opinion. One parent discovered that she still saw her sixteen-year-old son as "an absent-minded, head-in-the-clouds" type. When he was twelve, he was always leaving the door open when he went out of the house. He would forget his lunch on the bus, his jacket at the playground, or would turn in the wrong assignment at school. When she wrote her descriptive letter she realized how much he had changed. He was responsible at home, got decent grades at school, had an after-school job, and paid for his own car. He was hardly the "absent-minded space case" that he had been at twelve.

To add to your description, check in with other people who know your child—teachers, friends, or friends' parents. You might be surprised (and delighted) by some quality that others notice that you never see at home. They might describe your daughter as a real leader or a team worker. They might describe her as someone who is helpful, sensitive, or funny. Make this description a treasure hunt of her talents. Look for the seeds of potential. Be honest about her limits, annoying habits, and sources of conflict.

2. Now go through the description and underline your child's positive and negative qualities. You will construct two lists. The first will have all the positive qualities, talents, abilities, interests, and potential areas of growth that you want to nurture. The other list will include negative qualities, limits, potential problems, and bad habits.

This is a partial list written about Jane, a twelve-year-old gymnast who is popular with her friends.

Positive Qualities	*Negative Qualities*
Funny	Overactive—can't sit still
Creative	Easily frustrated
Determined	Poor math skills
Very coordinated—good at sports	Fights with sister
	Sloppy
Outgoing—social	Forgetful
Artistic—drawing, clay, dress	Very easily influenced by friends
	Deals poorly with changes in plans

Looking at the Positive

First, look at the list of positive qualities and pick out two or three items that you want to reinforce right away. Make sure that these qualities are really strengths or abilities or areas of special talent that are already present in your child—not something that you *wish* were true for him or her. Every time that you reinforce this behavior (by praising, rewarding, or recognizing it) you make it more likely that your child will want to do it again. Reinforcing real positive qualities is an important strategy in building self-esteem.

Here are three things you can do to reinforce positive qualities.

1. *Notice examples of ability* (talents, skills, interests, and the like) in many different circumstances. How does your child show it at school? How does he or she show it at home? *Point it out to him or her.* Your child might not be able to see these abilities on his or her own. "You are sure a good problem solver." "You arranged the flowers like a real artist, it's beautiful." "It took someone with a lot of coordination and balance to climb that tree and unsnag the kite."

2. *Find occasion to frequently praise your child.* (And don't forget to praise him or her to others for his or her ability.) The language of praise will be discussed later in this chapter. Display your child's work, trophies, stories, or playdough sculptures. Tell the story of a dilemma and how he or she solved the problem. Recount how patient, inventive, determined, or creative he or she was. Make your child the hero of the story.

3. *Give your child an opportunity to show his or her ability frequently.* He or she needs many chances to develop it and prove it, strengthen it and count on it. To develop any ability a child needs lots of practice—be it swimming, reading, or thinking.

These three steps will reinforce positive behavior. Your child will learn to value these talents and see himself or herself as capable and special in these areas. Even when your child is struggling in other areas, he or she can still feel OK, since he or she is extra good at something.

After reinforcing these behaviors for two weeks, come back to the list and find two or three other items and reinforce them as well. Soon you will get used to finding the special positive qualities in your child's everyday life. Because you see your child in a positive way, your child will start to see himself or herself that way too. The internalized parental voices—the voices that nurture or destroy self-esteem—will be warm with praise and appreciation. And your child will develop the ability to nurture his or her own self-esteem.

Looking at the Negative

Every action your children make is an attempt to meet their needs. This is true whether or not the behavior is successful at meeting their needs. This is true whether or not the behavior is acceptable.

A child who picks fights with siblings, shows off in an obnoxious way, baby-talks, or acts regressive needs something! It might be more attention, or less pressure, or more challenge. A son who is defiant might need you to set consistent limits on his behavior—or he might need to make more choices in his life. A daughter who nags or whines might need your exclusive attention for a moment so that she can express what she really wants and feel that you are hearing her. In many cases, if you can determine what need is being expressed, you can help your child meet the need in a more appropriate way.

Try this exercise. For every item on the negative list, ask yourself these three questions:

1. What need is being expressed by this behavior?
2. Can I see a positive quality being expressed by this behavior?
3. How can I help my child express this quality and meet his or her needs in a more positive way?

One parent described his daughter as "stubborn and inflexible, willful and bossy." First he looked for a need that was being expressed by this behavior. He saw that his daughter had a great need to control what happened to her. Instead of seeing her with the negative label "stubborn and inflexible," the parent reframed her behavior in a positive way. He saw a determined and independent child who had a strong opinion about how things ought to be. After giving it some thought, he decided on three strategies to help this child express independence as well as meet her need for control.

1. Give her a choice whenever possible. ("Do you want to do your homework now or after dinner?" "You can watch one hour of TV. You decide what you want to watch.")
2. Reinforce the positive, appropriate ways she expresses her determination and independence. ("You really stick to your guns when you want something—I like that.")
3. Recognize how hard it is for her to accept disappointment. ("It took a lot of guts to keep trying even though the other kids were so much bigger. I'm so sorry you didn't make the team.")

Of course things won't always go her way just because she's determined, and at times she will have to go along with others even if she is independent. But disappointments and frustrations are easier to accept when children feel that their parents know and accept who they are and that their efforts and difficulties are being recognized.

Jamie's parents observed that she had a hard time settling down to do her homework or to practice the piano. She was always fidgeting, drumming, fighting with her sister, or finding any excuse at all to get up and move around.

What need was being expressed? Jamie had lots of physical and nervous energy. It was enormously hard for her to "just sit still." By the end of the school day she *needed* to run around. Instead of seeing her energy as a problem, her parents realized that it could be an asset if channeled in a positive way. If she had an opportunity to be really active after school, she might be better able to settle down to homework after dinner. Jamie's parents decided to initiate a number of changes to make sure that she met her needs and used her energy in a positive way. Jamie was encouraged to join an after-school soccer team where her energetic style of play was appreciated, and her success in this sport gave her better self-esteem and confidence. Jamie was allowed frequent breaks while she was doing her homework, since sitting longer than one half hour made her fidget. She actually got more done in less time because she had better concentration after taking a break. Instead of piano lessons, Jamie took drum lessons and on the weekend had a judo class. There she learned discipline and control, while using her energy in another positive outlet.

Behaviors to ignore. Look again at the items on the negative list. Are some of these items really a matter of taste, preference, or personal style? Don't waste your time or energy in changing these attributes. They are best left alone. No amount of nagging or reminding will make a shy child outgoing, or an awkward child graceful. Forget about hairstyles, clothes, taste in music, and so on. Harping on these things won't produce change. Instead, you are likely to spoil your relationship with your child. Some of the behaviors that annoy you may be related to your child's age or to the culture he or she lives in. For instance, eight-year-old boys imitate macho super heroes. Twelve-year-old girls are often "boy crazy." Teenagers commonly push the limits in their quest for autonomy. Nagging about how your teenager looks or decorates his or her room creates more conflict and little change. Do set limits to protect your child, and save your sanity, but focus on the more important issues.

A Special Challenge—The Child Who Is Different

You might have the feeling that one of your children would have fit better in a different family. "Where did he come from?" you ask yourself. He or she is the sensitive artist in a family of athletes, the shy one in a family of outgoing social butterflies, the slow learner in a family of scholars. It's a real challenge to see your child for what he or she is and not just for what he or she is not. If you try to make him or her "fit the mold," your child will feel frustrated and unhappy and end up believing that something is wrong with him or her. If you recognize and value his or her unique talents, a child who doesn't fit in can still feel good about himself or herself and have high self-esteem.

Martin was an unathletic child in a family of all stars. His father was a local football hero and coached the school team. His brother won three school letters for track, baseball, and football. His sister competed in track and swimming. Though Martin was not athletic, he was very talented mechanically and he loved music. When he was young, he would take things apart and try to fix them. He was always asking how something worked. When he was ten, he fixed an old record player and gathered a collection of opera records from garage sales and junk stores. He built his own radio to listen to concerts and over the years taught himself the great operas and a lot about classical music. But his parents never knew about these accomplishments. His father felt frustrated. He was available to help Martin with batting practice and weight training, but since Martin wasn't interested in these things father and son had little contact. Despite his abilities, Martin grew up with poor self-esteem because he felt like a failure in *that* family. Although his parents didn't "put him down," they never really "put him up." It took many years for him to find himself and find others like himself who valued and encouraged his natural ability.

If your child's strengths are really different from the family norm, it may be difficult for you even to recognize them. Martin's dad thought he was "moping around in his room instead of getting out in the sun and playing sports." He also felt inadequate when Martin asked him questions that he couldn't answer ("How does the radio work?"). He never had a chance to share his knowledge about sports with his son.

Exercise. If one of your children seems not to fit the family norm, try this exercise. Write a brief description of the "ideal kid," the one who would fit the family norm more closely. What does this child look like? How does he or she excel? What are his or her interests, personality traits, likes and dislikes? List this ideal child's qualities and compare them to qualities you listed for your real child. Put an "A" next to the qualities that are alike and "D" next to the qualities that are different from the ideal child. (Note that "different" does not mean "negative." An attribute can still be a positive one even though it is different from your ideal.)

1. Look at the items marked and see if you can change your focus from what your child *isn't* into what he or she *is*. If your son doesn't like things you'd prefer, record what he does like. If he's not good at skills you value, write down what he is good at. If your daughter is weak in math, find out what subject she excels in. English? Debate? Track? Music?
2. Do your child's different qualities have something you value at their root? For instance, both Martin and his dad were very analytical. Martin's dad was analytical in the ways he observed his students—that's what made him such a good coach. He

could watch a kid pitch a baseball and tell him how he needed to change his stance, his arm, or his focus in order to be a better pitcher. Martin expressed his analytical ability in another way. By the time he was fifteen he could fix just about anything mechanical and diagnose what was wrong with a car by listening to the engine.

3. Revise your child's positive and negative lists to include your new discoveries.

When children are different from the family norm, it is especially important to recognize, reinforce, and acknowledge their differences in a positive way. To not recognize a child's potential can make him or her miss an important opportunity for self-esteem and accomplishment.

Nancy's parents never valued her ice skating; instead, they thought of it as babyish and self-indulgent, a waste of time and money. Nancy's ability as a skater won her a scholarship, and she started to compete in local meets. Nancy's parents never attended the meets and resented the time it took from her academic work. They often threatened to make her quit if she neglected her studies. With her parents' support and acknowledgement, she could have "been a contender," but without it she was discouraged and dropped out without ever realizing her potential.

When you are reinforcing the positive qualities in a child who is different, make sure that you include some qualities or talents that *are* different from the family norm. Tell your child how he or she is special in his or her differences. "You're the one who can fix anything—I'm all thumbs." "You're the one in the family who can be really creative. What would we do without you?"

You can also emphasize the ways that he or she is "alike" or similar to the family, even if he or she expresses that quality differently. It will enable him or her to feel less like an outsider even if he or she is different. "We are a family of artists—three musicians and one dancer." "We all like to learn new things—some of us learn better from books, and some from experience."

A Child in Your Own Image

Your child might remind you of yourself—either how you are now or how you used to be. If your child has your negative qualities, you might be excessively sensitive to them. As a parent you should be careful not to fall into the trap of focusing on the negative behaviors that are a matter of taste or preference or something that your child has little control over.

Ann was a fat child. After years of dieting, she has finally managed to keep her weight down, proudly wearing a size seven. When her daughter Heather started getting chubby at eight years old, Ann had a hard time not nagging and reminding her about food at every meal. Ann did take steps to eliminate junk food from the house and provide good low-cal meals at home, but she realized that Heather would deal with her tendency to gain weight in her own time.

If your children have your positive qualities, you might have a strong reaction when they don't achieve or apply themselves or accomplish the things that they are capable of. In reinforcing positive qualities in children who are very much like you, include the ways that they are different and the ways that they express similar qualities in a different way.

For example, Clara is smart like her mom and does well in school, but she is more interested in science than history and better at verbal skills than writing skills. These differences should be noticed and reinforced. All children want to be seen as unique and feel that they have permission to grow in their way.

Listening

"I never tell my mom anything," says sixteen-year-old Carla. "She's hopeless. I come home from school, and she's usually reading the paper or doing the crossword puzzle. She asks me how my day was, but I can see she's not really listening. She says she can listen and read at the same time, but I know that's a load of crap. Sometimes I'm tempted to tell her that I was kidnapped and stabbed at lunch just to see if she'll look up from her paper. Sometimes she'll get up and walk into the kitchen to start dinner right in the middle of our 'conversation.' It really turns me off!"

Carla's mother is not alone. Many well-meaning parents find themselves listening with half an ear. You get home from work, and there are so many things competing for your attention: the other kids, the chores, the phone, the dog. You might just be too tired to be a good listener.

Yet it is essential for the self-esteem of your child that you do find the time to listen, and to listen in a way that communicates your interest and caring. When you stop and listen to someone, you are saying to that person, "You are important. What you say matters to me. You matter to me."

How To Listen to Your Kids

1. Make sure that you are ready to listen. You might need a half hour to catch your breath after coming in from work in order to feel centered. You might be worried about having just chipped a tooth, or you might be absorbed in the sports page. You might be watching the last few minutes of your favorite TV program. You need to be able to take care of some of your own needs before you can be a good listener.

2. Give your child your full attention. Even if it's for five minutes of checking in after school before he or she runs out to play, put the paper down, turn off the TV, sit down, and be there.

3. Minimize distractions. If the phone rings, answer quickly and arrange to call the person back. Tell the other kids, "Phil and I are talking now, I'll help you find your sweater in a little while." Your child might need privacy, away from the other kids, if he or she is telling you something personal or embarrassing. If you can't eliminate distractions, then tell your child so and plan a time to talk later. "I'm worried about Mindy; she's an hour late coming home from school. I just can't be a good listener now. Let's find a time after dinner when we can talk."

4. Be an active listener. Ask questions, clarify situations, respond, and look at your child. Give your daughter all the cues that you are interested in her story. Remember the names of her friends and the names of their pets. Ask for updates on the previous day's concerns. She will feel important because you listen to her and remember the things that concern her.

5. Invite your child to talk. Some kids will pounce on you as you walk in the door; they are full of news and chatter. But there may be at least one child in a larger family who has difficulty competing for verbal space. Even if this child doesn't demand your attention, he or she may still need it. Make a special time together devoted to him or her alone. Start the ball rolling by asking some open-ended questions, then follow your child's lead. This is not the time to discuss his or her poor grades or complain about his or her messy room.

What To Listen for

1. Listen for the point of the story. As your son is talking to you, ask yourself, "What is the reason this is important to him? What is he trying to tell me?" Is he telling you about his plans? Or that he was successful in solving a problem? Is he telling you that he was strong and brave? Or that he was embarrassed, angry, and confused? Give feedback to the point of the story and don't distract yourself with the details.

Fourteen-year-old Suzie tells her mom about the day at school. She's very excited and talking a mile a minute. "I was late for my second period class because I forget my math book in art class. So the teacher told me I'd have to make up the quiz during lunch period, which was really a drag because that meant I wouldn't be able to find Kim, who owed me lots of money. Now I was stuck without lunch money or a lunch period. So I decided to go back to the gym to try to find the jacket I left there yesterday, and I saw this guy practicing free throws all alone on the basketball court. I sat and watched him for a while and he seemed to like having an audience. So I stayed. After a while we started talking and I told him how bummed out I was about missing lunch and losing my jacket. Anyway, he had a coke and he shared it with me. He's rad, I hope he liked me.''

Listening to the story, Suzie's mom might easily miss the point. She might be dismayed at Suzie's forgetfulness (forgotten math book, lost jacket!). She might be angry at her missing a quiz. She might be irritated at her losing her lunch, lending money to Kim, going hungry, hanging out in the boys' gym, and the rest. But the *point* of Suzie's story is that she met a nice guy. She was excited and wanted to share her excitement with her mom.

2. Don't feel that you have to fix things. The hardest challenge in listening to kids is to keep from making suggestions, giving advice, or solving the problem. You know how annoying and frustrating it is to talk to someone who interrupts mid-sentence with the "solution." You feel cut off. You aren't able to ventilate feelings or share the excruciating details of your problem. Besides, you are robbed of the opportunity to figure out your own solution. Yet when kids are relating a problem, it is all too common for parents to jump in too soon with a solution. You want to "fix it and make it better," or you fear your children are too young or too inexperienced to generate their own answers. The odds are that your child is not so much asking for a solution as wanting to share the experience.

If appropriate, *after* your child has had plenty of time to ventilate, you can help him or her explore solutions to a problem. If your child is able to come up with his or her own solution, it will do more for his or her self-esteem than having you fix it. Besides, this problem may not have a solution, or the solution may be more obvious later, after he or she is feeling less angry or disappointed.

3. Listen and respond to the feelings. When you're listening to your daughter, pay attention not only to the words, but also to the feelings that she is expressing. Watch also for cues in her physical posture and tone of voice. Is she excited and happy? Does she sound disappointed or dejected? Is she sitting up, pacing and jumping, or lying sullenly on the couch? Respond to the feelings you observe as well as the story you hear. "I can see how excited you are about the party. You can hardly sit still. Why is it so special to you?"

For a young child, it will often be necessary to help him or her find the words to describe what he or she feels. "It sounds like you are angry because you didn't get a turn. Angry and sad, is that what you feel?''

Accepting Your Child's Negative Feelings

It's very upsetting to hear your child express feelings that you wish were not true. Your son hates his brother or his stepfather or he is angry at you. Your daughter rebels against what you think she ought to do and rejects what you feel is important. It's tempting to try to cut your child off when he or she is expressing any strong negative feelings, but putting a lid on a boiling cauldron of feelings will not make them go away.

Children are often afraid of their own strong feelings. They sometimes become overwhelmed by anger or frustration, jealousy or fear. If their feelings are labeled "bad" or if they are made to repress, deny, or cover up their feelings, the result can be: (1) lowered self-esteem ("I must be bad to feel this way."), (2) inauthentic behavior ("I have to put on an act to be acceptable to my parents. If they knew how I felt they might abandon me."), and (3) losing touch with all feelings—the positive as well as the negative. Joy, excitement, affection, and curiosity will be muted along with anger, jealousy, and fear. Remember that feelings can't be created on demand or banished when inconvenient. A child whose strong negative feelings are acknowledged and who is given support to express them in an acceptable way can eventually let go of those feelings. He or she doesn't have to sulk, hold a grudge, or brood about things. It is only when bad feelings have room for expression that good feelings can be fully enjoyed.

Here are five common reactions that parents have that make children deny their feelings.

1. Deny that the feeling exists. "Your elbow doesn't hurt—it was just a little bump."
2. Say what the child *should* feel. "You should love your brother."
3. Compare a child with others. "Jimmy doesn't act that way at the dentist. What's the matter with you?"
4. Respond with ridicule or sarcasm. "Are you going to cry again just because you can't do it? What a baby!"
5. Use threats and punishment. "If you feel that way every time you strike out, then you should just forget little league this year."

Here are some ways you can help your child deal with strong negative feelings.

1. Encourage your children to express their true feelings in a safe, accepting environment. Provide the privacy and time to let

them tell you how angry, sad, or frustrated they are. If your son is angry at you, try not to get defensive or talk him out of it. You can acknowledge feelings without apologizing or giving in. "I hear how angry you are at me. I know you don't like to be told what to do." "I hear how much you want to sleep overnight at Sheila's house, but you can't go tonight."

2. Help your children find different ways to ventilate. Encourage little children to growl, hit a pillow, or stamp their feet to express angry feelings. A child often needs to tell a story over and over again for real catharsis. Older children might draw a picture or write a letter or telephone a sympathetic friend to tell them what happened. Sports and strenuous physical activities can provide another outlet for strong feelings.

3. Encourage your children to use their imaginations to express their feelings. "What do you wish you could have said or done to that bully?" "How big will you have to be to run faster or jump higher than she can?" "Do you want her to disappear? Be invisible?"

4. Share a story about yourself in a similar predicament, feeling similar things. "I remember when I was your age, my sister used to sneak into my drawers and borrow things. I was so mad." Your child can feel that he or she is not alone in his or her feelings and take comfort that you understand. (But be careful when sharing a story about yourself that you don't become the focus of the conversation, or that you use the story to minimize your child's distress.)

5. Be a good role model in how you deal with your own strong feelings. Share some of your own coping skills.

6. Help your children feel good about themselves even in the face of defeat or disappointment. "You didn't win the race, but your butterfly stroke has really improved. Once you get more speed you will be unstoppable." "Even though you were lost and scared, you had the good sense to ask the saleslady for help. How did you think of that?"

The Language of Self-Esteem

The most powerful tool you have as a parent to build good self-esteem is the language you use. Every day, in the hundreds of interactions you have with your children, you mirror back to them who they are. Like a sculptor's tools on soft clay, your words and tone of voice shape their sense of self. For this reason, it is vital that the feedback you give, both praise and correction, is couched in the language of self-esteem.

Feedback that enhances self-esteem has three components.

1. A description of the behavior. The language of self-esteem is a language of description. You *describe* the behavior without *judging* the child. In this way, you distinguish between the child's worth and his or her behavior. This is an important distinction. Your son is not a good boy because he shares his toys. He is not a bad boy because he hits his brother. He is good because he exists, because you love and care for him, because he is special to you. Sometimes he is able to *do* good (helping or sharing or achieving). Describing behavior (what you see, what you hear, what happened) gives children accurate feedback about how they act and how their actions affect others. But by not labeling children bad or good, you uncouple such appraisals of their behavior from their basic value and worth.

2. Your reaction to the behavior. The language of self-esteem is a language that shares something about yourself. You share your appreciation, enjoyment, and delight, or your disapproval, annoyance, or anger. You communicate your reasons for wanting something done or your reaction to a situation. It is easier for children to meet expectations and avoid conflict when they know why people around them react as they do.

3. Acknowledgement of the child's feelings. The language of self-esteem validates your child's experience. Your daughter's efforts are appreciated, whether successful or not. You've acknowledged her predicament and motives, her confusion or carefulness. She feels seen and understood even when being corrected.

In the sections that follow, these three components of feedback are applied to the process of praising and correcting your child.

Praise

Your approval is what shapes behavior. Pleasing you is what motivates your children to learn everything from language to table manners. When you praise your kids, they get the message that they're OK and that what they do is acceptable and appreciated.

But using the language of self-esteem in praising children does far more than communicate approval. It gives your children something to take away with them. Your children learn to recognize what is special, what they did that they can take pride in. They can learn to praise themselves and to recognize and value their own efforts and talents.

Consider the case of Joey. He proudly shows his dad a painting that he made in school. His dad is effusive. "What a gorgeous painting. I love it. You're terrific." But Joey never learns what his dad likes about the painting. As a result Joey can't later remember and say to himself what was good about his accomplishment. Using the language of self-esteem, Joey's dad might have said something like this: "This is terrific. I see a house and a boy in bright flowers (*description*). I like the colors you chose and those swirling clouds, and I see how carefully you drew in the pockets on the boy's pants (*reaction*). You must have worked very hard on it (*acknowledgement*). Let's hang it up and show mommy."

Sharing feelings when you praise. If you share something about yourself with your children, they begin to learn what is important to you. They know more about your needs and moods, and they know how to please you, or avoid you when you're on the war path. For instance, you appreciate that your son makes his bed in the morning—you like a neat room. You are glad when your daughter is able to occupy herself when you are on the phone—you hate being interrupted. Sharing reactions such as these with your child makes you understandable, rather than arbitrary. You cease to be an unpredictable person blowing hot and cold without reason.

Arlene is waiting for David, her fourteen-year-old, to get home from school. She needs him to babysit so that she can leave for a dental appointment. As David walks in the door, Arlene speaks sharply: "Glad you're home in time. I was sure you'd forget. I've got to go now, bye." David can see that his mother is nervous, and he wonders why. He didn't forget and he got home on time, so what's bugging her? If Arlene had remembered to use the language of self-esteem, she would have shared more of her feelings. "Thanks for getting back in time (*description*). I was so afraid you'd forgotten (*reaction*). I know you'd rather hang out with your friends after school (*acknowledgement*). I especially appreciate it today because I have a dental appointment and I always get so nervous (*reaction*)."

This form of praise enables David to learn something about his mom and himself. Mom was nervous and edgy this morning because of her dental appointment. His success in remembering to get home and the sacrifice of leaving his friends was recognized. He also gets to see himself as a dependable person who comes through when needed.

Be generous with your praise. Find as many opportunities to sincerely praise your children as you can. Praise helps kids see themselves in a most positive way, not just how they are, but how you believe they could be. They get validation for their best selves.

Overpraise makes children uncomfortable. Your daughter knows that she is not the "smartest kid in the class, a real genius." She may have been able to do well in the math test today, but your overpraise makes her feel pressure to shine every day. When she eventually gets a B or C on a test, will that make her "stupid, a real dunce"?

Some parents report they resist praising their children for something good because as soon as they draw attention to what the child did well, he or she will do the opposite. This phenomenon is due to overpraising. The tension of being overpraised is too much to bear. Your daughter is more comfortable being "herself" than the "best little girl in the world."

Consider the case of Suzie. Molly and her mom are visiting Suzie's house. When Molly walks in, Suzie hands her a doll. Suzie's mom is delighted. "What a generous girl you are! You're the most generous girl I've ever seen. You're an angel." This form of praise can make Suzie anxious. Suzie knows she isn't the most generous girl in the world. Maybe she was feeling generous, or just distracting Molly from a more precious toy, or maybe softening her mother up so that she will let Suzie buy ice cream later. In any case, when Suzie doesn't share, does that make her the most selfish little girl in the world? If Suzie were praised using the language of self-esteem, it might sound like this: "How nice. I appreciate your letting her play with your doll (*description, reaction*). Sometimes it's hard to share special toys (*acknowledgement*)." This kind of praise allows Suzie to feel good about sharing without feeling that her identity is at risk if she doesn't share.

Avoid backhanded praise. A backhanded compliment mixes praise with insult. It gives children praise for what they did well, but at the same time reminds them of earlier failures. No wonder it doesn't make them feel good to receive it.

> *Backhanded praise:* "Your hair certainly looks better than it did this morning."
> *Real praise:* "I like the way you've combed your hair."

> *Backhanded praise:* "That's pretty good considering how you waited to the last minute."
> *Real praise:* "You did a good job, and you did it very quickly."

> *Backhanded praise:* "It's about time."
> *Real praise:* "I'm glad you got it done."

> *Backhanded praise:* "You did it, boy was I surprised."
> *Real praise:* "Congratulations, I knew you had it in you. Good job!"

Correcting Your Child

Nowhere is the careful use of language more important than when correcting a child's problematic behavior. Children who are spoken to abusively tend to verbally abuse others, including their parents. Children who are given corrections without reasons tend to be less reasonable. Children whose efforts are not recognized resent being "misunderstood." Children who are not given clear statements of what is expected of them feel defeated and hopeless about doing anything right. It is very difficult for a child to develop a sense of worth when his or her behavior has inspired anger or annoyance from others.

Parents are teachers as well as mirrors to their children. They need to teach their kids to control impulses, take responsibility, resist pressure, and be considerate of others. This learning process depends on your ability to use the language of self-esteem in all your feedback. If corrections take place in the form of rejection or insult, your child won't be open to new information or have any desire to do the behavior right. Although your child might "obey," he or she will feel resentful, defeated, resistant, and angry.

Giving correction using language of self-esteem allows your children to get the point of correction and change their behavior without having to feel like a bad person. The language used in correcting children is very similar to the language used in praising children. It involves these four steps.

1. *A description of the behavior* (in nonjudgmental language). "The room is still not straightened." "The dishes were still in the sink this morning." "The report card indicated you cut English class nine times."
2. *A reason for behavior change*. Make it simple and to the point. "I'm tired now." "I worry when you're late." "She is expecting us on time."
3. *Acknowledgement of the child's feelings* (or effort, predicament, or motive). "I see how angry you are." "Maybe it seemed like the only choice you had." "You must have felt really pressured by them."
4. *A clear statement of what is expected*. "I need you to come help me now." "Do not take things from your sister's room without asking." "I expect you to be home on time."

The following examples contrast an attacking feedback style with the language of self-esteem. Each of the five typical angry reactions is followed by examples of how you can change the statement so that you can get your point across clearly and respectfully, without insult, anger, or rejection.

Attacking communication: What a mess! You live like a pig. (*Negative labels*)

Language of self-esteem: I see clothes, books, and records all over the room (*description of behavior*). When your room is straightened, you'll have more room to play (*reason for behavior change*). You probably don't know where to start (*acknowledgement of feelings*). I want the clothes in the hamper, books on the desk, and records put away in the next half hour (*statement of expectation*).

Attacking communication: Stop bugging me! Can't you ever play by yourself? (*Rejection*)

Language of self-esteem: You've been following me around the house (*description of behavior*). There's a very important call I have to make (*reason for behavior change*). I know I promised we'd go buy school supplies today right after work (*acknowledgement of feelings*). I need you to play quietly while I'm on the phone, and then we can go shopping (*statement of expectation*).

Attacking communication: Stop that, you little monster! (*Negative label*)

Language of self-esteem: You're hitting Suzie (*description of behavior*). That hurts her (*reason for behavior change*). I see that you get angry when she takes your toys (*acknowledgement of feelings*). Hitting is not allowed here (*statement of expectation*).

Attacking communication: Can't you be quiet? Keep this up and we'll have an accident. (*Threat*)

Language of self-esteem: There's a lot of jumping around and noise in the car (*description of behavior*). I can't drive safely with all this distraction (*reason for behavior change*). I know that it's hard to sit still for such a long time (*acknowledgement of feelings*). I expect you to put on your seat belts and talk quietly until we stop for lunch (*statement of expectation*).

Attacking communication: All you ever think about is yourself. (*Overgeneralization*)

Language of self-esteem: You promised you'd babysit tonight, but now you want to go to Connie's party (*description of behavior*). Dad and I have tickets for tonight and we are counting on you (*reason for behavior change*). I can see how disappointed you are about missing the party (*acknowledgement of feelings*). But I expect you to keep your promise and stay home with your brother (*statement of expectation*).

By following the four steps in giving corrections, you'll often avoid struggles and resistance, and you'll be demonstrating a style of clear communication to your children. Later, when your children are grown, their internalized parental voices will be more supportive. And when you hear your kids using the language of self-esteem to others, you'll know they have learned a valuable life skill.

Language styles to avoid. When correcting your child, make every effort to avoid the following destructive language styles. They are guaranteed to tear down self-esteem.

1. *Overgeneralizations.* "You *always* do it wrong." "You *never* think before you act." "*All* you care about is your friends." Overgeneralizations are untrue because they emphasize the negative behavior and ignore the positive. Eventually a child will believe the negative generalization and feel hopeless about ever doing things right.

2. *The silent treatment.* If you're very angry or distracted, it can be useful to delay your interaction—but be sure to schedule a time to talk the problem out with your child. "I'm so angry right now I need to be alone for a bit. We'll talk when I get back." Refusing to talk or even look at a child for misbehaving makes him or her feel personally rejected, with no way to make it up or do better.

3. *Vague or violent threats.* "Wait till I get you home." "Try that again and you'll see what will happen." "If I catch you at it again I'll break your neck." "I'll spank you so hard you won't be able to sit down for a week." These kinds of threats give children a sense of dread. Young children take things literally, and in their imaginations the violent act (a broken neck, a bottom so sore they cannot sit down) may be extremely frightening. They must be *very* bad to deserve such punishment. Older children know you don't really mean it, and tune you out. Either way the children don't learn anything except that you are angry and they are bad.

Changing the way you give children correction might not come easily at first. You may find yourself slipping into the same old style of labeling, judging, threatening, or nagging. Don't be discouraged. As you become proficient with the language of self-esteem, your relationship with your kids will improve and you'll feel increasingly free of the old conflicts, impasses, and resistances of the past.

The following three exercises will help you tune in to how you use language and help you learn new habits of communication to build self-esteem.

1. Listen to child-parent interactions wherever you find them—in the playground, at the supermarket, or visiting friends or relatives. Listen not only to the words, but also to the tone. Do you hear description or judgment? Is the adult validating feelings or putting the child down? Does the adult seem reasonable or arbitrary? Do you hear a clear statement of expectations? Decide if the interaction is likely to enhance or endanger the child's self-esteem.

Make note of three such interactions you have observed. Then mentally rewrite the scene using the four steps in giving corrections based on the language of self-esteem. (Practice using *all* the steps, even if the result sounds a little stilted).

2. Pay attention in the same way to your interactions with your own children. When you successfully use all the steps in giving corrections, notice the difference in their response. Is there less conflict, less arguing, less resistance? Notice the difference in how you feel when you acknowledge their feelings. Are you less angry? When you give a reasonable explanation for why you want something done, do you feel more justified? When you make a clear statement of expectation, do you feel more in control?

3. Note the times when you have the most difficulty using the language of self-esteem. It may be when you are especially angry or under a lot of stress. Or your old responses may be triggered by areas of chronic conflict. When you do "blow it," review the interaction later and mentally rewrite the scene using the steps you have learned. You may find it helpful to plan ahead when you anticipate a conflict situation around lateness, bedtime, chores, or homework. Rehearse your communication using all four steps you have learned.

Discipline

Discipline is any instruction or training that corrects, molds, or perfects mental faculties or moral character. As a parent, you are by definition an instructor and trainer, and you teach your children most of the skills they need to live in the world—impulse control, social skills, decision making. Whether you have many or few rules matters less than how those rules are presented and enforced. If the rules are fair and predictable and your children feel accepted as persons even when their behavior is not acceptable, then they can learn and grow with good self-esteem. If the rules are arbitrary and inconsistently enforced, or if your children feel shamed, blamed, overpowered, or humiliated, then they will learn that they are worthless and lose confidence that they can ever do things right.

It is a mistake to think that children who are never corrected or limited can grow up with high self-esteem. In fact, the opposite is true. Children raised without discipline have lower self-esteem and tend to be more dependent, achieve less, and feel that they have less control over their world. The world is full of unhappy surprises as they run into the disapproval of their teachers and the cruel feedback of peers. They tend to be more anxious because they never know exactly what the limits are and when they'll run into trouble (since even the most sanguine parents finally reach the end of their patience). These children often feel unloved because they lack the physical and emotional protection of rules and limits. "If it doesn't matter what I do, then they must not care about me."

Discipline needn't be an assault on self-esteem. It can be the means of creating a safe, supportive home environment where learning takes place. It starts with building a good relationship with your children, a relationship where they know what is expected of them and the consequences of misbehaving are predictable, reasonable, and fair.

The Case Against Punishment

Punishment is defined as "enforcing obedience or order" and implies external control over a person by force or coercion. You have a lot of power in the relationship with your child. You are physically stronger and more intelligent and experienced. You control the resources; the children live in your house. Since your children depend on you for support, approval, love, and feelings of worth, you have the power to intimidate and force them to obey. "Do it because I said so." "I'll make you sorry." "Don't you dare." "You better not."

If the reason for punishment is to teach children to behave differently, then punishment does *not* work. In fact, it distracts children from feeling sorry for what they did or didn't do. They become involved in feelings of defiance, guilt, and revenge. All they remember is "I'll get even," "she'll be sorry," "next time I won't tell her and she'll never find out." To the child who is punished, the parent is seen as unfair. You are the bully, and he or she is the victim. At the same time the effect on self-esteem can be devastating. The child feels humiliated, belittled, powerless, and bad. He or she gets the message that to be accepted, he or she has to do it your way and forget his or her needs. "My needs are unimportant and so am I."

Finally, it is very unpleasant to be the punishing parent. You never get the good family feeling of cooperation and support, and the negative feelings drain the joy from your relationship. Punishment starts a negative cycle of misbehavior, punishment, anger, revenge, and misbehavior again. You are as trapped as your child.

There is an alternative to punishment in handling discipline problems. It entails more thought and planning than punishment, but the rewards are great for both you and your family. It starts before any misbehavior occurs, before there is any need for discipline. You begin by creating and preserving a good relationship with your child. This relationship is the most powerful tool that you have to motivate your child to change his behavior. If kids want to please you, if they want your approval, they are less likely to misbehave.

But how do you keep a good relationship when you are correcting them, limiting them, and disciplining them? You do that by using the same communication skills that you use when dealing with any other person around conflict.

- Don't let old resentments build up.
- Don't martyr yourself or overextend beyond what you feel comfortable doing for another.
- Communicate clearly using the language of self-esteem, without accusing or attacking.
- Avoid mind reading—guessing another's motivation or needs.
- Deal with one problem at a time—avoid throwing in the kitchen sink.
- Acknowledge the other person's feelings, problems, or needs.

Make It Easy To Do It Right

When you make it easy for children to behave well, their self-esteem grows. They learn to see themselves in a positive light, as cooperative and helpful, and they feel successful in being able to please you. Here are some suggestions to help your child meet your expectations.

1. *Be sure that your expectations are reasonable and appropriate for your child's age.* It is not reasonable to expect that your three-year-old daughter won't spill her drink. Her coordination is simply not that well developed. Nor would you leave your twelve-year-old son alone in the house all weekend; it's not reasonable that he would be able to handle that kind of responsibility. Having reasonable expectations for the child's level of maturity avoids conflicts and disappointments.

2. *Plan ahead.* When you know that a situation will be difficult for your children, do what you can to help them cope. A long car ride can be made more bearable for everyone if you take along some toys and a snack. Children are less likely to be patient, pleasant, or flexible when they are tired or hungry. If you plan ahead and anticipate their needs, you make it more likely that they will be cooperative.

3. *Be clear about your expectations.* Your daughter is more likely to meet your expectations if you define clearly what you mean by "be good at grandma's house." Be sure to tell her specifically not to jump on the furniture, touch the knick-knacks, or fight with her brother.

4. *Focus on the positive.* Use every opportunity to praise and reinforce "good behavior" and effort. When correcting a child, point out the good as well as the bad. Acknowledge what your son did right as well as what still needs doing. If he feels that he is partially successful already, it will be easier for him to try harder to get it right. "I really liked your short story about our trip, but your handwriting makes it hard to read. I want

you to copy it over in your very best handwriting so that your
teacher will enjoy reading it tomorrow.''

5. *Provide choices when possible.* Providing choices gives children a sense of control. As a consequence, they resist less. ''We
have enough time to go on one more ride before we go home.
You decide which one it will be.''

6. *Provide rewards.* Getting to stay up a little later or going out
for a special dessert can be just the added incentive to help a
child change an old habit. ''If you wake up on time for a whole
week we can go out for sundaes after school on Friday.'' ''If
you can keep a B average this quarter, I'll pay for half of your
ski trip at Christmas.'' The goal that the child is working
towards should be achievable with reasonable effort. The
reward needn't be extravagant. Even a gold star or a decorative
decal on the top of a good science quiz can be an effective
incentive.

Involve Your Child in Solving Problems

What are the chronic behavior problems or conflicts in your
family? For some families bedtime is a problem, and for others the
morning routine of getting the kids up, dressed, fed, and out the door
is a struggle. Some families have difficulty getting their children to finish
their homework. Others struggle with siblings who borrow from each
other and don't return possessions. There might be conflicts over use
of the family car, phone, or stereo equipment.

Sometimes you can simply ask your children if they have any suggestions about how a problem could be solved. You might be surprised
at the creativity of their solutions. By just making your children part
of the process, you will change their perspective about the problem
and make them more interested in resolving it.

Another way to involve a child in the problem-solving process is
through a family ''brainstorming'' meeting. The goal of the meeting
should be to find a solution that everyone can live with, so the session should not become a gathering where you lay down the law. Even
young children can be successfully engaged in this process with good
results.

First notify everyone in the family ahead of time that you want
to discuss the problem, and then set a time when everyone can be present. Suggest that they think about the problem before the meeting
so that they can be ready to find a solution. At the meeting, take lots
of time to present everybody's needs, including your own. Don't jump
to a solution too fast. Make sure that everyone gets a turn to talk. Write
down *all* suggestions without making judgments. You can eliminate
the unreasonable suggestions later. If kids have trouble getting started,
give a few suggestions first and write them down. Continue by giving

the children lots of time to participate and add to the list. Next, help them narrow the list down to reasonable suggestions until everyone is in agreement. Be sure that everything is spelled out in the final plan—the what, when, where, how, and who of the solution. This includes what to do if someone does not follow the plan. Before you end the meeting, plan to get together again within a set time (one week, one month) to evaluate how the plan is working and to make any necessary changes.

Julia had a terrible time trying to get her two sons (ages eight and eleven) out the door in the morning. It took a half hour just to get the boys out of bed, and then they argued about what clothes they wanted to wear. They complained about the lunches she packed and then would often forget to bring them to school. Julia felt that she met with resistance at every step and found herself nagging, threatening, and finally screaming. All three were emotionally distraught by the time they piled into the car. Their family meeting resulted in the following agreement.

1. The boys would make a list of the kinds of foods they liked for lunch.
2. The boys would select and lay out the clothes they would wear the night before.
3. The boys would pack up their school bags and leave them by the front door the night before.
4. Julia would buy them their own clock radio.
5. The boys would set their own clock radio to wake them up at seven. If they were out of bed in fifteen minutes, Julia would pack a dessert with their lunch.
6. Julia would make their lunches and leave them on top of their school bags by the front door.

This solution solved many problems of their morning routine. The children enjoyed the use of their own clock radio, tuned to their favorite station. They were motivated to get out of bed by the promise of a treat for lunch. Julia no longer was the one who nagged and reminded them. The clock woke them at seven. The clock told them that it was 7:15 and they had better be out of bed if they wanted a treat for lunch. The boys enjoyed the increased independence of making decisions about what they wanted for lunch and what they wanted to wear. Julia made it easier for them to remember their lunches by leaving them by the front door with their books.

The Facts of Life—Consequences

Teach your children the real facts of life. Every act has its consequences. If you speed in your new sports car, you will get a ticket. If you insult someone, they will not want to be your friend. If you're late at the bus stop, you miss your bus.

Natural consequences are those that are not imposed by any authority. There are many instances when allowing the natural consequences of your child's behavior to occur is the best method of learning. If your son doesn't eat his lunch now, he'll be hungry later. If your daughter doesn't study, she won't pass the test. If your youngest doesn't keep a C average, the coach won't allow him on the team.

By allowing consequences to occur, you make your child responsible for his or her own actions. You are not the bad guy who nags, punishes, and berates. You can even be sympathetic and supportive. But your child gets the point: bad things happen when he or she acts in certain ways. By preventing the consequences from occurring, you keep your child from learning and remove all incentive for behavioral change.

Sometimes it is not reasonable to allow certain consequences to occur. You can't risk that your child will learn by natural consequences to stay out of the street or not play with matches. The lesson might be fatal! For these and other situations where natural consequences should not occur, you need to *create* consequences for misbehavior. The following rules will help you create effective and fair consequences.

1. Consequences should be *reasonable.* Match the severity of the consequence to the importance of the offense. If your child is a half hour late coming home, a reasonable consequence would be that he has to be a half hour earlier tomorrow. It is not reasonable that he be grounded for a week.
2. The consequence should be *related* to the event. If your son leaves his bike out in the rain, then the consequence will be more effective if it relates to his use of his bike, rather than to his use of the phone. When Dave did the dishes, he did them so poorly they had to be rewashed. His mom reacted by no longer asking him to wash the dishes at all. Dave learned that the consequence of doing a poor job was to get out of doing it all together. Why should he ever improve his dishwashing skill? When his mom made him rewash the dishes himself, Dave's dishwashing technique quickly became flawless.
3. Consequences should occur *close in time* to the events. Limit TV on the same night your child loses his jacket, not a week later. By then the consequence will seem too arbitrary and unfair.
4. Consequences should be enforced *consistently.* This is probably the hardest rule, but the most essential. If your children know that you are not consistent, they won't be motivated to change their behavior. If your son is running around in a restaurant, be clear that you will leave. Then do it! You'll probably only have to go through this inconvenience once before the behavior

ceases to be a problem. Resolve to be consistent even when you are tired, even when grandparents are visiting, even when you are on the phone. Choosing reasonable consequences in advance, when you are calm and not angry, will make it easier to be consistent.

5. Consequences should be understood in advance by both you and your children. They can then take responsibility for their actions, and you are relieved of the pressure to create reasonable consequences when you are stressed or angry. Eight-year-old Len had been told many times not to play ball close to the house lest he break a window. When his mother heard the unmistakable sound of broken glass, she was furious. If she had had to create a consequence on the spot, she might have threatened to "take that bat away for good!" But Len had been told in advance that if he broke a window he would be expected to pay for it from his allowance; if his allowance was not sufficient, he would have to "earn" the extra money by doing chores on the weekend. Len didn't have to argue or explain, and his mother didn't have to nag or threaten.

Allowing your children to experience the consequences of their acts teaches them to take responsibility for what they do. Taking that responsibility builds self-esteem because it gives them control. They are not attacked or berated, and they don't have to feel guilty. Their relationship with you is not on the line. You accept them and care about them even though they have made a mistake.

Autonomy

Nancy was talking about how she felt when leaving the hospital with her new baby. "I remember feeling overwhelmed with the responsibility. The baby seemed so vulnerable, and there were so many dangers. Even the sound of the cars on the street seemed too loud, too close. How were we going to provide for his needs—keep him safe, keep him alive. He was totally dependent on us."

Frank talks about his eighteen-year-old daughter going away to college for the first time. "I look at her and see a young woman starting out in life. Sure, for the past eighteen years she's had the security and support of a father who loves her, but the lessons she needs to learn now are the ones I can't teach her. She needs to learn to get along with others, schedule her time, budget her money, take care of herself. I know she's capable of living on her own, but she needs to do it in order to prove it. I'll be the safety net for the next few years, but she's the one on the high wire."

Teaching kids the skills and knowledge they need to leave the nest is the basic task of parenting. You want them to be capable of caring for themselves and sufficiently confident to meet challenges. You want them to fit in socially, but not lose their sense of identity; to be generous enough to give and trusting enough to take in close relationships. Somehow, during the intervening years between first holding your fragile infant and watching him pack up to move away, your child achieves autonomy. And a sense of autonomy is essential for good self-esteem.

If you spend some time with toddlers, you see the innate drive to achieve autonomy in its rawest form. You see their incredible drive to learn and master skills both physical and intellectual. They'll climb, reach, touch, and taste any new object in their environment. They'll struggle to acquire language, and then use their first words (''no'' being most important) to begin affecting their world.

The process of promoting a child's autonomy is continuous. You provide a balance between the opportunity to explore and the security of your protection. This balance between safety and growth is constantly changing. But despite the fluctuations, the trend is always toward autonomy. It's like watching the tide come in. Not every wave comes closer to you than the last, but in an hour's time you can see that there is less beach and more ocean and it's time to move the blanket or you'll soon be wet. As your children grow, by providing more challenges, allowing more choices, and expecting more responsibility, you function as a positive mirror in building their self-esteem. You trust them, you believe them capable. Your approval of their drive toward autonomy assures them that it is safe to grow up and grow away.

Promoting Confidence

1. *Teach skills necessary for independence.* From tying their shoes and dressing themselves to helping fix the car and cook a dinner, everything your children learn that helps them function independently will increase their confidence that they are competent and can make it in the world.
2. *Keep track of their history.* Just as you measure your daughter's physical stature on a growth chart on the wall, keep track of her progress in other areas. Remind her how much more capable, more skillful, more understanding, more adventurous she is compared to last year (or last month). That's how she learns to recognize and trust her developing skills.
3. *Give your child responsibilities in the family.* No matter how young a child is, it is a great boost to self-esteem to feel that he or she can make a contribution to the family. Young children can set the table, pick up toys, turn on the garden hose, or put

water out for the dog. Older children can assume responsibility for a whole project, from assessing what is needed to taking charge of how it is to be done. Of course, in the beginning it is often easier (and faster and neater) to do things yourself. But your children will never learn important skills. More importantly, they'll be cheated out of the self-esteem-enhancing experience of being needed and having their efforts recognized and appreciated.

Promoting a Feeling of Success

When a child tries something new and faces a challenge successfully, his or her self-esteem grows. You can help your children have the courage to try new experiences by providing these four conditions.

1. *Let a child know what to expect.* A young child's first trip to the dentist can go more smoothly if he or she knows what the office looks like, what the dentist does, what it might feel like, how long it will take, where you will be, and so on. You might practice at home by sitting the child on a high chair and holding a pretend mirror on a stick. A child prepared in this way can look forward to a new experience. Many potentially scary or intimidating events can be turned into adventures by making sure your child knows what will happen.

2. *Let your child practice the necessary skills.* Ten-year-old Ethan wanted to help his dad paint a dresser, but in a few minutes Ethan and the brushes were swimming in paint. His dad felt irritated and started barking commands and suggestions at Ethan. ''Don't dip the brush so deeply in the paint. Use the drop cloth. Watch your shoes. Don't touch that.'' Hurt and defeated, Ethan tried to clean up in the bathroom, where he managed to smear paint on the sink, rug, and towels. Now both his parents were disgusted with him. What started out as an adventure ended up in a disaster. The chance that Ethan could have successfully helped his dad would have been greater if he had first practiced such necessary skills as putting just the tip of the brush in the can, wiping off the excess, moving the drop cloth, and brushing smoothly to avoid splattering.

3. *Be patient.* When possible, allow sufficient time for a child to go slowly while trying something new. Your son might need time to check out the new environment and people before he feels comfortable enough to join the kids in a karate class. He might need to get the feel of a new bike before he takes off down the street. Pressure to perform before he's ready will make him shy away from new challenges.

4. *Make it safe to fail.* The fact that your child is trying something new means that he or she is already successful. He or she has succeeded in accepting a challenge. If a child doesn't feel pressure to do something well the very first time that he or she tries it, then he or she is more likely to accept a challenge or try again until he or she masters it. By praising your child's willingness to try, rather than the result of a first attempt, his or her self-esteem will be nourished.

Promoting Success in School

The lessons learned at school are not just reading and math skills or knowledge of history and science. When children are able to finish assignments on time, with reasonable neatness and care, they learn some very important life skills. They learn to organize, plan ahead, follow through, and exercise some self-control. Reasonable grades also support self-esteem. Your son sees stars and smiling faces at the top of his homework papers, that his teacher is pleased and friendly towards him, and that other children see him as competent.

The child who is allowed to continue to do poorly in school faces daily assaults on his or her self-esteem. Poor grades, disapproval from the teacher, and even social ostracism are the painful burdens that he or she bears. A child's self-esteem can take a beating as he or she falls further and further behind.

Of course, there are many reasons why children do poorly in school. Your son may have difficulty seeing or hearing the teacher. Or he may have a learning disability (aphasia, dyslexia, hyperactivity). Your daughter may be bored because she's not challenged or frustrated because she can't keep up. Or she may be distracted by friends who sit nearby.

Whatever the problem, you need to deal with it early in a child's school career—before he or she begins to think of himself or herself as a failure, and before he or she suffers years of disapproval from frustrated teachers.

Check it out. Check with your child first. Have you son tell you what he sees as the problem and what he thinks is needed to solve it. Check with his teachers. From them you'll learn about any problems before they get out of hand, and you'll also let the teachers know that you're an interested parent and that your child is trying. Look at parent-teacher conferences as an exchange of information. The teacher needs to know if there is some situation at home that's affecting your child: the birth of a sibling, a recent move, the death of a grandparent or a pet, a family illness or marital problem. You need to know what is expected of your child and how well he or she is meeting those expectations.

Listen to how the teacher perceives the problem. Does his or her perception sound reasonable? Is your son restless or distractable? Does he fail to finish assignments? Does he forget his books? Does he work too slowly or freeze up during exams? Look at his tests, his artwork, his desk, and his notes. Ask about his friendships and participation in class. Try to get a sense of what your child's experience in school is. Don't leave until you have a good idea about what the problem is and have agreed on a plan to solve it. Follow up by checking back in a few weeks to see if there is any improvement.

Marco was a bright but often bored fourth grader. When his math grades fell from his usual A's to C's, Marco's father asked him what he thought the problem was. Marco claimed that he understood the math, but thought it was stupid and boring. His father had a conference with the teacher. Once his father saw his son's math tests and worksheets, he could see where the problem was. Marco's handwriting was so sloppy that his sevens looked like nines and his fives looked like eights. Some mistakes were clearly due to transcribing the numbers incorrectly. The teacher pointed out that in working word problems Marco seemed to understand how the problems were done, but would skip certain steps. They agreed that the father would check Marco's homework each night for accuracy and legibility. He would also check that Marco didn't skip steps when solving word problems. Marco's teacher agreed with the father that Marco might be bored in math. She therefore began saving some fun math games for him to work on after he finished his regular assignments. This simple intervention got Marco back on track, and his math grades improved. More importantly, his self-esteem improved as well. He was getting positive feedback from his teacher for improved handwriting, plus he was given extra attention and the challenge of math games.

You and the teacher should be *partners* in helping your child do well, feel good about himself, and be successful in school. If you feel that the teacher has labeled and dismissed your child (as a "slow learner, hopeless, a wall climber, a troublemaker" and the like) and that he or she is not willing to work with you in a positive way, try to have your child moved to another class.

Promoting Social Skills

Let your children spend time with other children. Social skills are only learned through practice. Kids need to learn to share, take turns, cooperate and negotiate. They learn how to get along and predict how others will react to them. They need other kids to practice how to handle their anger, how to compromise, how to get their own way. Getting along with peers is a very different skill from getting along with adults, and the social lessons of childhood are essential for a child to be successful socially, as a teen and as an adult.

For very young children, play groups or nursery school, even for a few mornings a week, are valuable. Encourage after-school activities where kids learn to enjoy team spirit and companionship. Encourage their friends to visit your home and let your child visit others after school. Take a friend along on an outing. Exclusive one-on-one contact during a trip can cement a friendship which might carry over to the school environment. This is an especially helpful opportunity for shy children.

Be aware of the tremendous pressure your children are under to be like other kids. From riding their bike in the street to dating and curfew restrictions, kids are going to want to do what ''everybody else is doing.'' What everybody else is doing will be different in different communities, and will almost certainly be different from your expectations. Hair style, dress style, and music are classic battlegrounds for family conflict during adolescence. But being part of a group identified by a distinctive style and philosophy gives teens a ready-made identity and the safety of the group while they struggle to find out who they are and what they want. As a parent, you are faced with a delicate balance between accepting their need to establish an independent identity and firmly setting limits in areas that relate to your child's physical and psychological safety. If your son or daughter has enough experience and feels competent socially, he or she will have a better chance to resist the pressures to ''go along'' with the crowd when going along exposes him or her to danger.

Modeling Self-Esteem

Children learn to value themselves by the example you set. When you have the self-esteem to forgive yourself, they learn to forgive themselves. When you talk about your appearance and behavior with acceptance, they learn to do the same. When you have the self-esteem to set limits and protect yourelf, kids model on your example. They learn to set limits and protect themselves as well.

Modeling self-esteem means valuing yourself enough to take care of your own basic needs. When you put yourself last, when you chronically sacrifice for your kids, you teach them that a person is only worthy insofar as he or she is of service to others. You teach them to use you and make it likely that later on they will be used. Setting consistent, supportive limits and protecting yourself from overbearing demands sends a message to your child that both of you are important and both of you have legitimate needs. You show your son or daughter that each person in a relationship has value and that a balance must be struck to meet the important needs of each one.

The Martyr Myth

The image of the self-sacrificing parent is often held up as an ideal. The good father gives all for the children no matter what the cost. The good mother never takes a break and has no outside friendships or activities. The good parents have needs that can be ignored, delayed, and forgotten. Is this the ideal?

In fact the opposite is true. Overstressed and overextended parents are often irritable, resentful, and depressed. Just as you can't keep driving a car without ever stopping for gas, you can't keep giving to kids without ever refueling emotionally. Taking care of yourself provides you with the capacity for taking care of your children. An afternoon out with friends for lunch, an evening dinner out with your husband or wife, a weekly exercise class, or even an hour alone in the tub with a good book can enable you to return to your parenting job with more energy, interest, and patience.

Bibliography

Barksdale, Lilburn S. *Building Self-Esteem.* Idyllwild, California: The Barksdale Foundation, 1972.

Berne, Patricia H. and Savary, Louis M. *Building Self-Esteem in Children.* New York: Continuum Publishing, 1985.

Brandon, Nathaniel. *The Psychology of Self-Esteem.* New York: Nash, 1969.

Briggs, Dorothy Corkille. *Celebrate Yourself.* Garden City: Doubleday, 1977.

Briggs, Dorothy Corkille. *Your Child's Self-Esteem.* New York: Doubleday, 1970.

Browne, Harry. *How I Found Freedom in an Unfree World.* New York: Macmillan Publishing, 1973.

Burns, David D. *Feeling Good.* New York: Signet, 1981.

Coopersmith, Stanley. *The Antecedents of Self-Esteem.* San Francisco: W. H. Freeman, 1967.

Durrell, Doris. *The Critical Years.* Oakland, California: New Harbinger Publication, 1984.

Faber, Adele and Mazlish, Elaine. *How to Talk So Kids Will Listen & Listen So Kids Will Talk.* New York: Avon, 1982.

Faber, Adele and Mazlish, Elaine. *Liberated Parents/Liberated Children.* New York: Avon, 1975.

Isaacs, Susan. *Who's in Control?* New York: Putnam, 1986.

McKay, Matthew, Davis, Martha and Fanning, Patrick. *Messages: The Communication Skills Book.* Oakland, California: New Harbinger Publications, 1983.

McKay, Matthew, Davis, Martha, and Fanning, Patrick. *Thoughts & Feelings: The Art of Cognitive Stress Intervention.* Oakland, California: New Harbinger Publications, 1981.

Rubin, Theodore I. *Compassion and Self-Hate.* New York: Ballantine, 1975.

Wassmer, Arthur C. *Making Contact.* New York: Dial Press, 1978.

Zilbergeld, Bernie. *The Shrinking of America.* Boston: Little Brown, 1983.

Zimbardo, Phillip G. *Shyness.* Reading, Massachusetts: Addison-Wesley, 1977.

Other New Harbinger Self-Help Titles